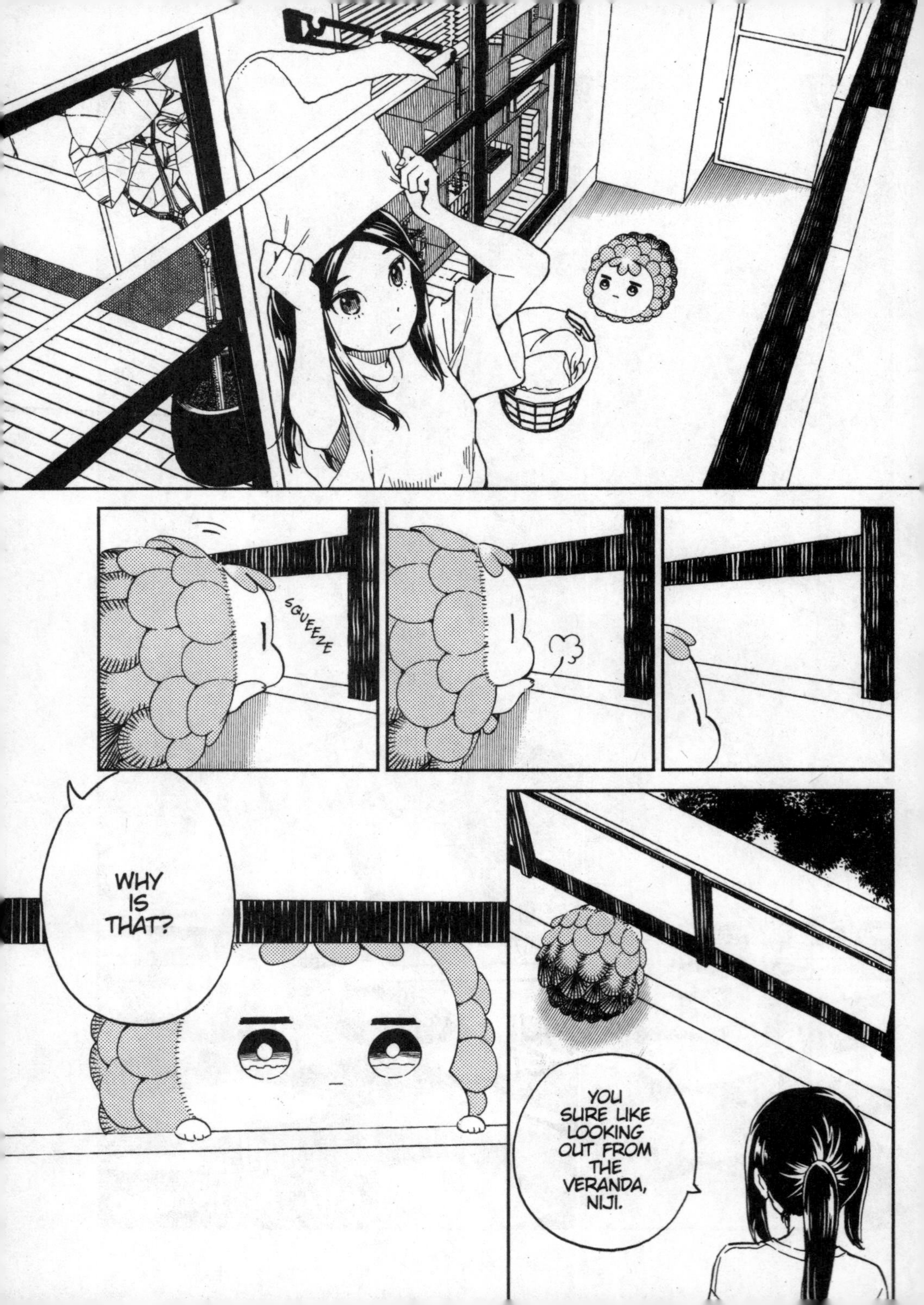
SQUEEZE
YOU SURE LIKE LOOKING OUT FROM THE VERANDA, NIJI.
WHY IS THAT?

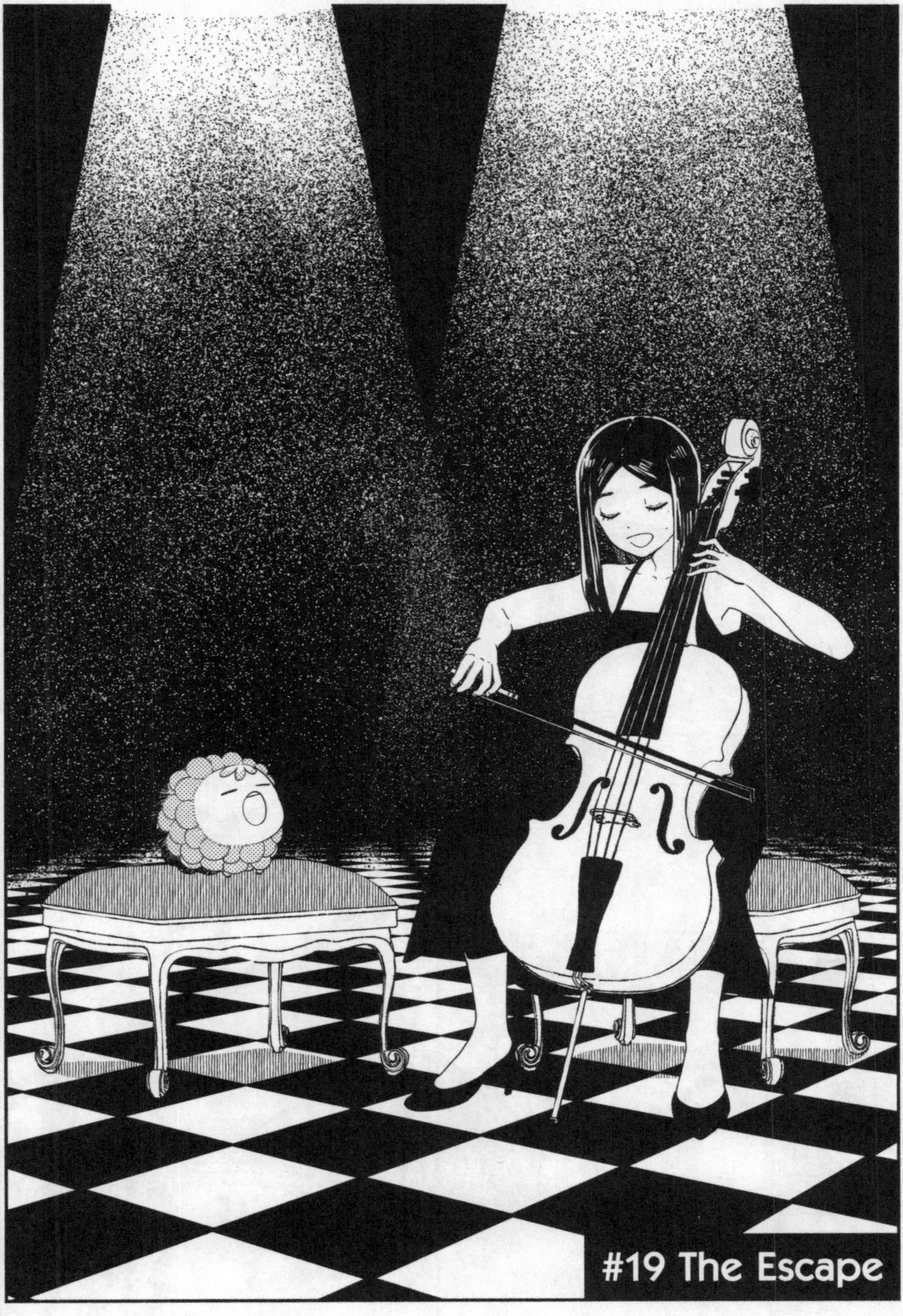
#19 The Escape

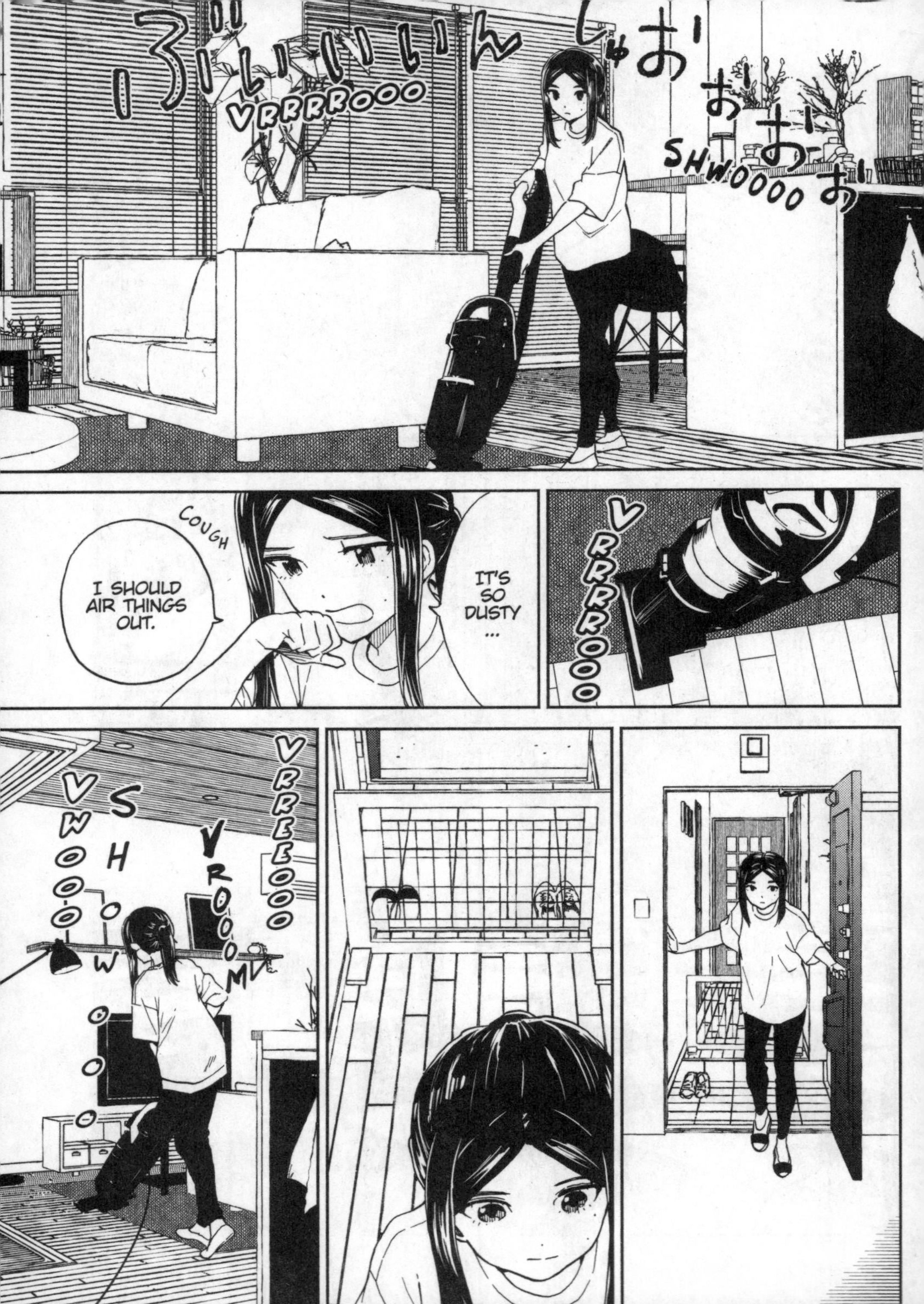

じゅおおおお
SHWOOOO
ぶいいいん
VRRRROOO
VRRRROOO
IT'S SO DUSTY ...
COUGH
I SHOULD AIR THINGS OUT.
VRREEOOO
VROOOOM
SHOWOOO
VWOOOOO

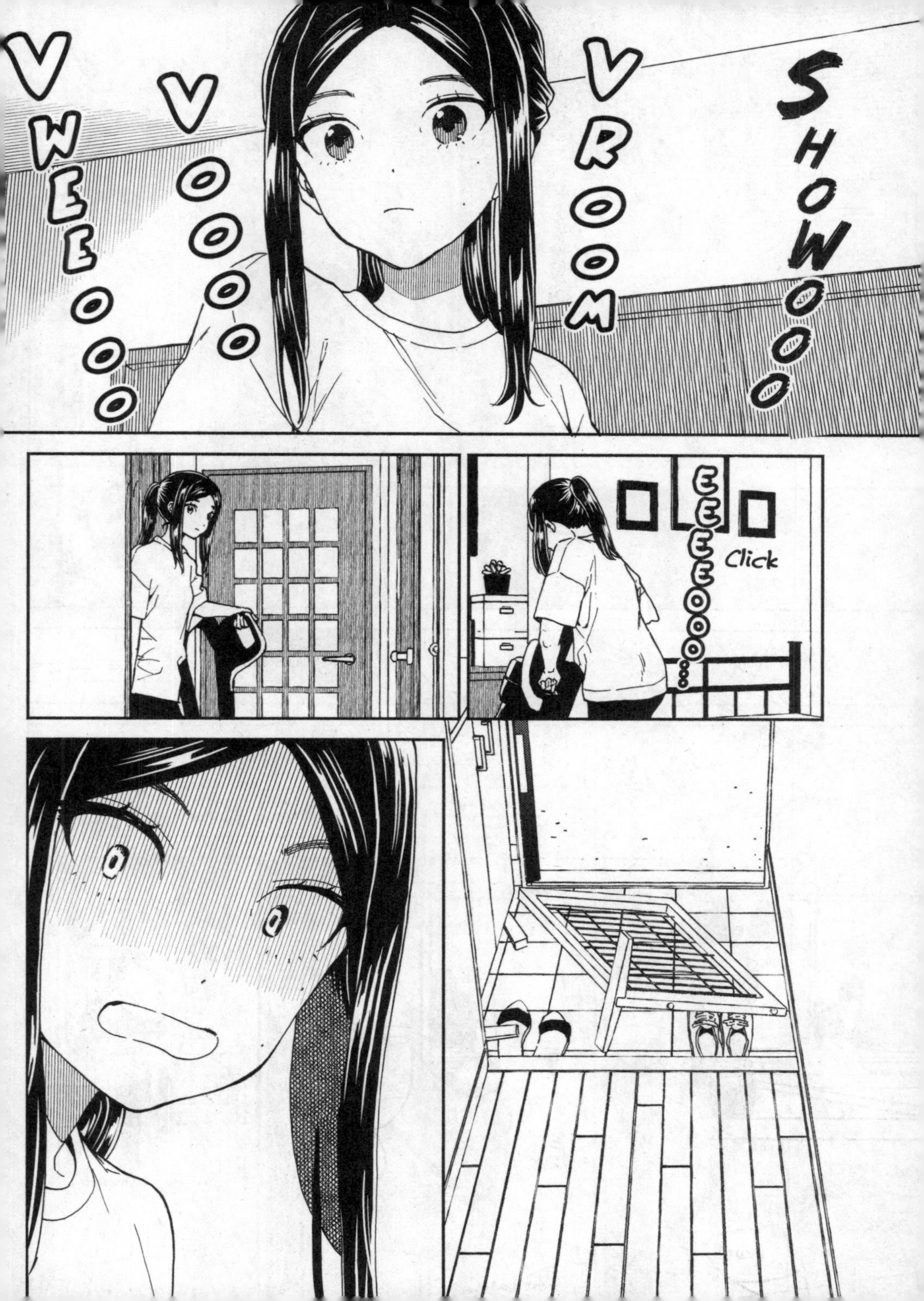
SHOWOOOO
VROOOM
VOOOOO
VWEEOOO
EEEEOOOO...
Click

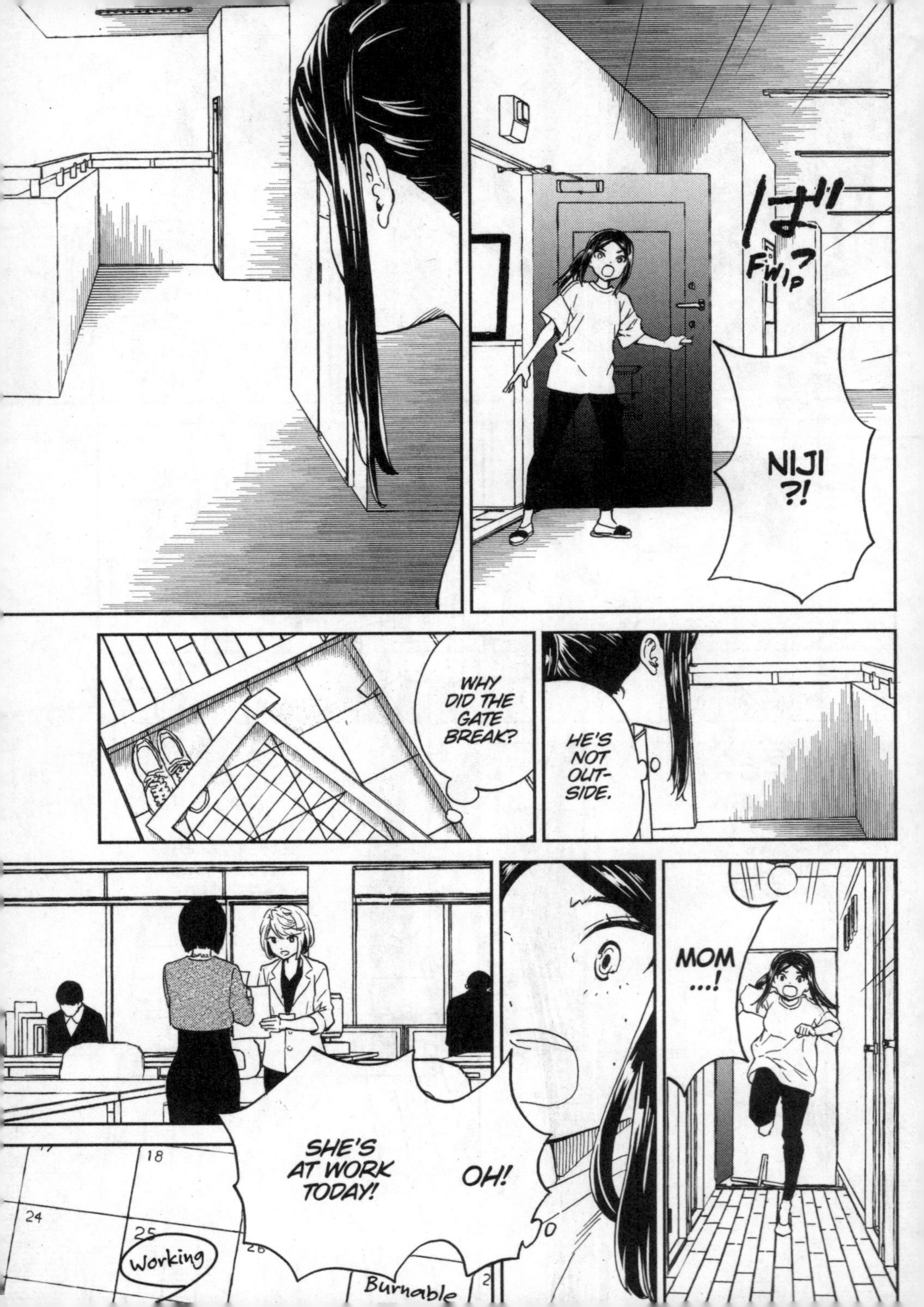
ば
FWIP?
NIJI ?!
HE'S NOT OUT-SIDE.
WHY DID THE GATE BREAK?
MOM ...!
OH!
SHE'S AT WORK TODAY!
18
24
25
Working
26
Burnable

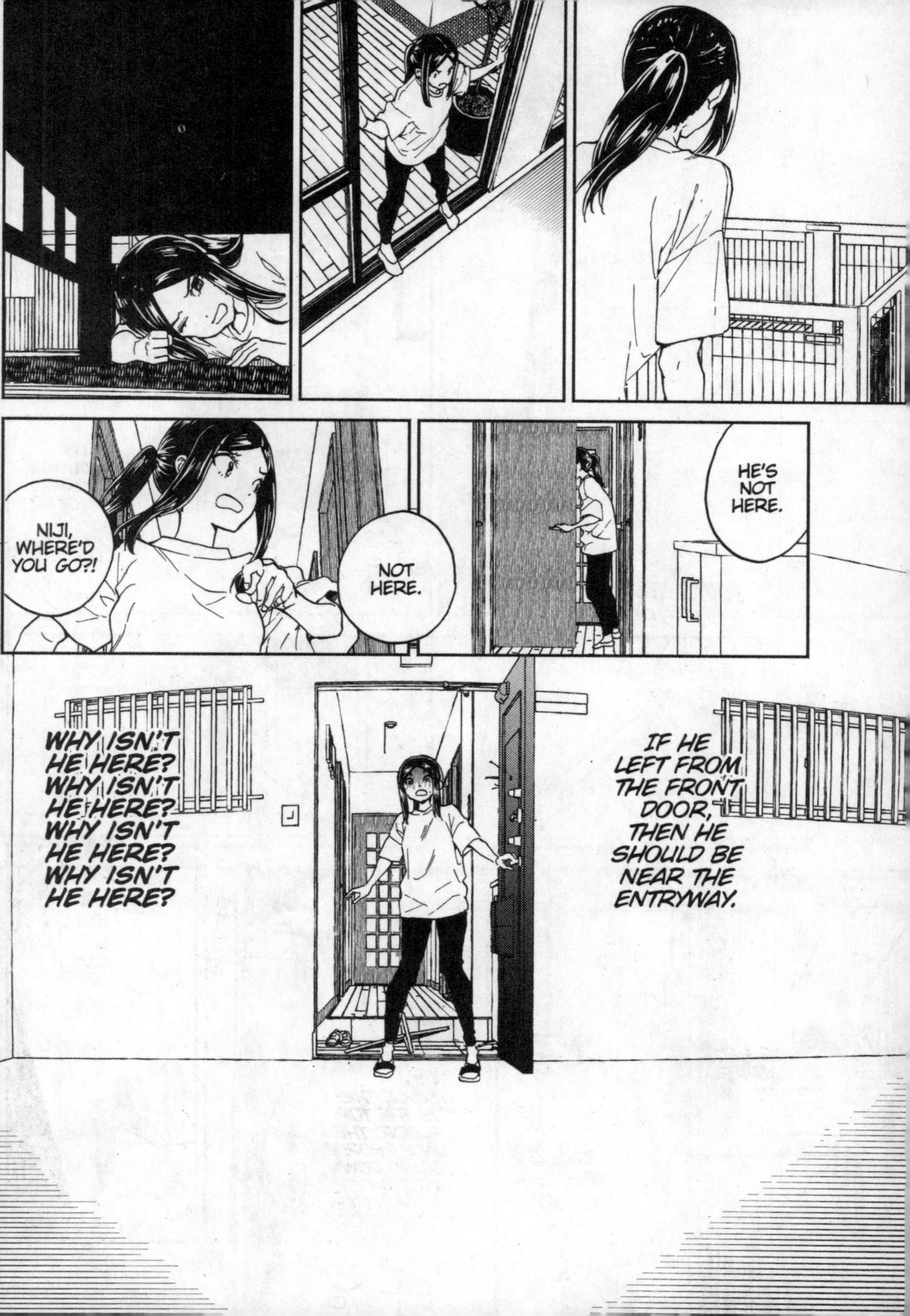
HE'S NOT HERE.
NOT HERE.
NIJI, WHERE'D YOU GO?!
IF HE LEFT FROM THE FRONT DOOR, THEN HE SHOULD BE NEAR THE ENTRYWAY.
WHY ISN'T HE HERE? WHY ISN'T HE HERE? WHY ISN'T HE HERE? WHY ISN'T HE HERE?

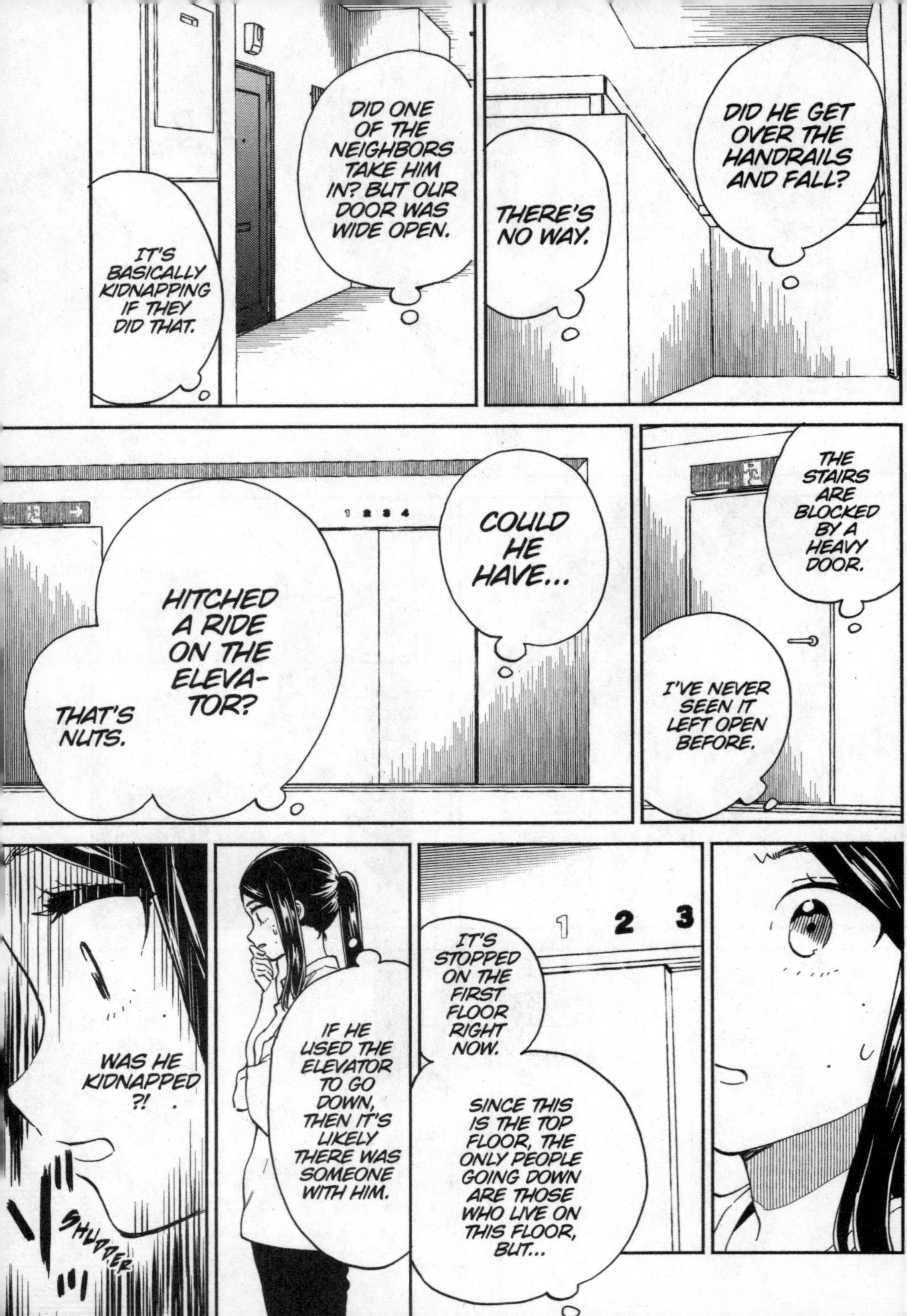
DID HE GET OVER THE HANDRAILS AND FALL?
THERE'S NO WAY.
DID ONE OF THE NEIGHBORS TAKE HIM IN? BUT OUR DOOR WAS WIDE OPEN.
IT'S BASICALLY KIDNAPPING IF THEY DID THAT.
THE STAIRS ARE BLOCKED BY A HEAVY DOOR.
I'VE NEVER SEEN IT LEFT OPEN BEFORE.
1 2 3 4
COULD HE HAVE...
HITCHED A RIDE ON THE ELEVATOR?
THAT'S NUTS.
1 2 3
IT'S STOPPED ON THE FIRST FLOOR RIGHT NOW.
SINCE THIS IS THE TOP FLOOR, THE ONLY PEOPLE GOING DOWN ARE THOSE WHO LIVE ON THIS FLOOR, BUT...
IF HE USED THE ELEVATOR TO GO DOWN, THEN IT'S LIKELY THERE WAS SOMEONE WITH HIM.
WAS HE KIDNAPPED?!
SHUDDER

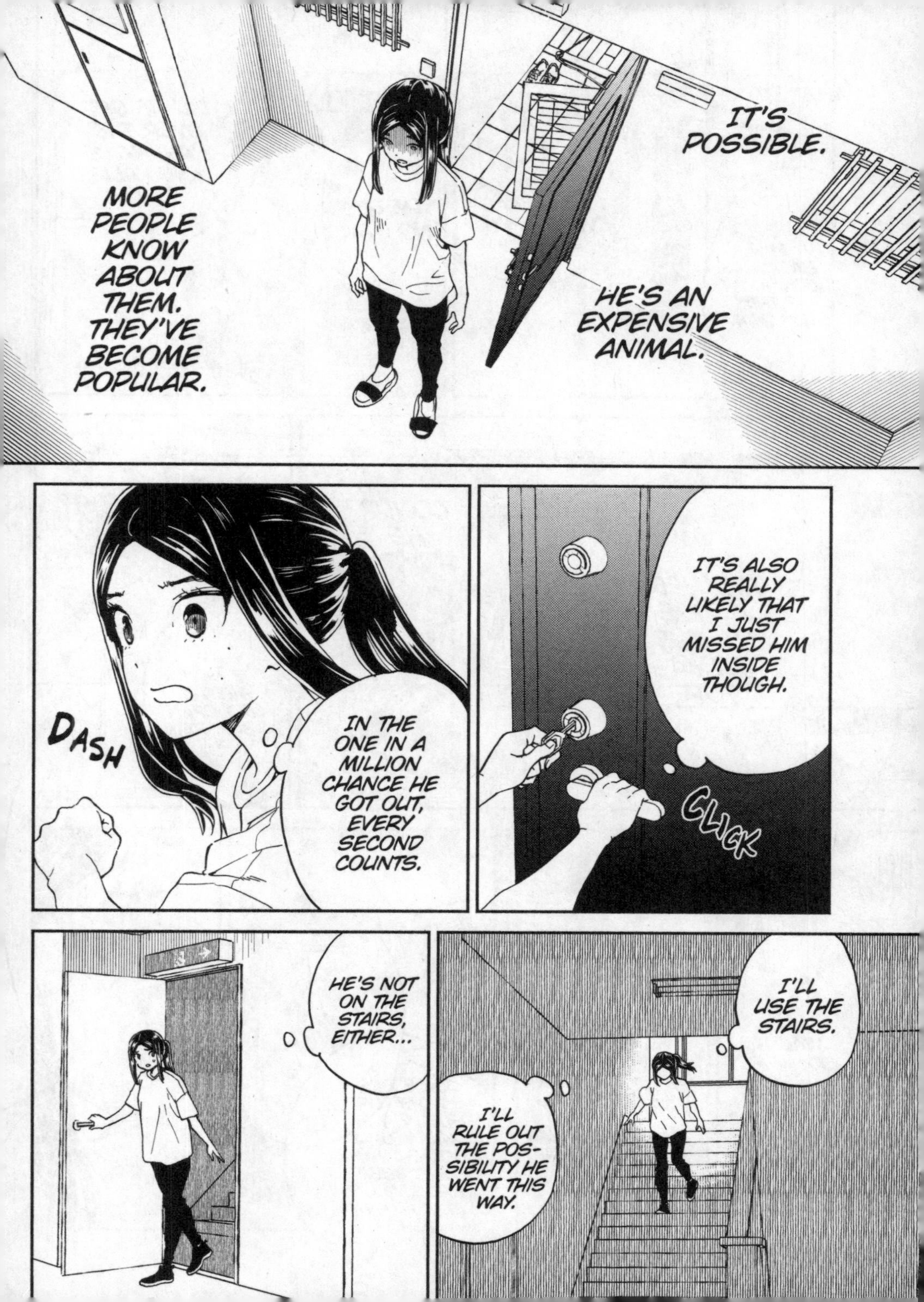
IT'S POSSIBLE.
HE'S AN EXPENSIVE ANIMAL.
MORE PEOPLE KNOW ABOUT THEM. THEY'VE BECOME POPULAR.
IT'S ALSO REALLY LIKELY THAT I JUST MISSED HIM INSIDE THOUGH.
CLICK
IN THE ONE IN A MILLION CHANCE HE GOT OUT, EVERY SECOND COUNTS.
DASH
I'LL USE THE STAIRS.
I'LL RULE OUT THE POS-SIBILITY HE WENT THIS WAY.
HE'S NOT ON THE STAIRS, EITHER...

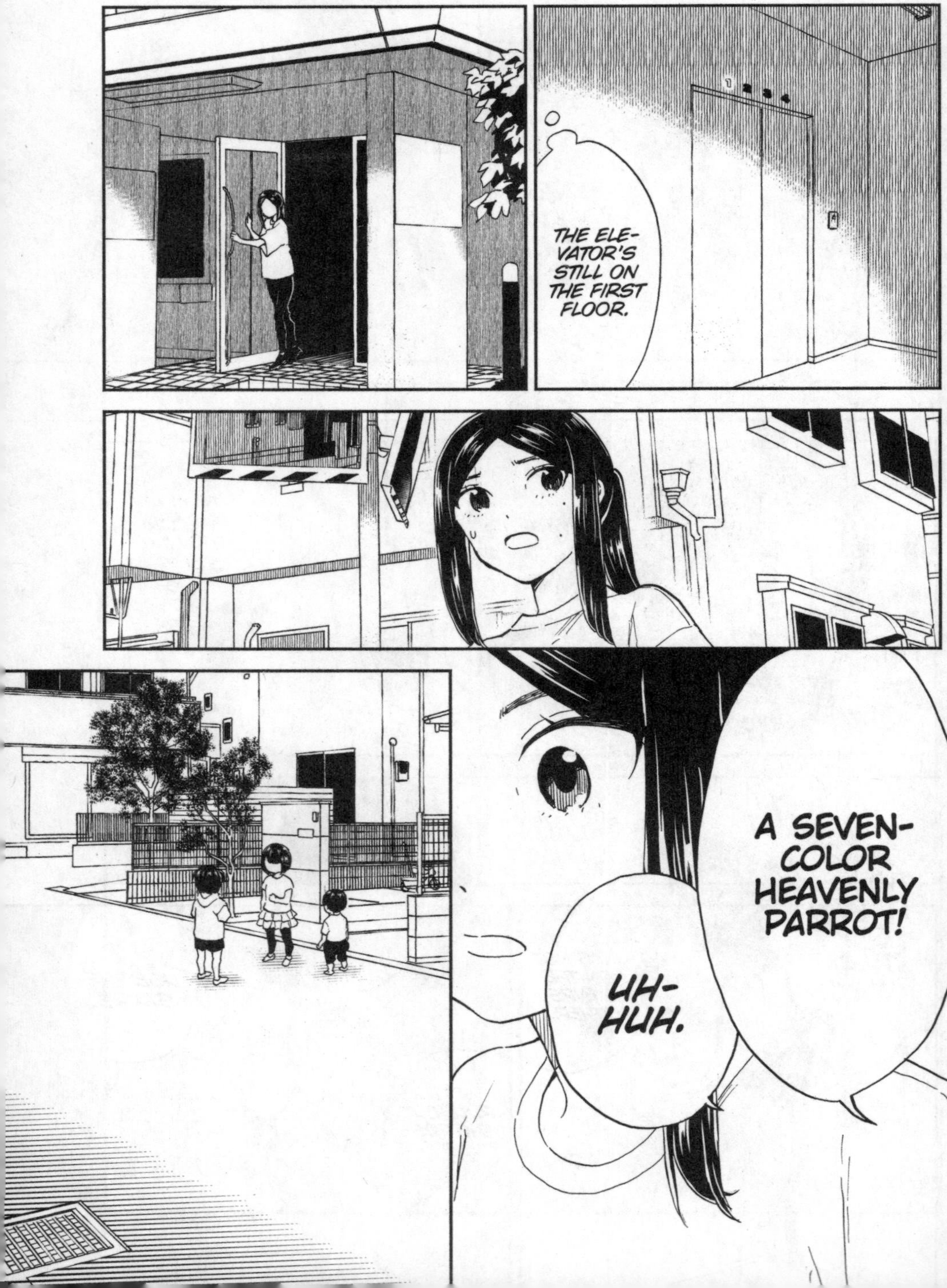
THE ELE-VATOR'S STILL ON THE FIRST FLOOR.
A SEVEN-COLOR HEAVENLY PARROT!
UH-HUH.

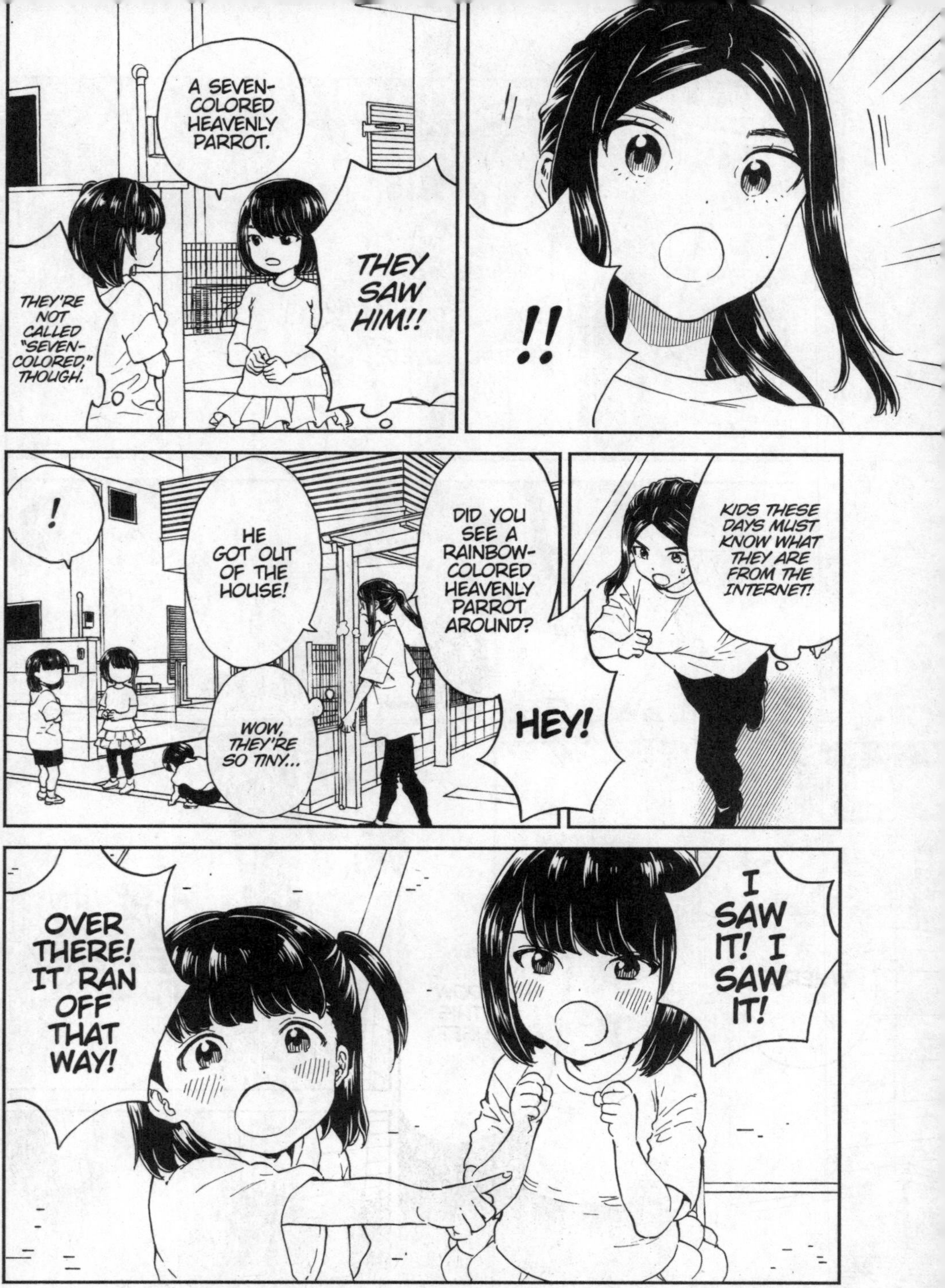
!!
A SEVEN-COLORED HEAVENLY PARROT.
THEY SAW HIM!!
THEY'RE NOT CALLED "SEVEN-COLORED," THOUGH.
KIDS THESE DAYS MUST KNOW WHAT THEY ARE FROM THE INTERNET!
HEY!
DID YOU SEE A RAINBOW-COLORED HEAVENLY PARROT AROUND?
HE GOT OUT OF THE HOUSE!
!
WOW, THEY'RE SO TINY...
I SAW IT! I SAW IT!
OVER THERE! IT RAN OFF THAT WAY!

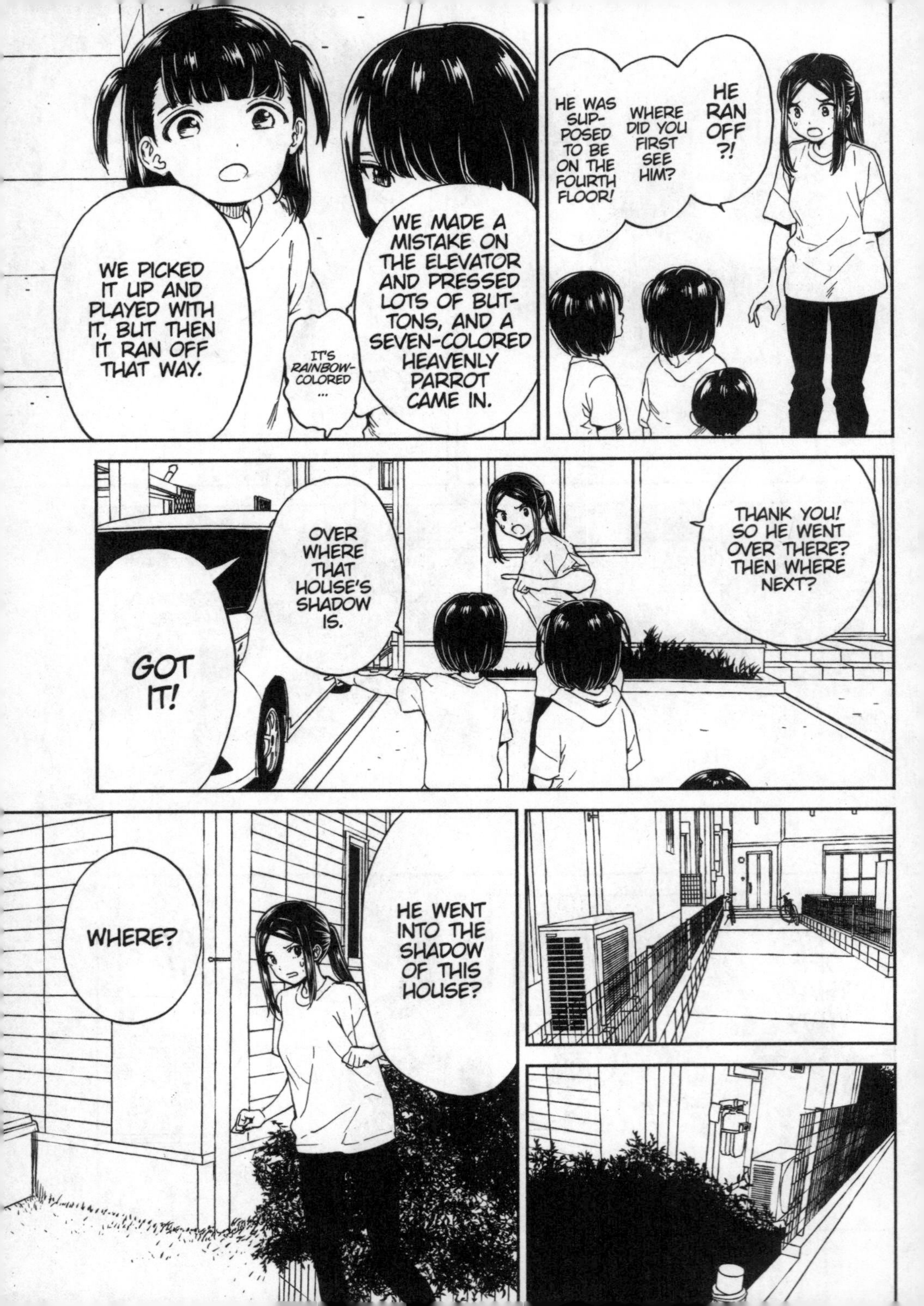
HE RAN OFF ?!
WHERE DID YOU FIRST SEE HIM?
HE WAS SUPPOSED TO BE ON THE FOURTH FLOOR!
WE MADE A MISTAKE ON THE ELEVATOR AND PRESSED LOTS OF BUTTONS, AND A SEVEN-COLORED HEAVENLY PARROT CAME IN.
IT'S RAINBOW-COLORED ...
WE PICKED IT UP AND PLAYED WITH IT, BUT THEN IT RAN OFF THAT WAY.
THANK YOU! SO HE WENT OVER THERE? THEN WHERE NEXT?
OVER WHERE THAT HOUSE'S SHADOW IS.
GOT IT!
HE WENT INTO THE SHADOW OF THIS HOUSE?
WHERE?

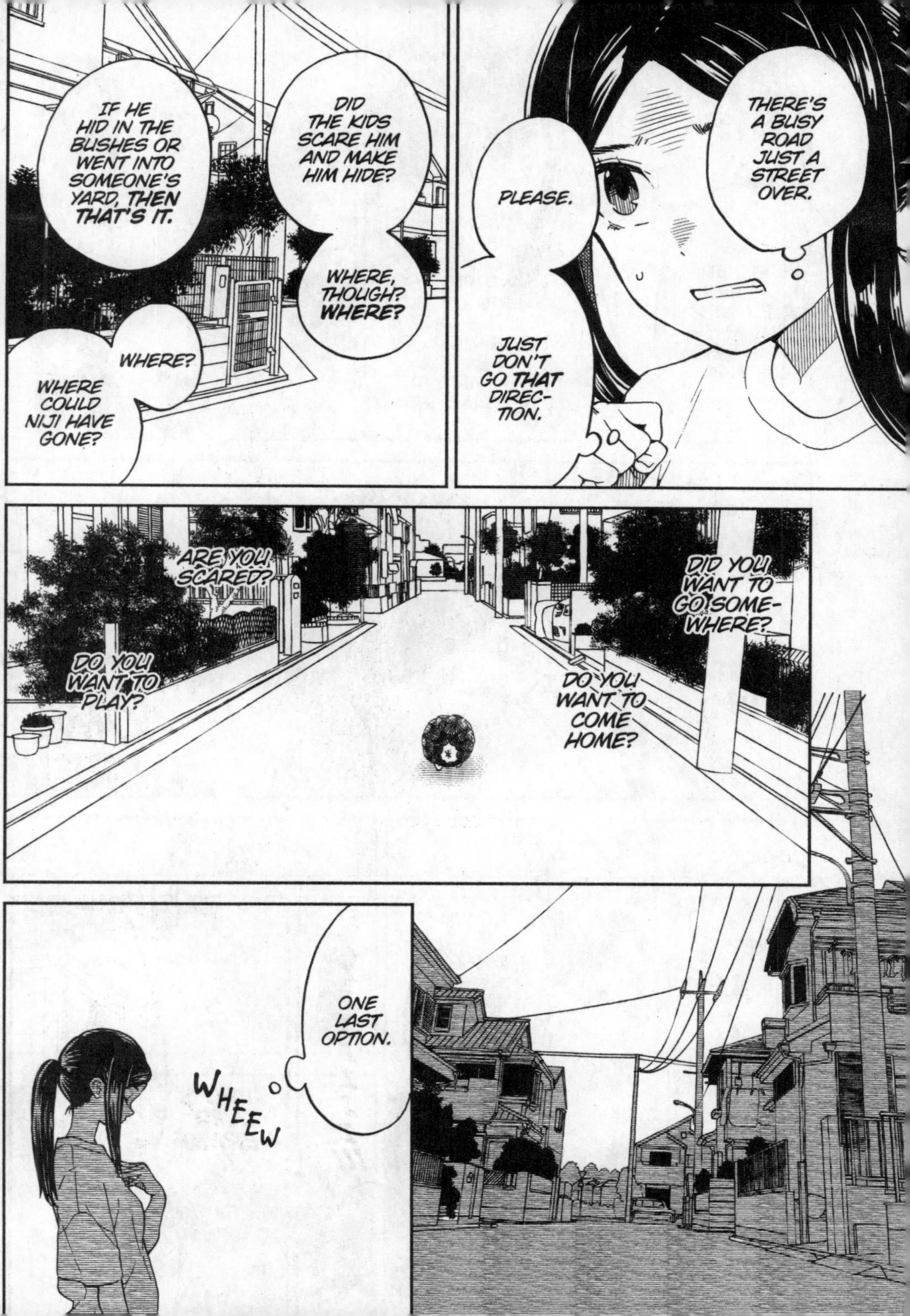
THERE'S A BUSY ROAD JUST A STREET OVER.
PLEASE.
JUST DON'T GO THAT DIRECTION.
DID THE KIDS SCARE HIM AND MAKE HIM HIDE?
WHERE, THOUGH? WHERE?
IF HE HID IN THE BUSHES OR WENT INTO SOMEONE'S YARD, THEN THAT'S IT.
WHERE?
WHERE COULD NIJI HAVE GONE?
DID YOU WANT TO GO SOMEWHERE?
DO YOU WANT TO COME HOME?
ARE YOU SCARED?
DO YOU WANT TO PLAY?
ONE LAST OPTION.
WHEEEW

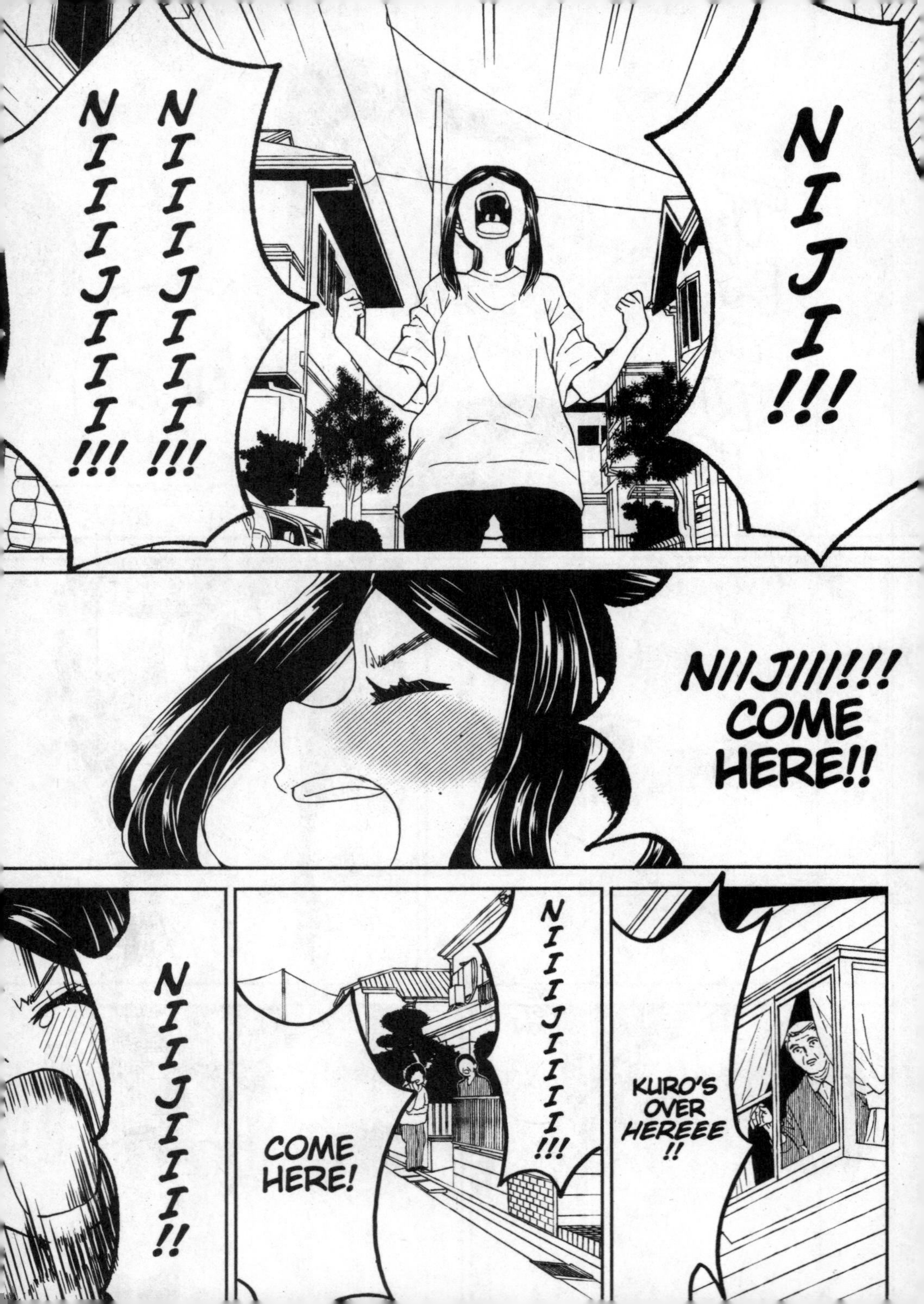
NIJI!!!
NIIIJIII!!!
NIIIJIII!!!
NIIJIIII!!! COME HERE!!
KURO'S OVER HEREEE!!
NIIIJIIII!!!
COME HERE!
NIIJIII!!

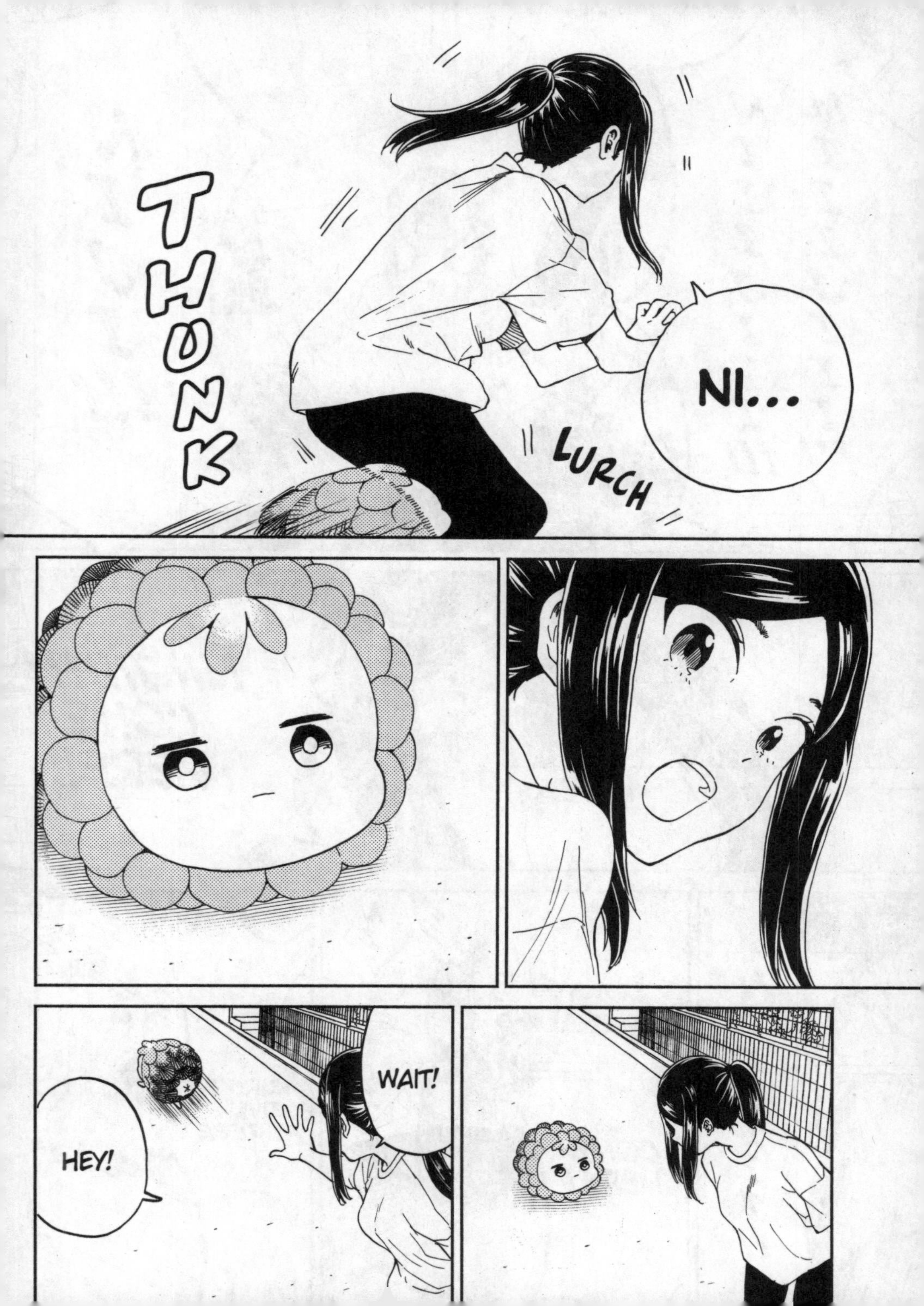
NI...
LURCH
THUNK
WAIT!
HEY!

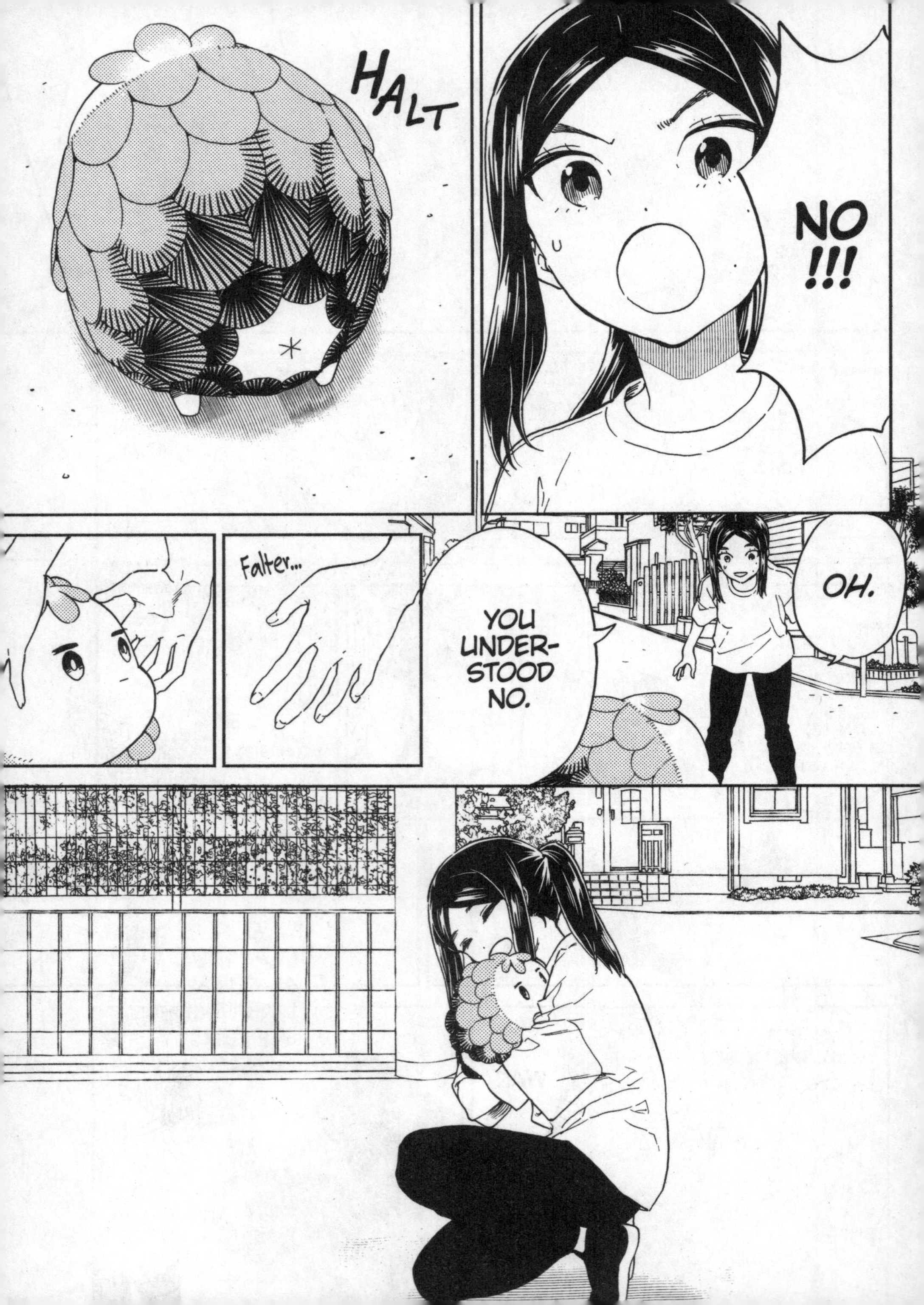
NO !!!
HALT
OH.
YOU UNDER-STOOD NO.
Falter...

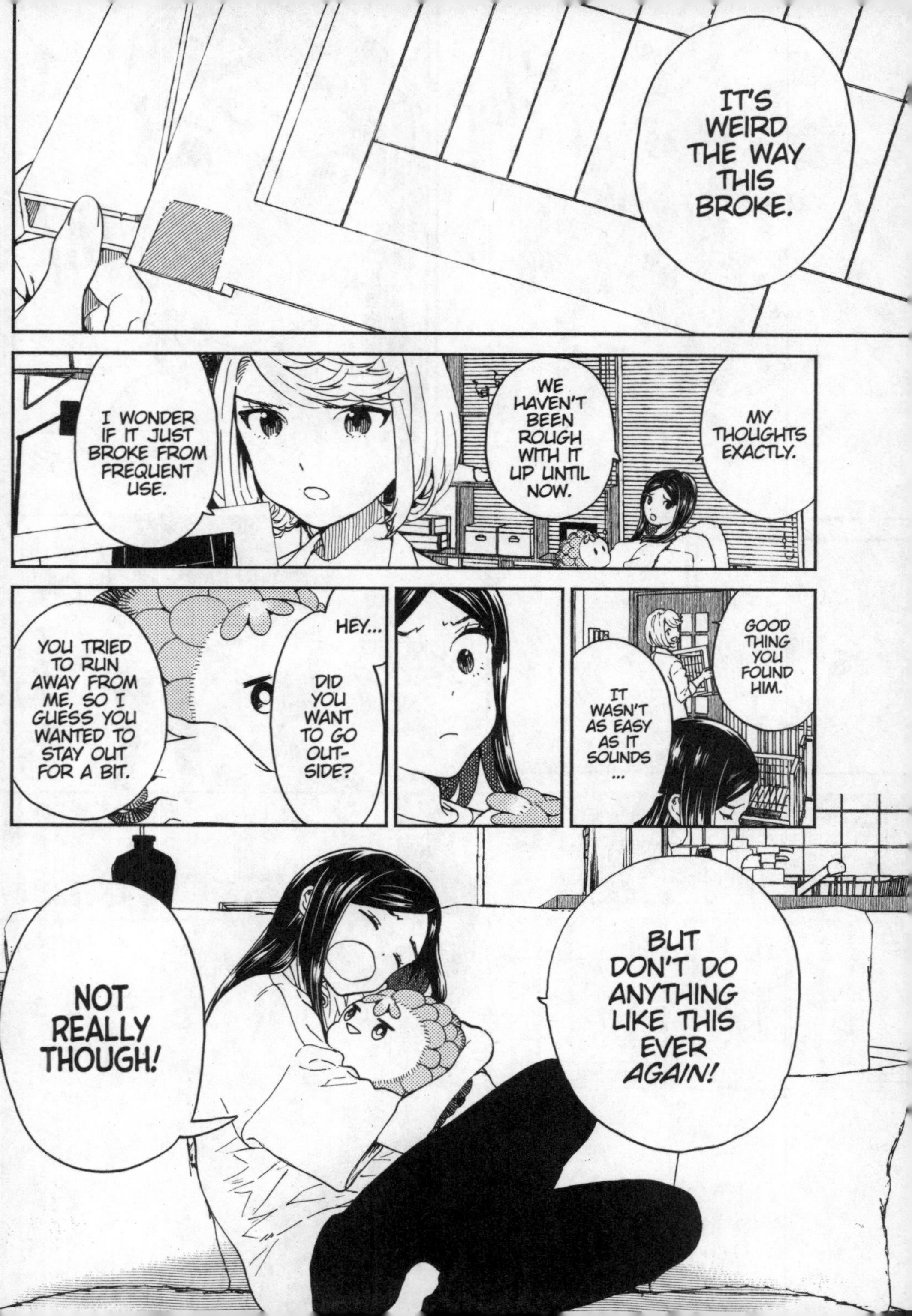
IT'S WEIRD THE WAY THIS BROKE.
MY THOUGHTS EXACTLY.
WE HAVEN'T BEEN ROUGH WITH IT UP UNTIL NOW.
I WONDER IF IT JUST BROKE FROM FREQUENT USE.
GOOD THING YOU FOUND HIM.
IT WASN'T AS EASY AS IT SOUNDS ...
HEY...
DID YOU WANT TO GO OUT-SIDE?
YOU TRIED TO RUN AWAY FROM ME, SO I GUESS YOU WANTED TO STAY OUT FOR A BIT.
BUT DON'T DO ANYTHING LIKE THIS EVER AGAIN!
NOT REALLY THOUGH!

Rainbow and Black

Story & Art by **Eri Takenashi**

NOW LOADING...

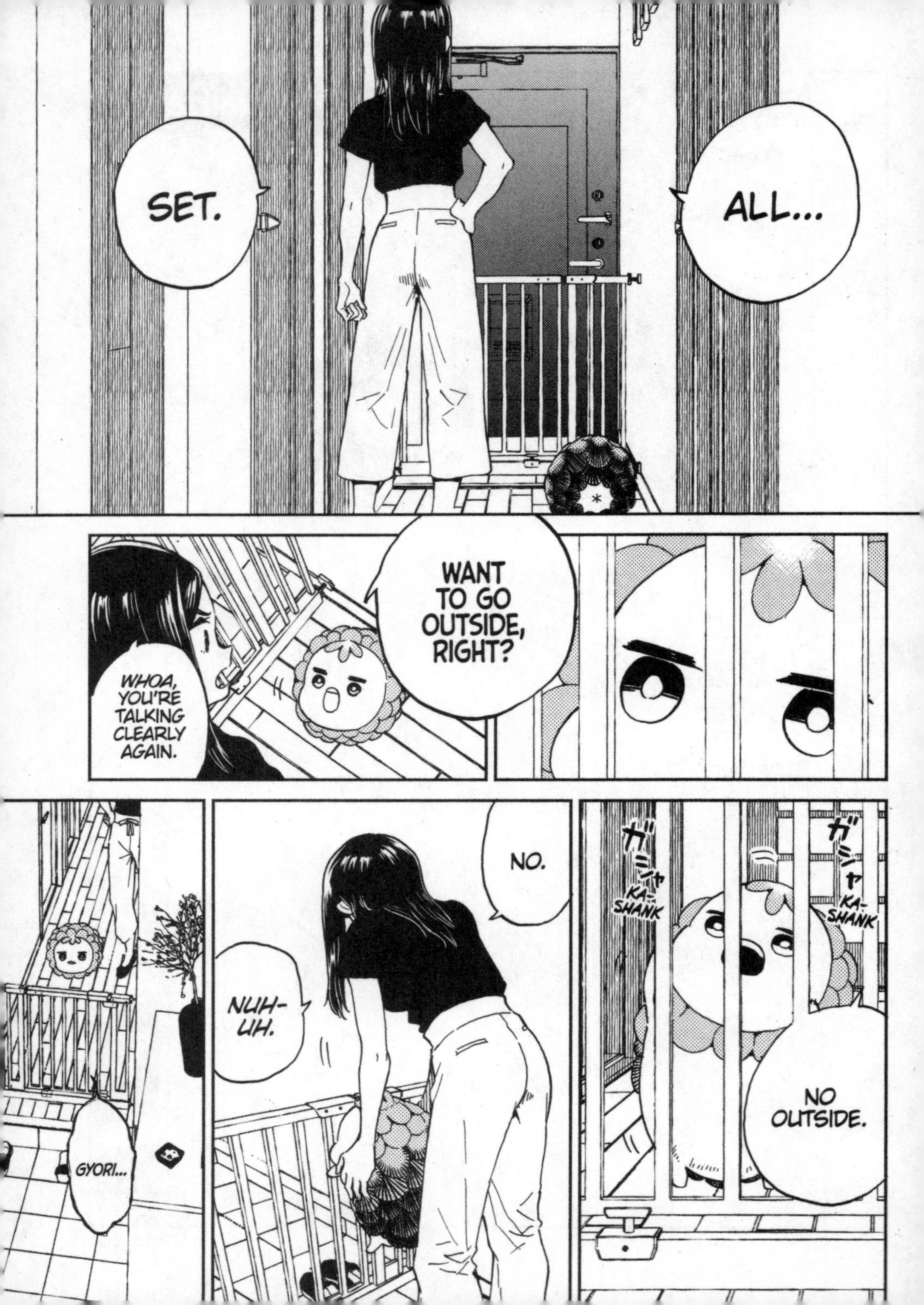
ALL...
SET.
WANT TO GO OUTSIDE, RIGHT?
WHOA, YOU'RE TALKING CLEARLY AGAIN.
ガシャ KA-SHANK
ガシャ KA-SHANK
NO OUTSIDE.
NO.
NUH-UH.
GYORI...

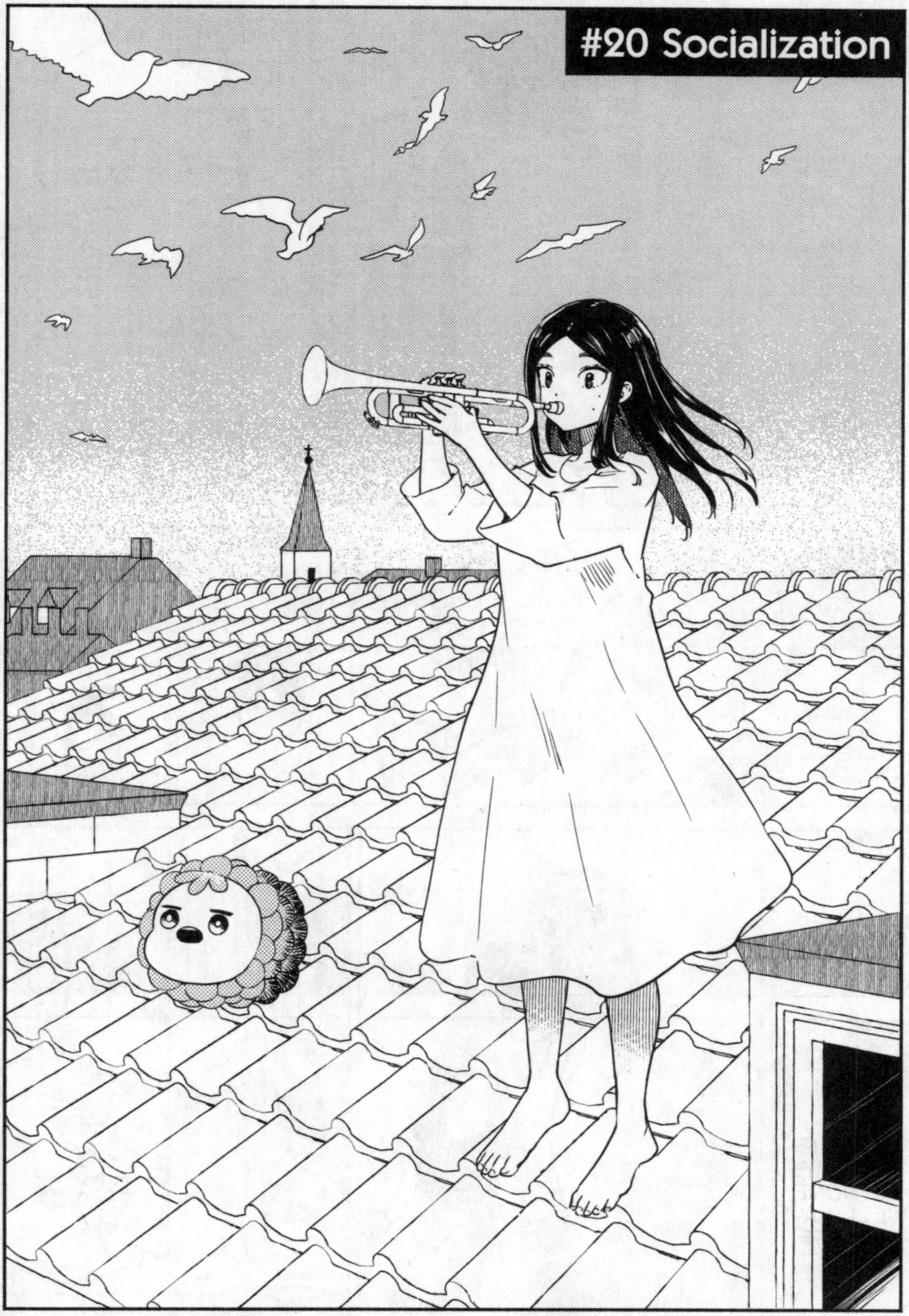
#20 Socialization

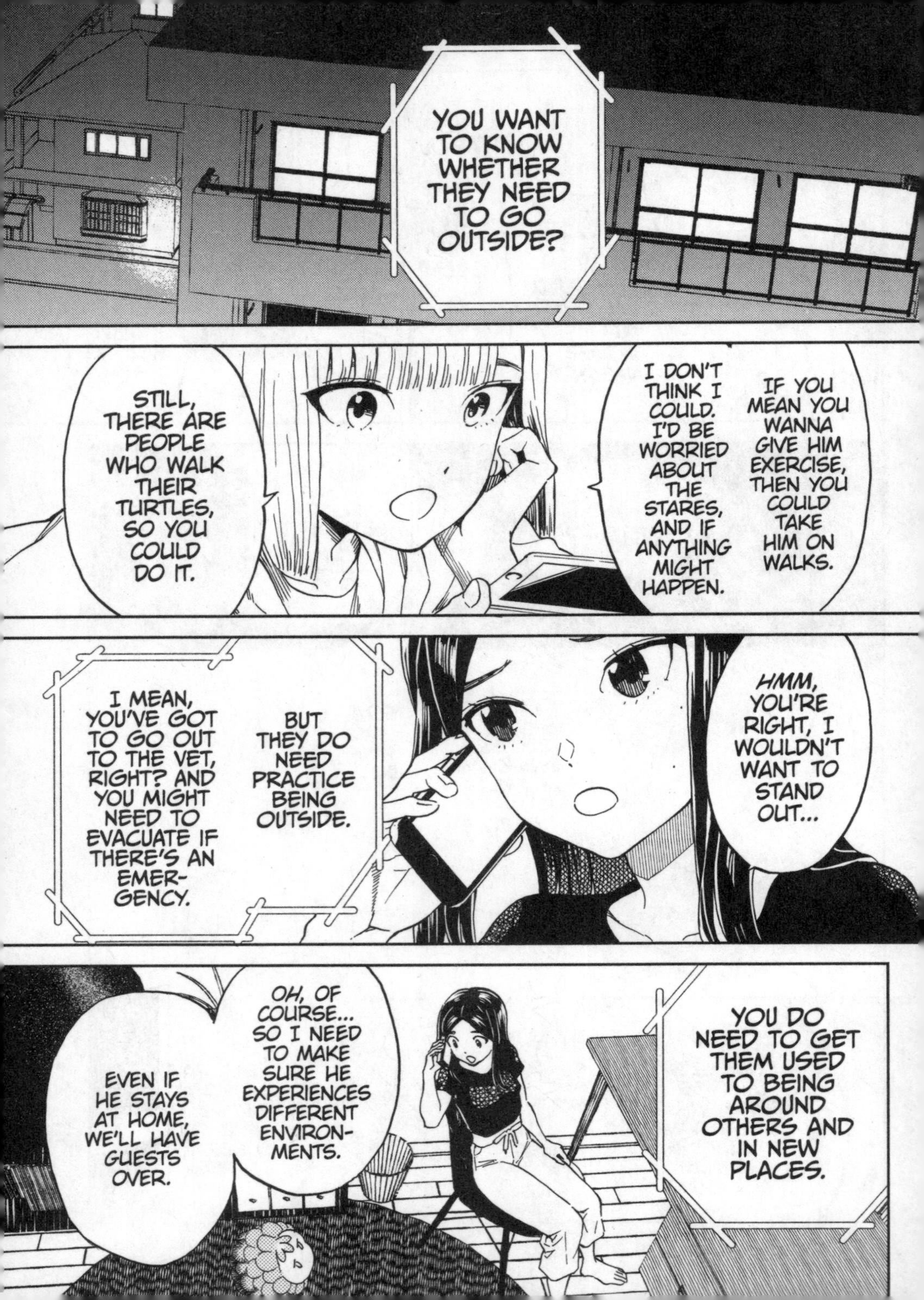
YOU WANT TO KNOW WHETHER THEY NEED TO GO OUTSIDE?
IF YOU MEAN YOU WANNA GIVE HIM EXERCISE, THEN YOU COULD TAKE HIM ON WALKS.
I DON'T THINK I COULD. I'D BE WORRIED ABOUT THE STARES, AND IF ANYTHING MIGHT HAPPEN.
STILL, THERE ARE PEOPLE WHO WALK THEIR TURTLES, SO YOU COULD DO IT.
HMM, YOU'RE RIGHT, I WOULDN'T WANT TO STAND OUT...
BUT THEY DO NEED PRACTICE BEING OUTSIDE.
I MEAN, YOU'VE GOT TO GO OUT TO THE VET, RIGHT? AND YOU MIGHT NEED TO EVACUATE IF THERE'S AN EMER-GENCY.
YOU DO NEED TO GET THEM USED TO BEING AROUND OTHERS AND IN NEW PLACES.
OH, OF COURSE... SO I NEED TO MAKE SURE HE EXPERIENCES DIFFERENT ENVIRON-MENTS.
EVEN IF HE STAYS AT HOME, WE'LL HAVE GUESTS OVER.

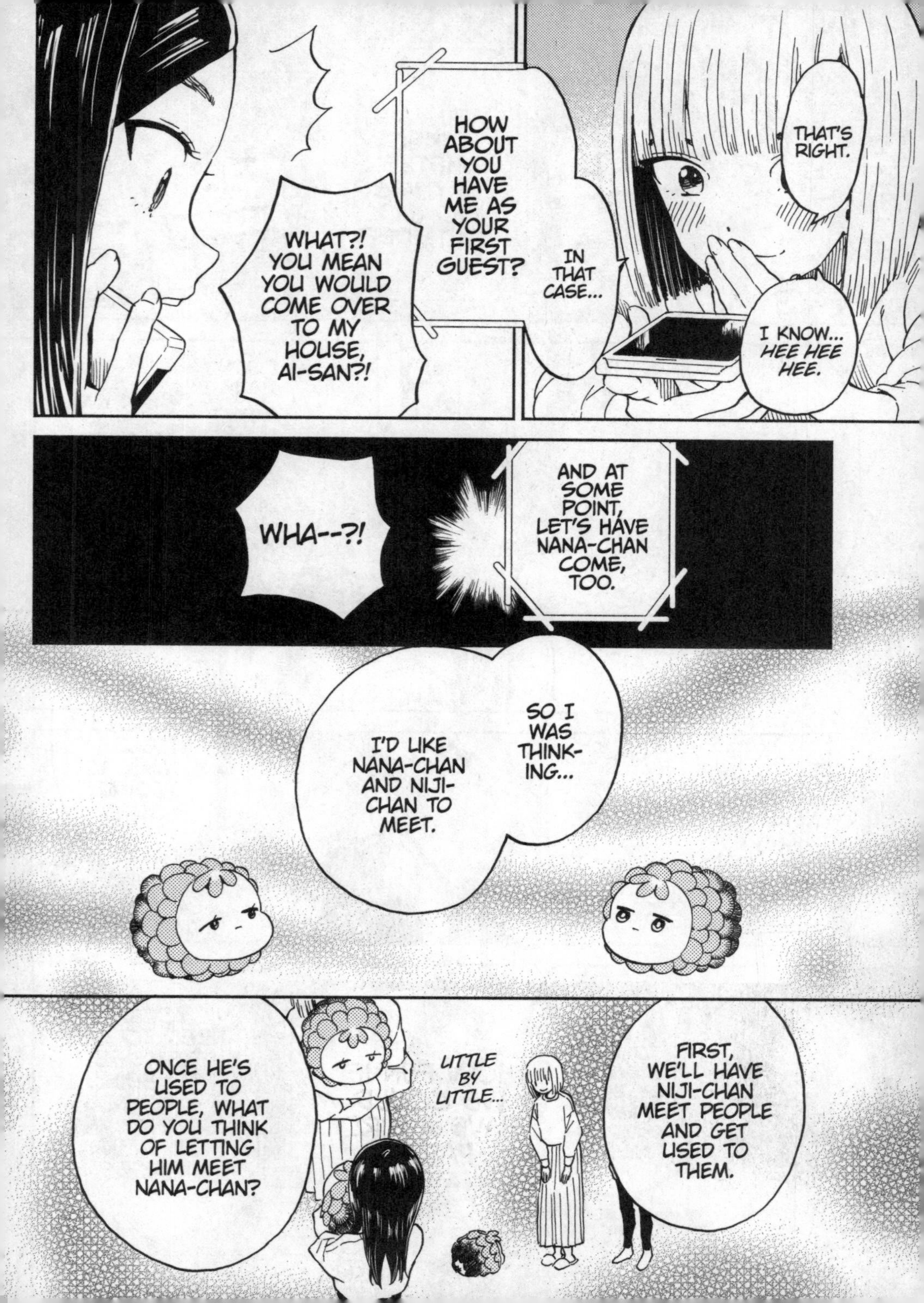
THAT'S RIGHT.
I KNOW... HEE HEE HEE.
IN THAT CASE...
HOW ABOUT YOU HAVE ME AS YOUR FIRST GUEST?
WHAT?! YOU MEAN YOU WOULD COME OVER TO MY HOUSE, AI-SAN?!
AND AT SOME POINT, LET'S HAVE NANA-CHAN COME, TOO.
WHA--?!
SO I WAS THINKING...
I'D LIKE NANA-CHAN AND NIJI-CHAN TO MEET.
FIRST, WE'LL HAVE NIJI-CHAN MEET PEOPLE AND GET USED TO THEM.
LITTLE BY LITTLE...
ONCE HE'S USED TO PEOPLE, WHAT DO YOU THINK OF LETTING HIM MEET NANA-CHAN?

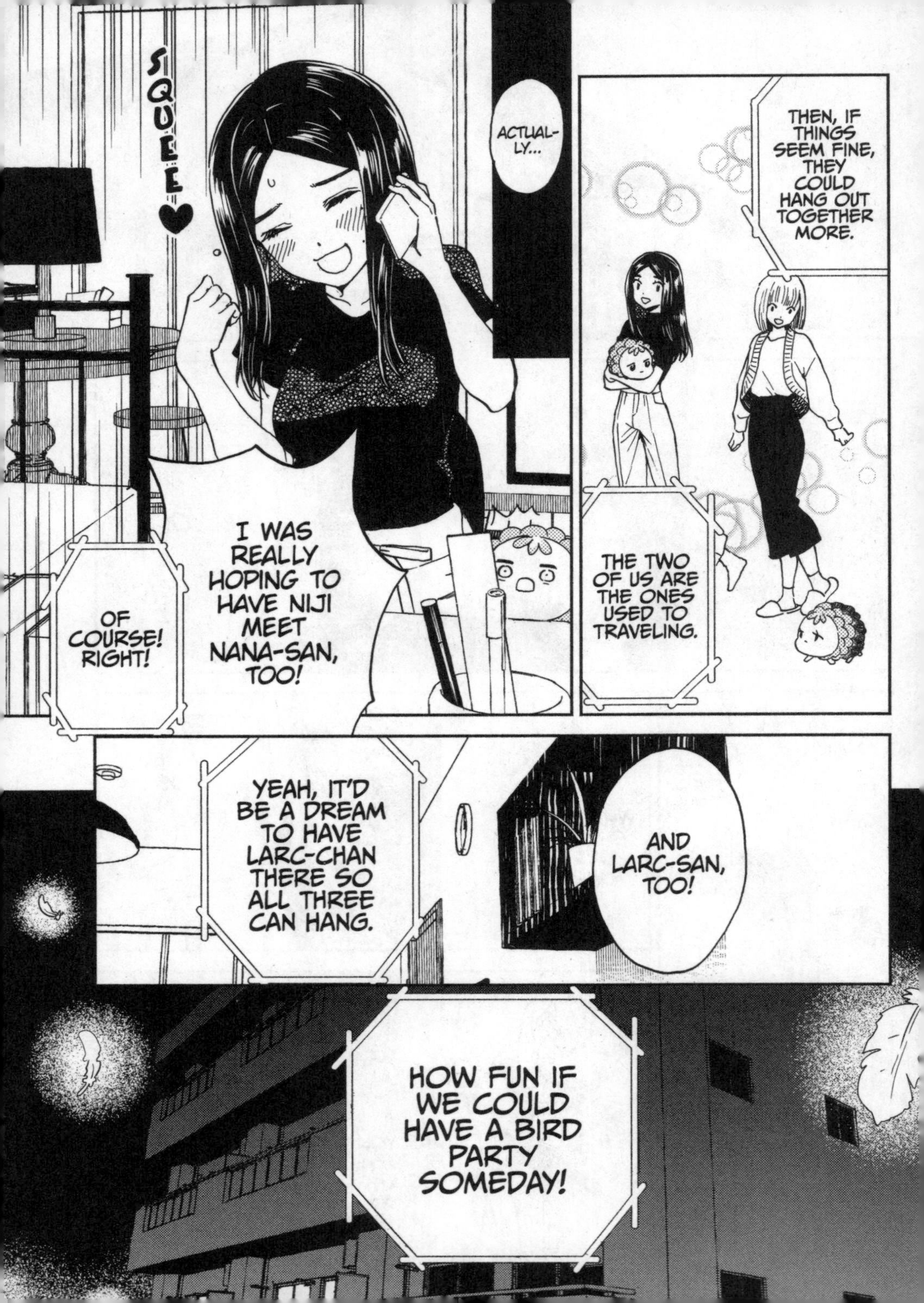
THEN, IF THINGS SEEM FINE, THEY COULD HANG OUT TOGETHER MORE.
THE TWO OF US ARE THE ONES USED TO TRAVELING.
ACTUAL-LY...
SQUEEE♥
I WAS REALLY HOPING TO HAVE NIJI MEET NANA-SAN, TOO!
OF COURSE! RIGHT!
AND LARC-SAN, TOO!
YEAH, IT'D BE A DREAM TO HAVE LARC-CHAN THERE SO ALL THREE CAN HANG.
HOW FUN IF WE COULD HAVE A BIRD PARTY SOMEDAY!

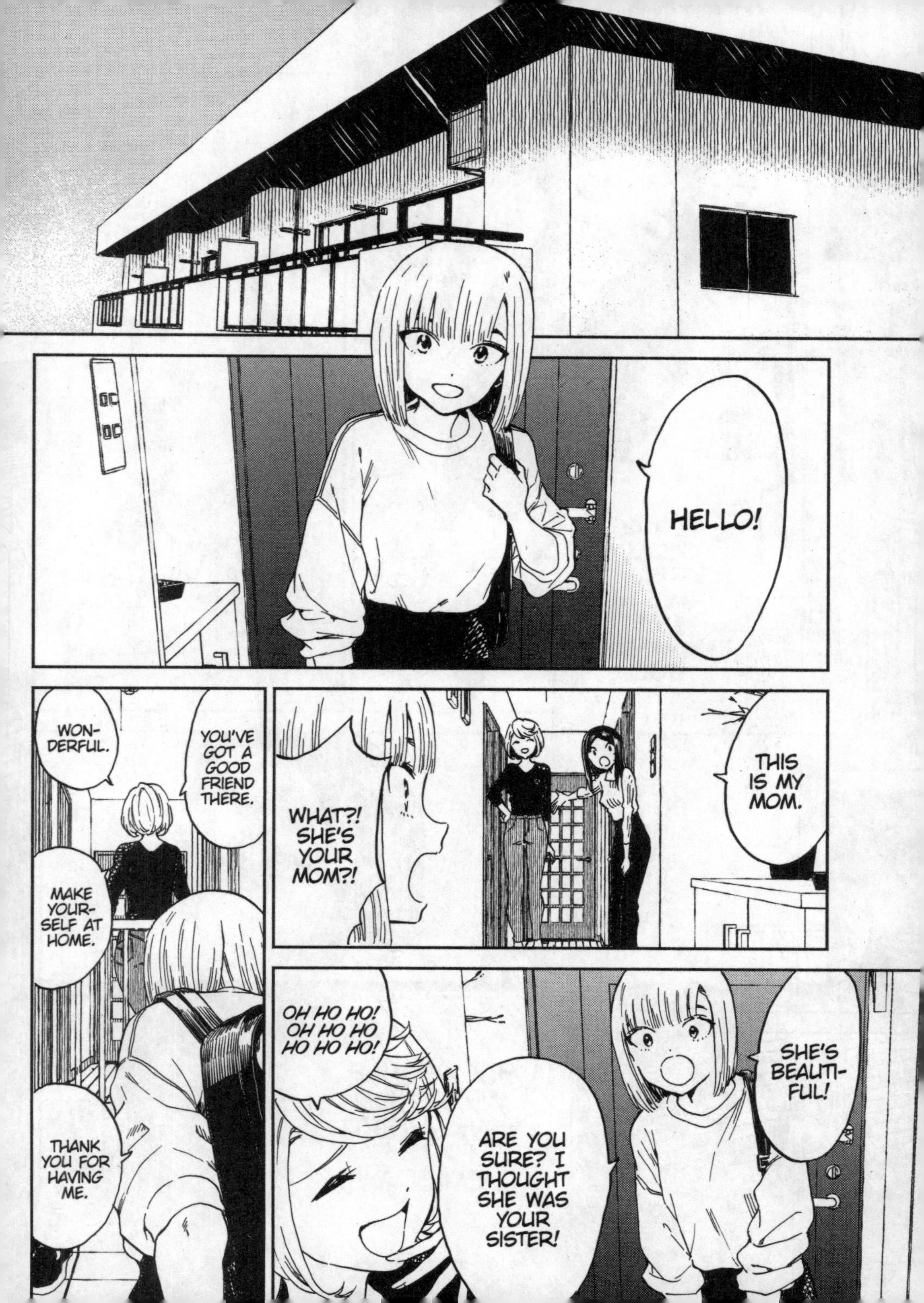
HELLO!
THIS IS MY MOM.
WHAT?! SHE'S YOUR MOM?!
SHE'S BEAUTIFUL!
ARE YOU SURE? I THOUGHT SHE WAS YOUR SISTER!
OH HO HO! OH HO HO HO HO HO!
YOU'VE GOT A GOOD FRIEND THERE.
WON-DERFUL.
MAKE YOUR-SELF AT HOME.
THANK YOU FOR HAVING ME.

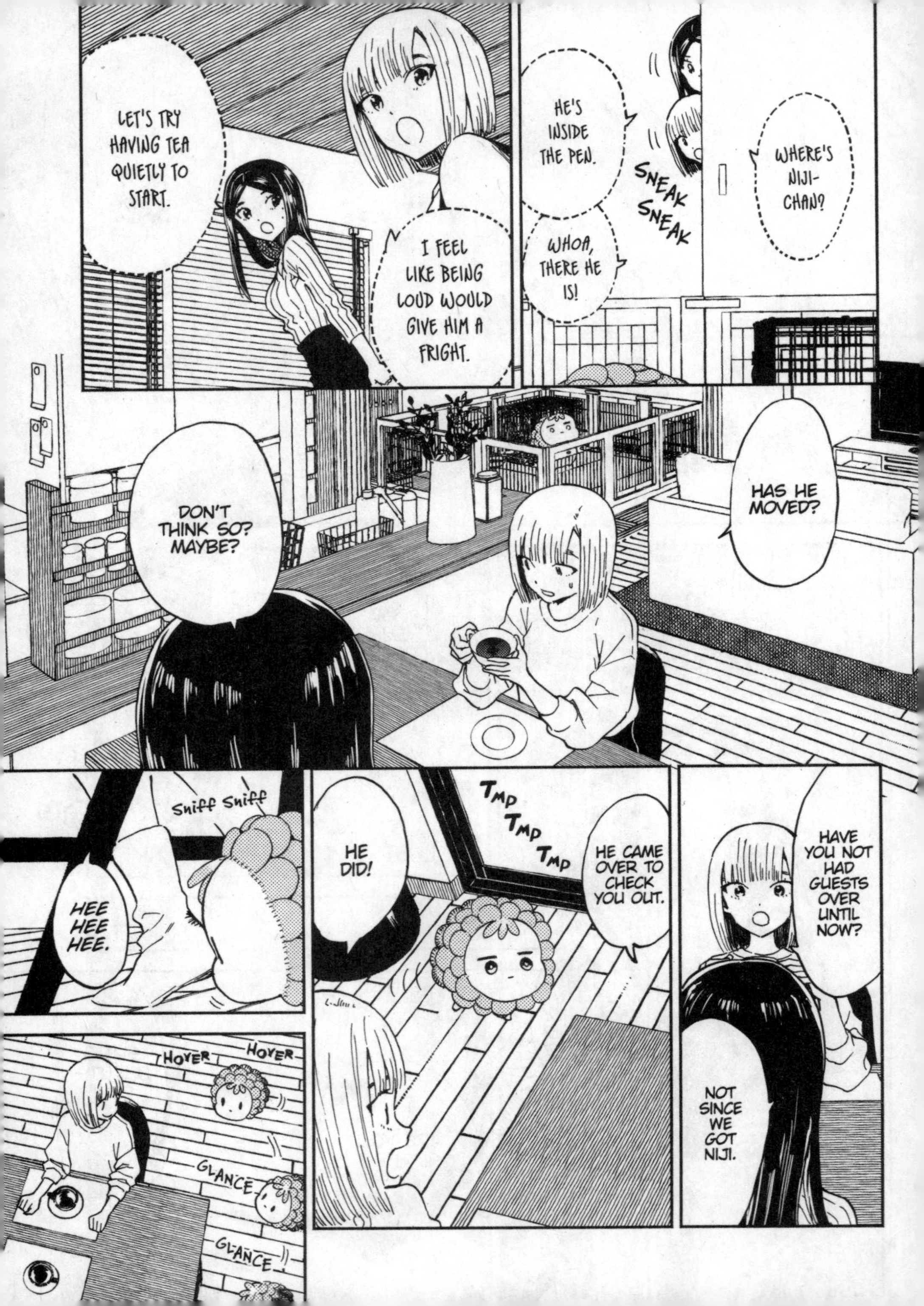
WHERE'S NIJI-CHAN?
SNEAK SNEAK
HE'S INSIDE THE PEN.
WHOA, THERE HE IS!
I FEEL LIKE BEING LOUD WOULD GIVE HIM A FRIGHT.
LET'S TRY HAVING TEA QUIETLY TO START.
HAS HE MOVED?
DON'T THINK SO? MAYBE?
HAVE YOU NOT HAD GUESTS OVER UNTIL NOW?
NOT SINCE WE GOT NIJI.
TMP TMP TMP
HE CAME OVER TO CHECK YOU OUT.
HE DID!
Sniff Sniff
HEE HEE HEE.
HOVER HOVER
GLANCE
GLANCE

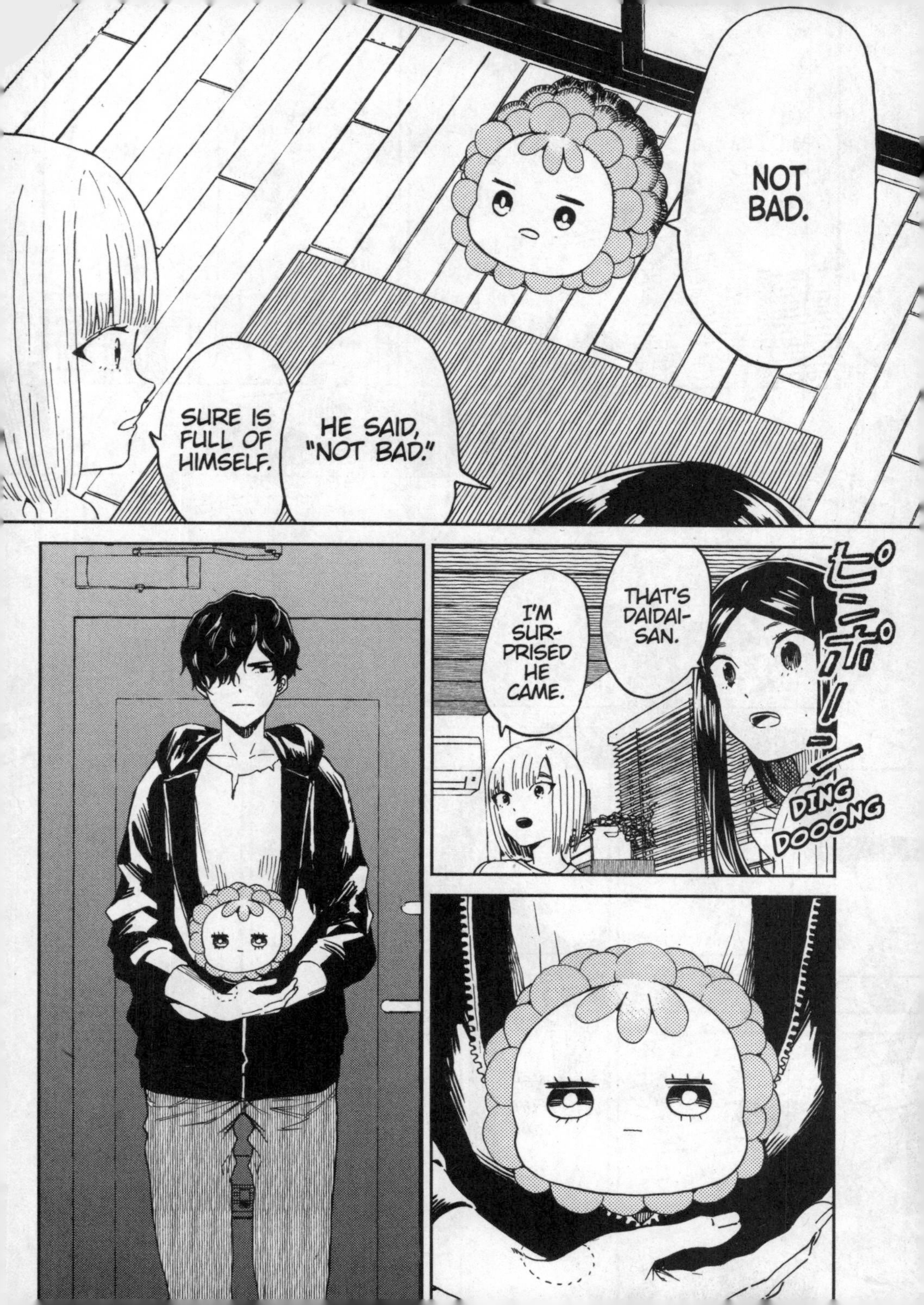

NOT BAD.
HE SAID, "NOT BAD."
SURE IS FULL OF HIMSELF.
DING DOOONG
THAT'S DAIDAI-SAN.
I'M SURPRISED HE CAME.

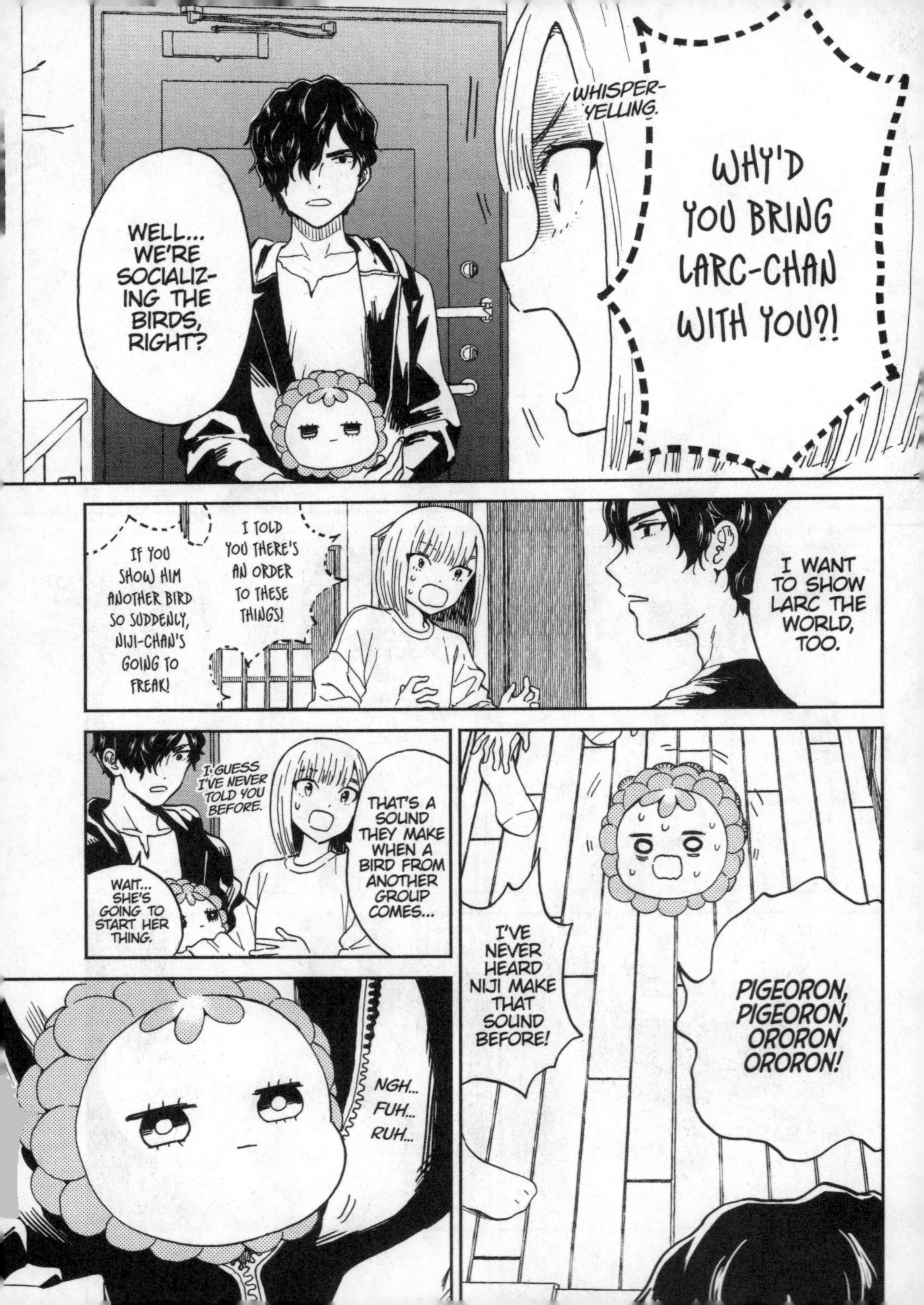
WHISPER-YELLING.
WHY'D YOU BRING LARC-CHAN WITH YOU?!
WELL... WE'RE SOCIALIZING THE BIRDS, RIGHT?
I WANT TO SHOW LARC THE WORLD, TOO.
I TOLD YOU THERE'S AN ORDER TO THESE THINGS!
IF YOU SHOW HIM ANOTHER BIRD SO SUDDENLY, NIJI-CHAN'S GOING TO FREAK!
PIGEORON, PIGEORON, ORORON ORORON!
I'VE NEVER HEARD NIJI MAKE THAT SOUND BEFORE!
THAT'S A SOUND THEY MAKE WHEN A BIRD FROM ANOTHER GROUP COMES...
I GUESS I'VE NEVER TOLD YOU BEFORE.
WAIT... SHE'S GOING TO START HER THING.
NGH... FUH... RUH...

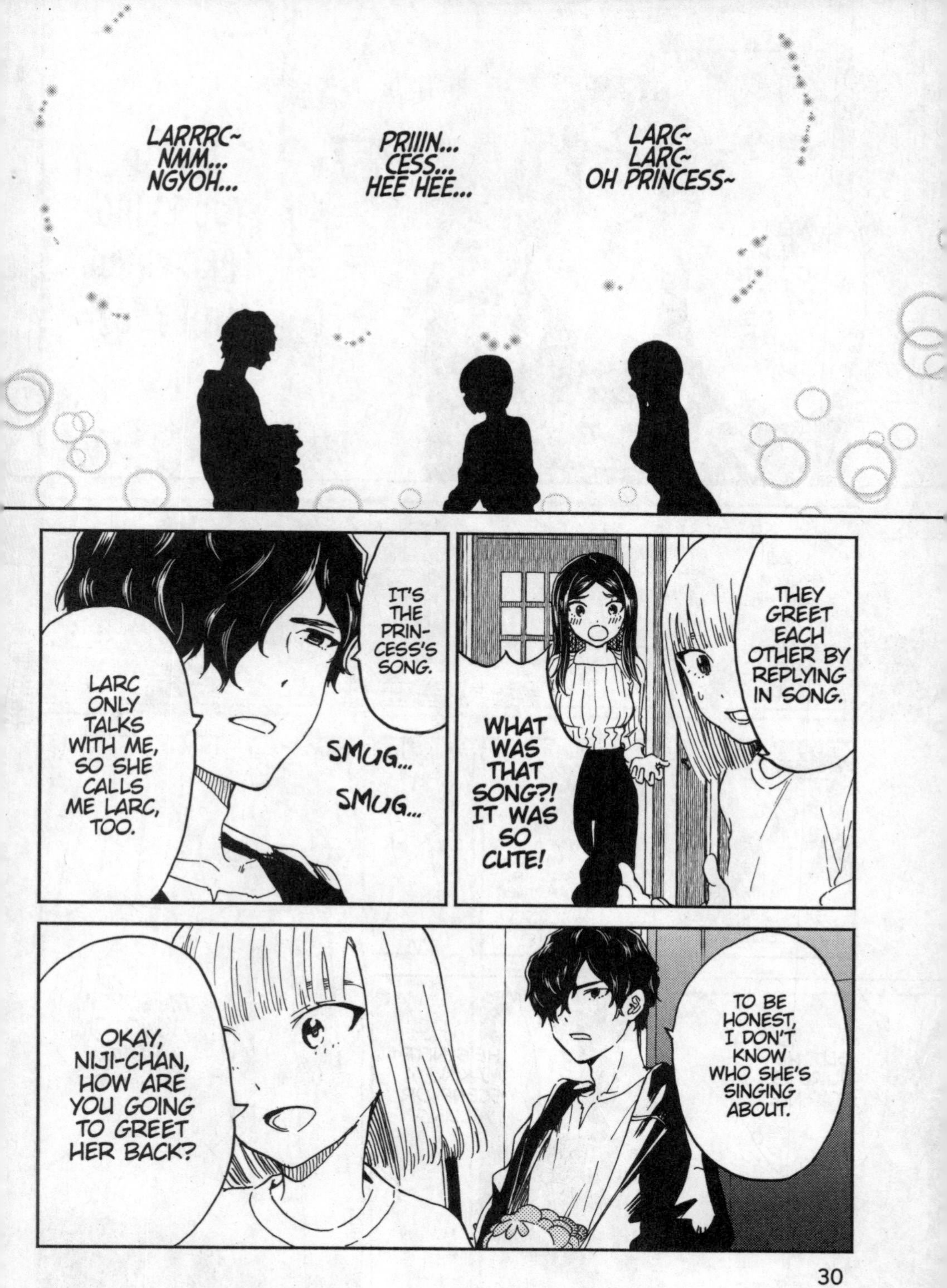
LARC~ LARC~ OH PRINCESS~
PRIIIN... CESS... HEE HEE...
LARRRC~ NMM... NGYOH...
THEY GREET EACH OTHER BY REPLYING IN SONG.
WHAT WAS THAT SONG?! IT WAS SO CUTE!
IT'S THE PRINCESS'S SONG.
SMUG... SMUG...
LARC ONLY TALKS WITH ME, SO SHE CALLS ME LARC, TOO.
TO BE HONEST, I DON'T KNOW WHO SHE'S SINGING ABOUT.
OKAY, NIJI-CHAN, HOW ARE YOU GOING TO GREET HER BACK?

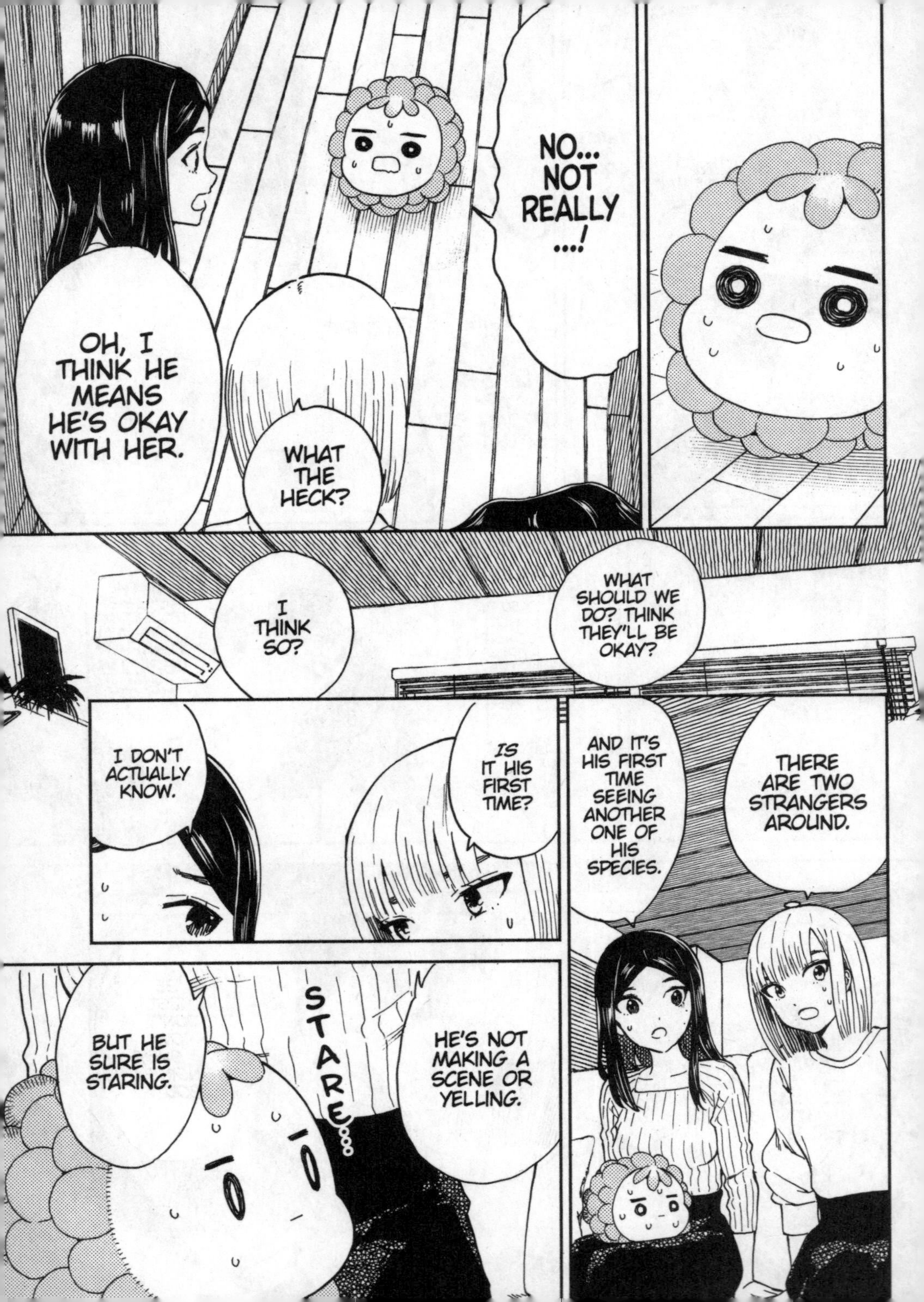
NO... NOT REALLY ...!
WHAT THE HECK?
OH, I THINK HE MEANS HE'S OKAY WITH HER.
WHAT SHOULD WE DO? THINK THEY'LL BE OKAY?
I THINK SO?
THERE ARE TWO STRANGERS AROUND.
AND IT'S HIS FIRST TIME SEEING ANOTHER ONE OF HIS SPECIES.
IS IT HIS FIRST TIME?
I DON'T ACTUALLY KNOW.
HE'S NOT MAKING A SCENE OR YELLING.
STARE...
BUT HE SURE IS STARING.

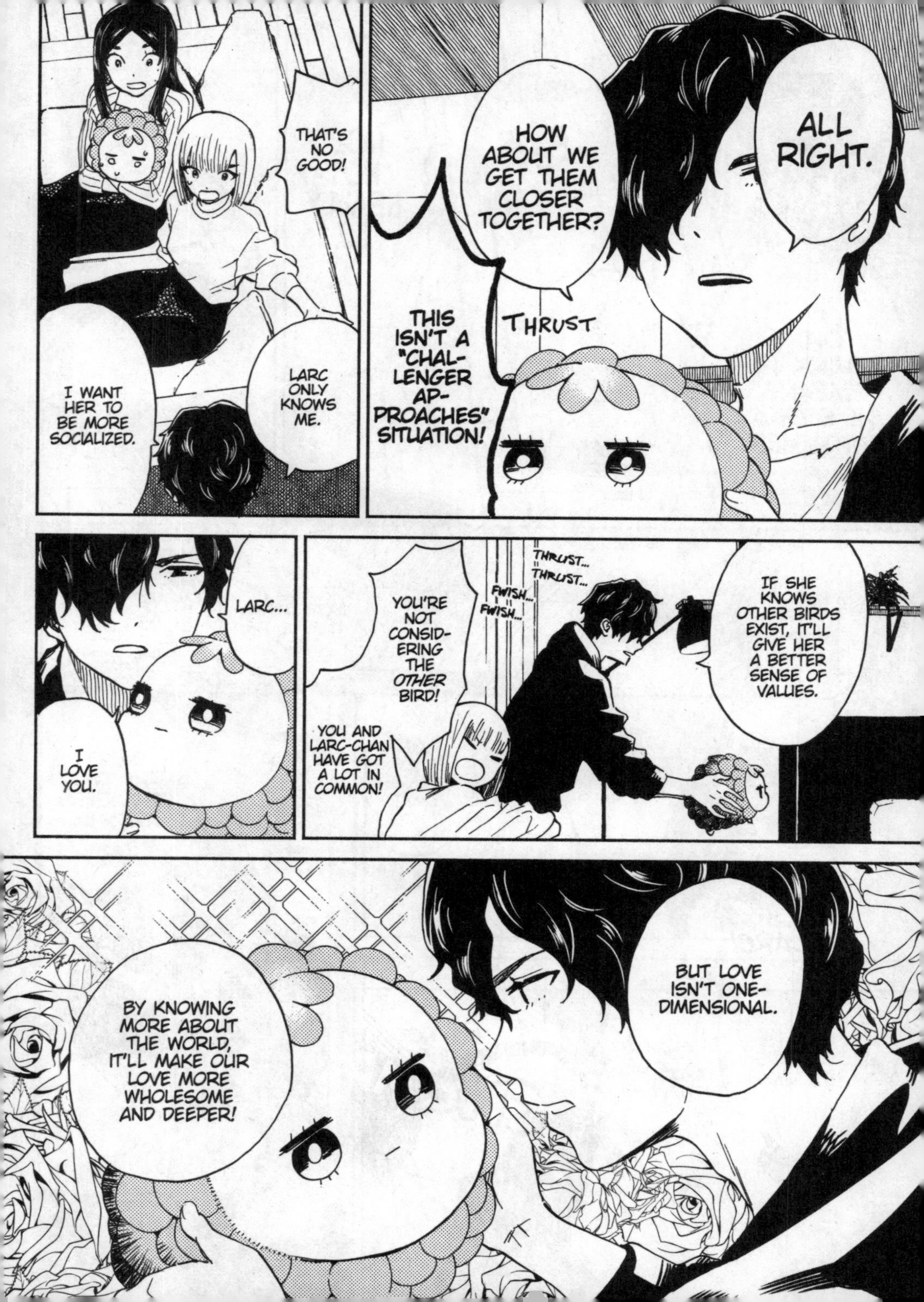
ALL RIGHT.
HOW ABOUT WE GET THEM CLOSER TOGETHER?
THRUST
THIS ISN'T A "CHALLENGER APPROACHES" SITUATION!
THAT'S NO GOOD!
LARC ONLY KNOWS ME.
I WANT HER TO BE MORE SOCIALIZED.
IF SHE KNOWS OTHER BIRDS EXIST, IT'LL GIVE HER A BETTER SENSE OF VALUES.
THRUST... THRUST...
FWISH... FWISH...
YOU'RE NOT CONSIDERING THE *OTHER* BIRD!
YOU AND LARC-CHAN HAVE GOT A LOT IN COMMON!
LARC...
I LOVE YOU.
BUT LOVE ISN'T ONE-DIMENSIONAL.
BY KNOWING MORE ABOUT THE WORLD, IT'LL MAKE OUR LOVE MORE WHOLESOME AND DEEPER!

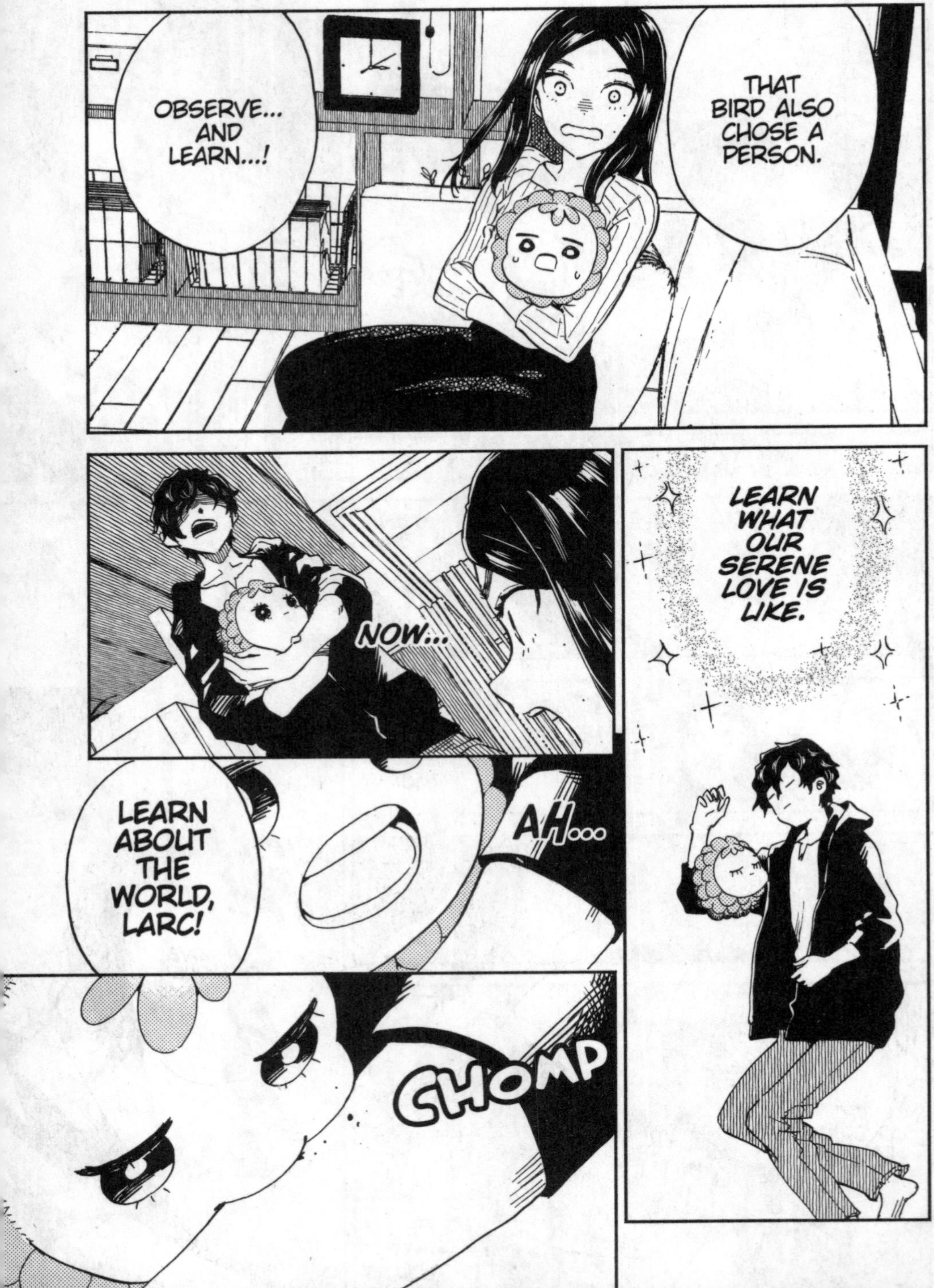
THAT BIRD ALSO CHOSE A PERSON.
OBSERVE... AND LEARN...!
LEARN WHAT OUR SERENE LOVE IS LIKE.
NOW...
AH...
LEARN ABOUT THE WORLD, LARC!
CHOMP

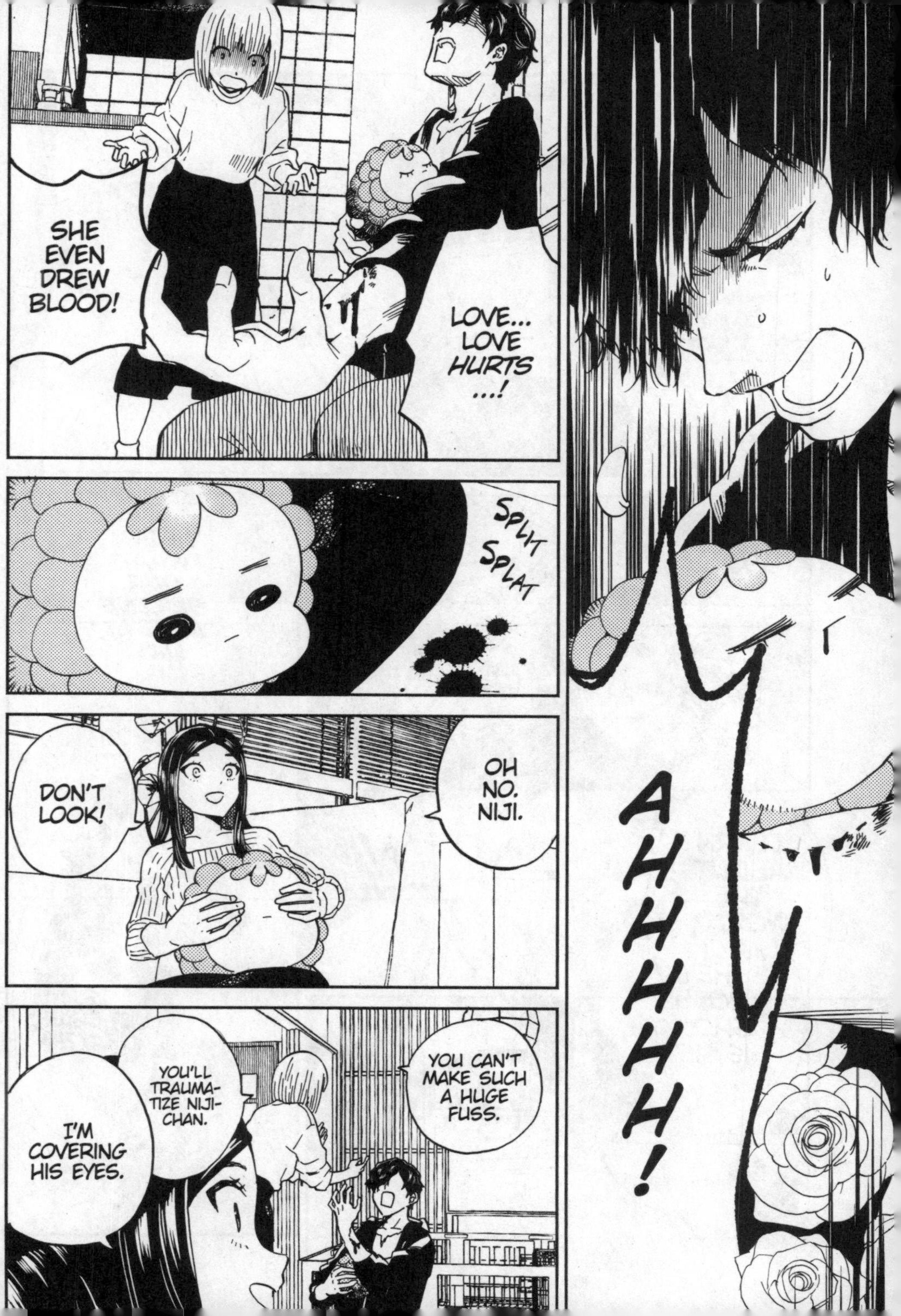
AHHHHH!
SHE EVEN DREW BLOOD!
LOVE... LOVE HURTS ...!
SPLIT SPLAT
OH NO. NIJI.
DON'T LOOK!
YOU CAN'T MAKE SUCH A HUGE FUSS.
YOU'LL TRAUMATIZE NIJI-CHAN.
I'M COVERING HIS EYES.

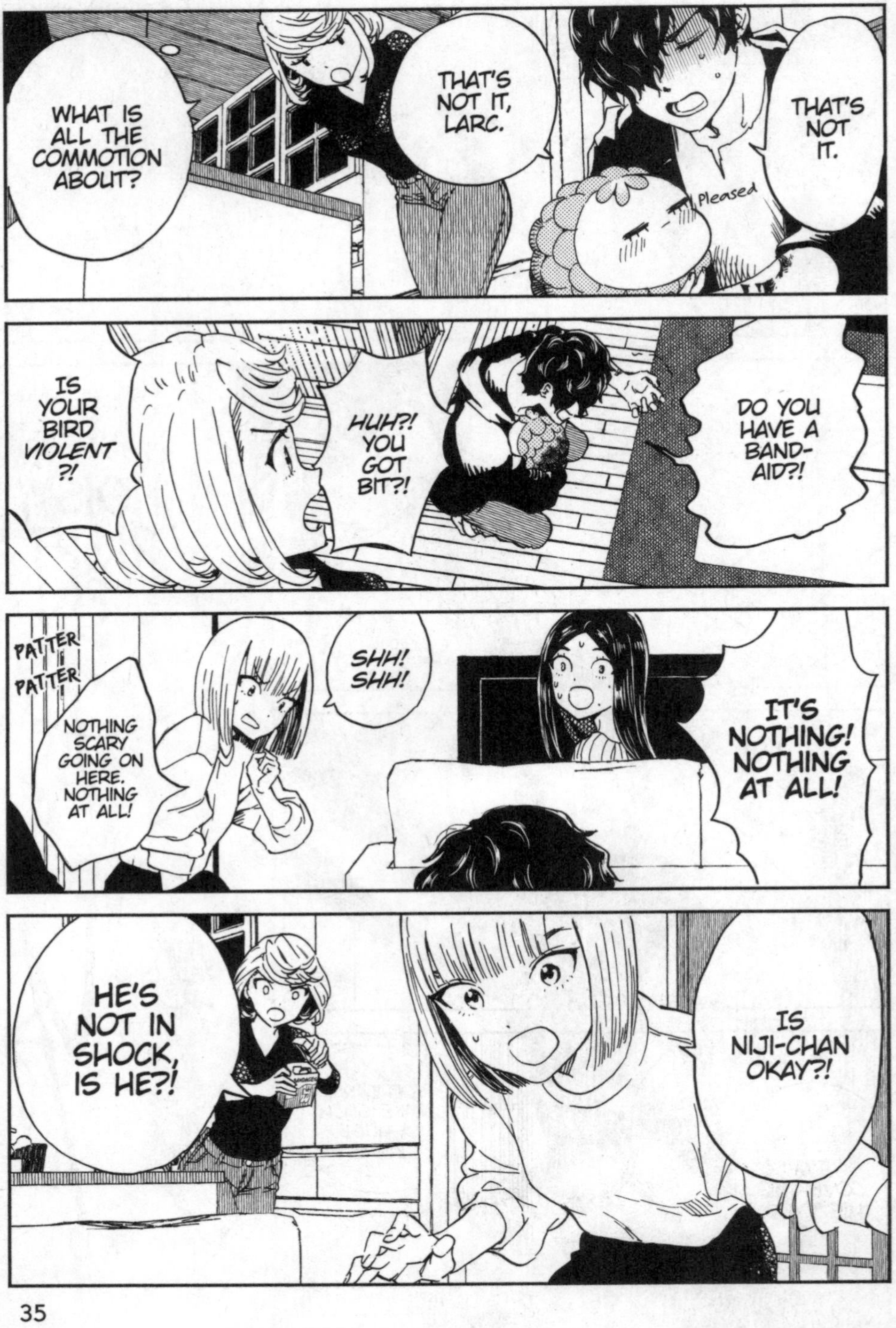
THAT'S NOT IT.
Pleased
THAT'S NOT IT, LARC.
WHAT IS ALL THE COMMOTION ABOUT?
DO YOU HAVE A BAND-AID?!
HUH?! YOU GOT BIT?!
IS YOUR BIRD VIOLENT?!
IT'S NOTHING! NOTHING AT ALL!
SHH! SHH!
PATTER PATTER
NOTHING SCARY GOING ON HERE. NOTHING AT ALL!
IS NIJI-CHAN OKAY?!
HE'S NOT IN SHOCK, IS HE?!

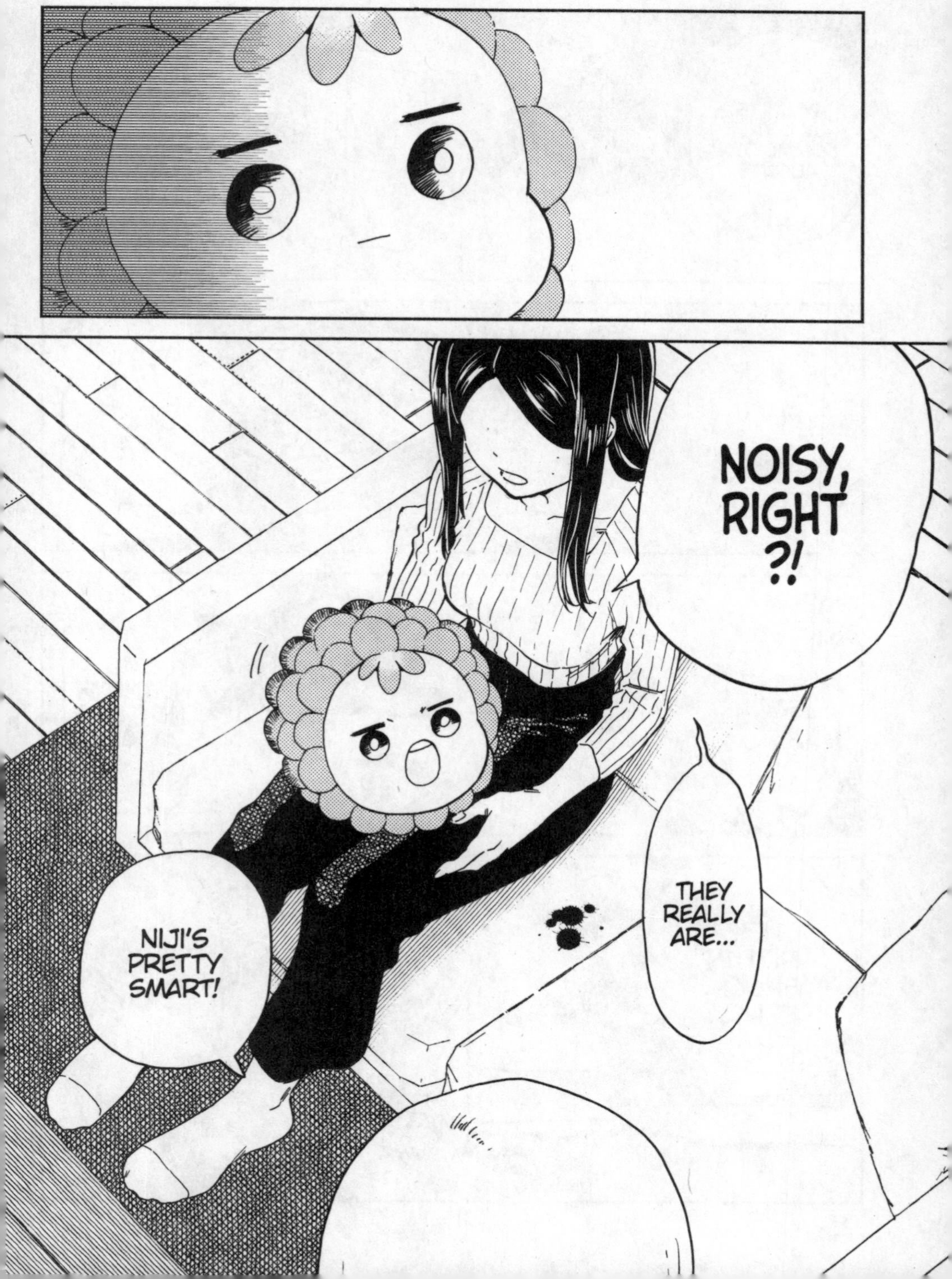
NOISY, RIGHT?!
THEY REALLY ARE...
NIJI'S PRETTY SMART!

Rainbow and Black

Story & Art by Eri Takenashi

NOW LOADING...

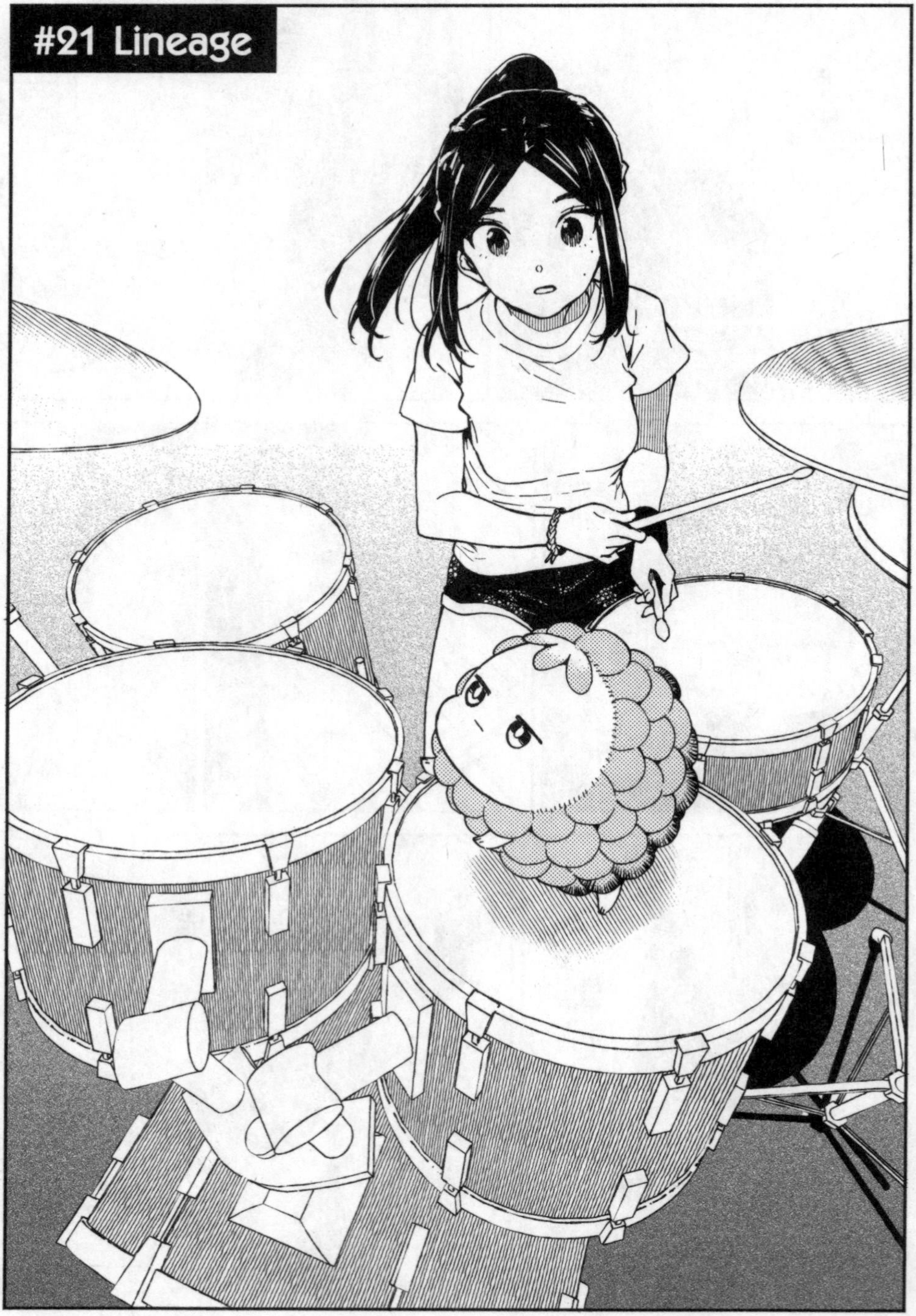
#21 Lineage

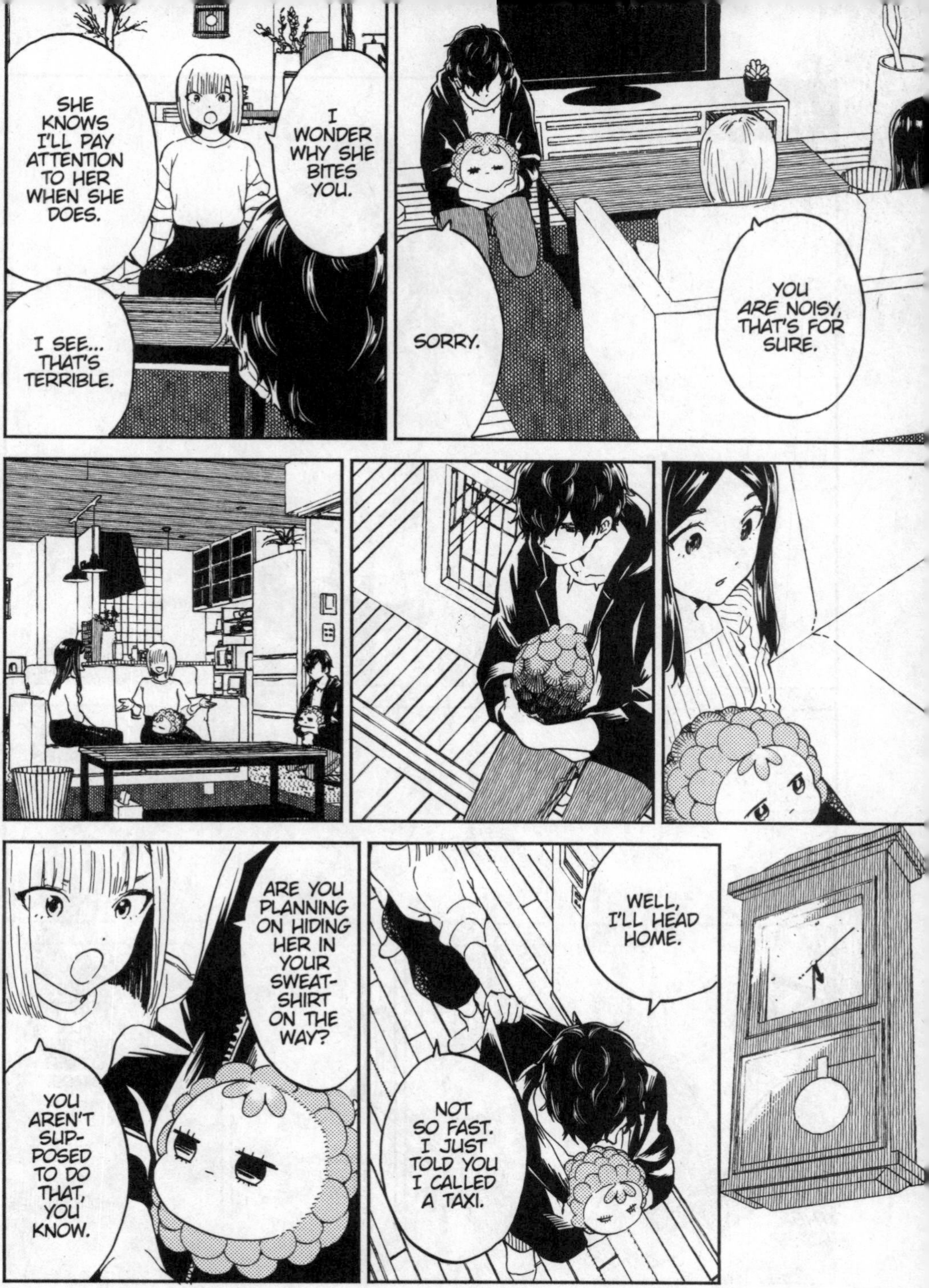
YOU ARE NOISY, THAT'S FOR SURE.
SORRY.
I WONDER WHY SHE BITES YOU.
SHE KNOWS I'LL PAY ATTENTION TO HER WHEN SHE DOES.
I SEE... THAT'S TERRIBLE.
WELL, I'LL HEAD HOME.
NOT SO FAST. I JUST TOLD YOU I CALLED A TAXI.
ARE YOU PLANNING ON HIDING HER IN YOUR SWEATSHIRT ON THE WAY?
YOU AREN'T SUPPOSED TO DO THAT, YOU KNOW.

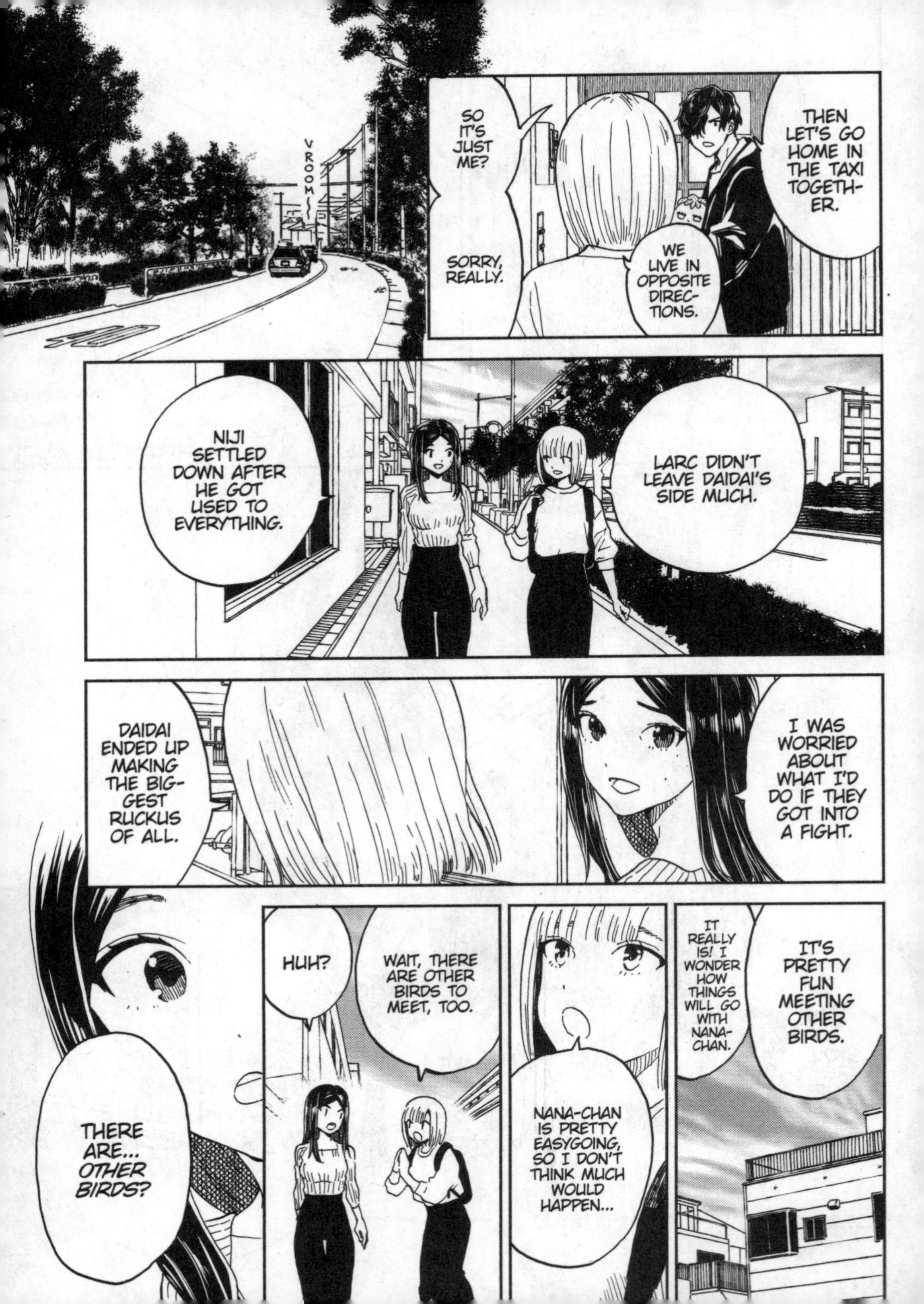
THEN LET'S GO HOME IN THE TAXI TOGETHER.
SO IT'S JUST ME?
WE LIVE IN OPPOSITE DIRECTIONS.
SORRY, REALLY.
VROOM~
LARC DIDN'T LEAVE DAIDAI'S SIDE MUCH.
NIJI SETTLED DOWN AFTER HE GOT USED TO EVERYTHING.
I WAS WORRIED ABOUT WHAT I'D DO IF THEY GOT INTO A FIGHT.
DAIDAI ENDED UP MAKING THE BIGGEST RUCKUS OF ALL.
IT'S PRETTY FUN MEETING OTHER BIRDS.
IT REALLY IS! I WONDER HOW THINGS WILL GO WITH NANA-CHAN.
NANA-CHAN IS PRETTY EASYGOING, SO I DON'T THINK MUCH WOULD HAPPEN...
WAIT, THERE ARE OTHER BIRDS TO MEET, TOO.
HUH?
THERE ARE... *OTHER BIRDS*?

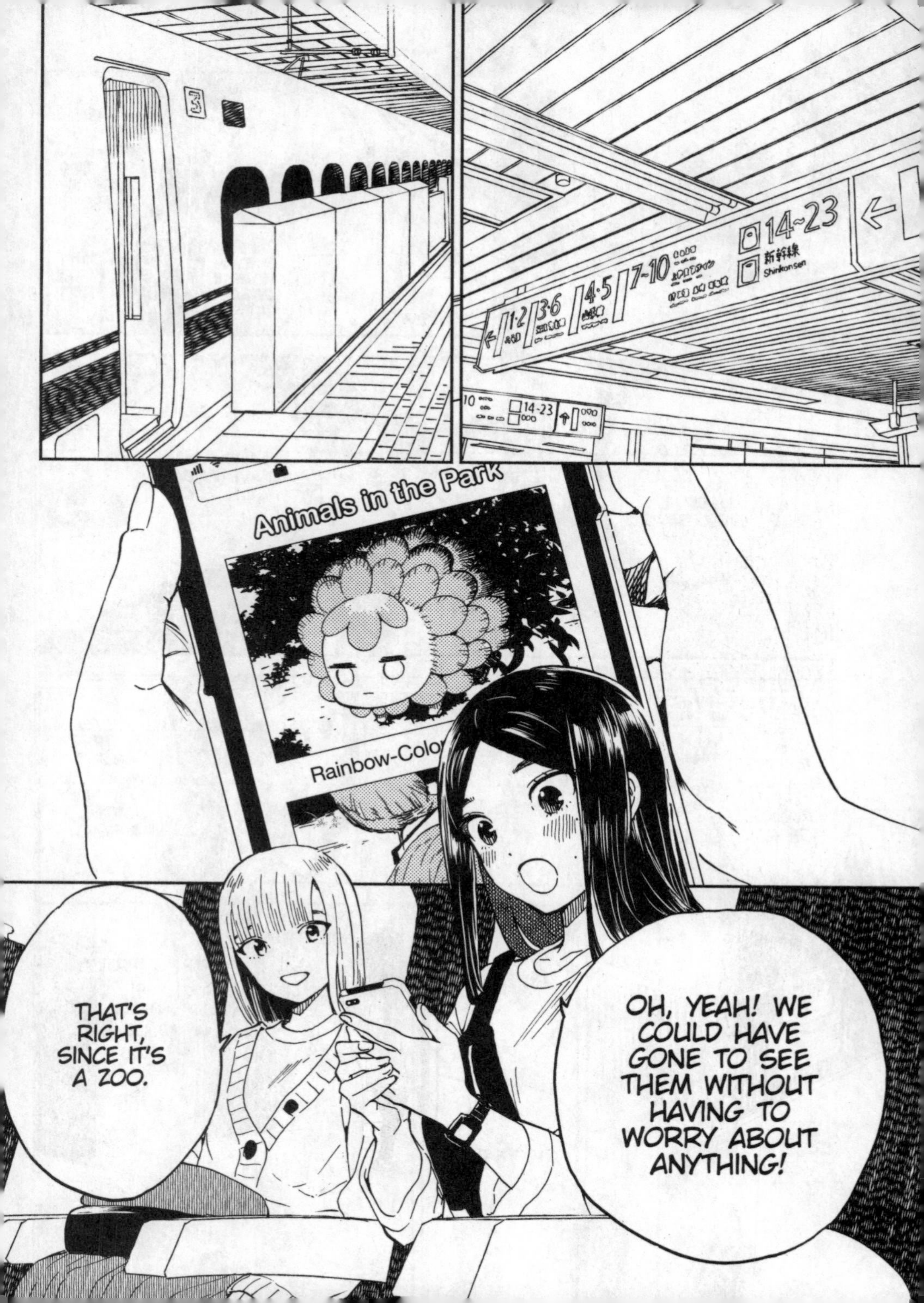
14~23
新幹線
Shinkansen
7-10
4·5
3·6
1·2
14-23
Animals in the Park
Rainbow-Colo
OH, YEAH! WE COULD HAVE GONE TO SEE THEM WITHOUT HAVING TO WORRY ABOUT ANYTHING!
THAT'S RIGHT, SINCE IT'S A ZOO.

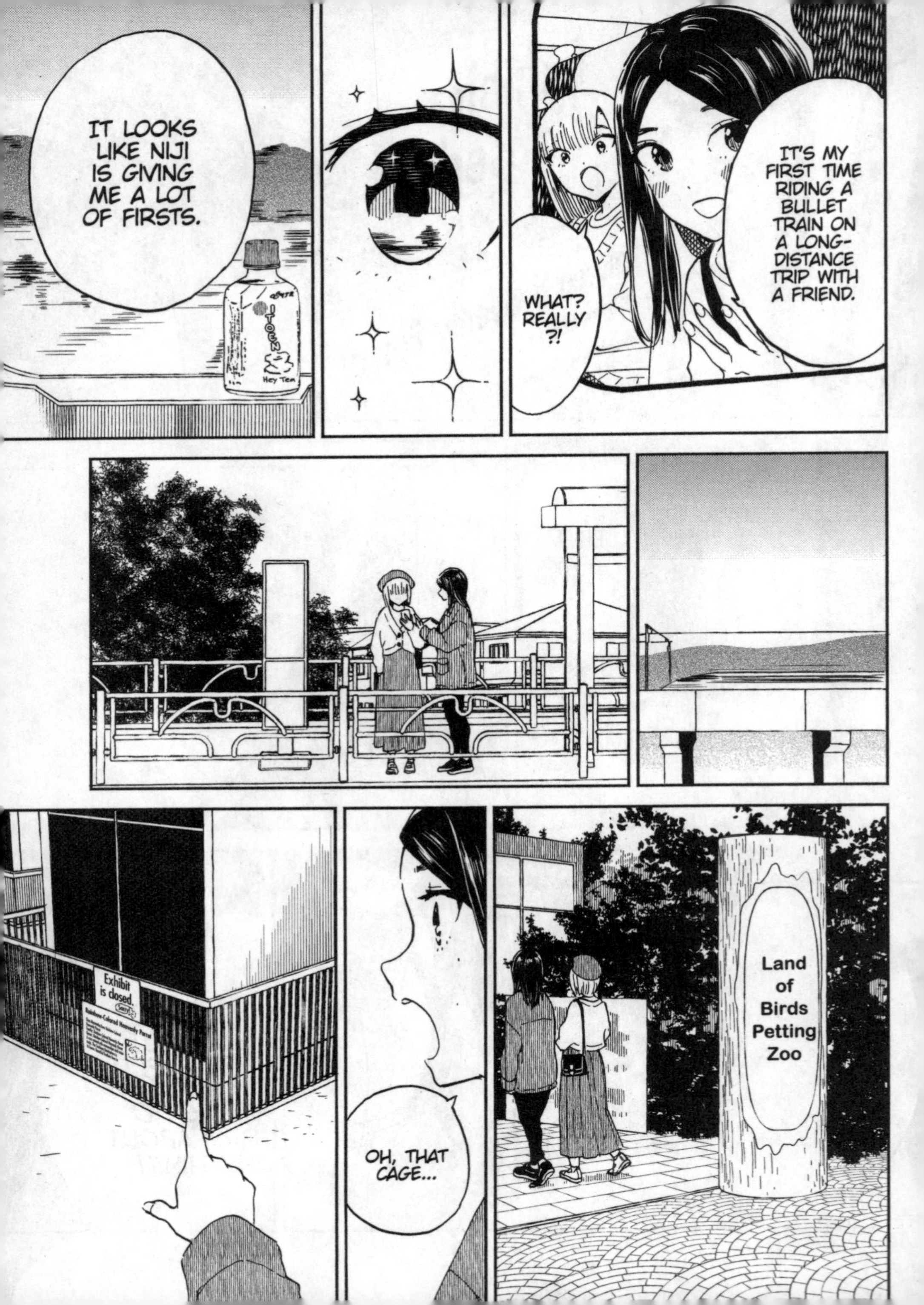
IT'S MY FIRST TIME RIDING A BULLET TRAIN ON A LONG-DISTANCE TRIP WITH A FRIEND.
WHAT? REALLY?!
IT LOOKS LIKE NIJI IS GIVING ME A LOT OF FIRSTS.
Land of Birds Petting Zoo
OH, THAT CAGE...
Exhibit is closed.

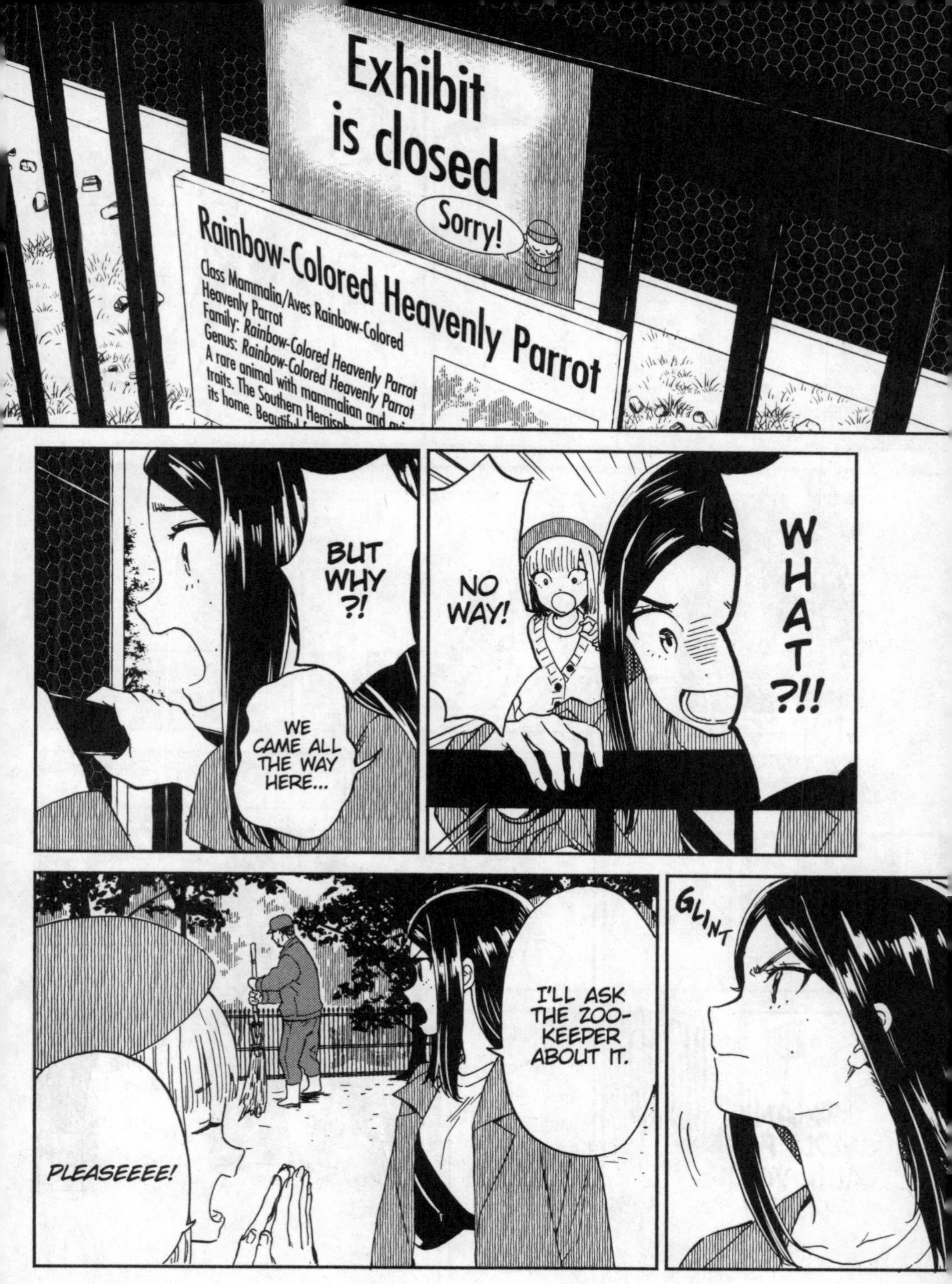
Exhibit is closed
Sorry!
Rainbow-Colored Heavenly Parrot
Class Mammalia/Aves Rainbow-Colored Heavenly Parrot
Family: *Rainbow-Colored Heavenly Parrot*
Genus: *Rainbow-Colored Heavenly Parrot*
A rare animal with mammalian and
traits. The Southern
its home.
WHAT?!!
NO WAY!
BUT WHY?!
WE CAME ALL THE WAY HERE...
GLINT
I'LL ASK THE ZOO-KEEPER ABOUT IT.
PLEASEEEE!

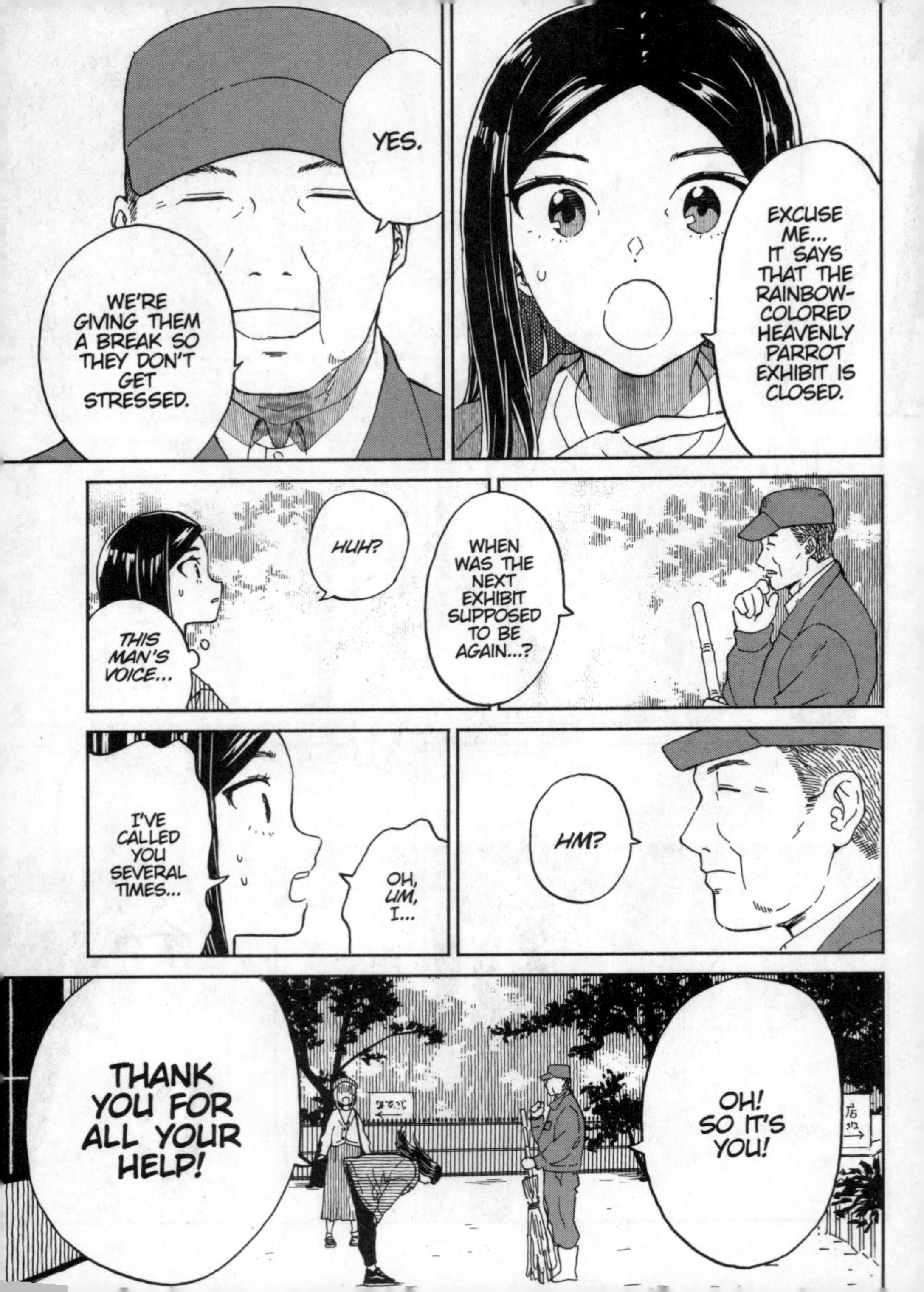
EXCUSE ME... IT SAYS THAT THE RAINBOW-COLORED HEAVENLY PARROT EXHIBIT IS CLOSED.
YES.
WE'RE GIVING THEM A BREAK SO THEY DON'T GET STRESSED.
WHEN WAS THE NEXT EXHIBIT SUPPOSED TO BE AGAIN...?
HUH?
THIS MAN'S VOICE...
HM?
OH, UM, I...
I'VE CALLED YOU SEVERAL TIMES...
OH! SO IT'S YOU!
THANK YOU FOR ALL YOUR HELP!

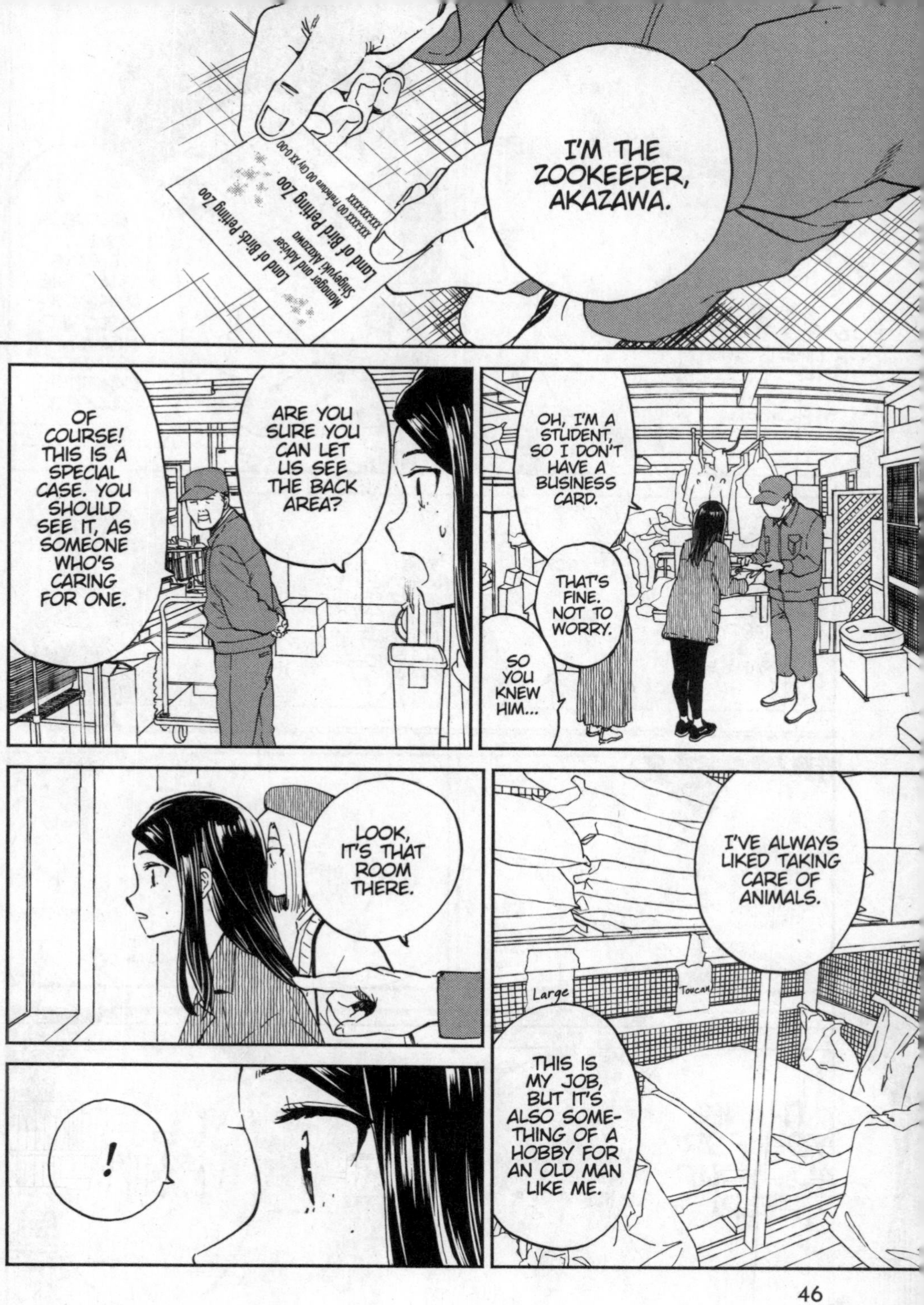
Land of Birds Petting Zoo
Manager and Advisor
Shigeyuki Akazawa
Land of Bird Petting Zoo
I'M THE ZOOKEEPER, AKAZAWA.
OH, I'M A STUDENT, SO I DON'T HAVE A BUSINESS CARD.
THAT'S FINE. NOT TO WORRY.
SO YOU KNEW HIM...
ARE YOU SURE YOU CAN LET US SEE THE BACK AREA?
OF COURSE! THIS IS A SPECIAL CASE. YOU SHOULD SEE IT, AS SOMEONE WHO'S CARING FOR ONE.
I'VE ALWAYS LIKED TAKING CARE OF ANIMALS.
Large
Toucan
THIS IS MY JOB, BUT IT'S ALSO SOMETHING OF A HOBBY FOR AN OLD MAN LIKE ME.
LOOK, IT'S THAT ROOM THERE.
!

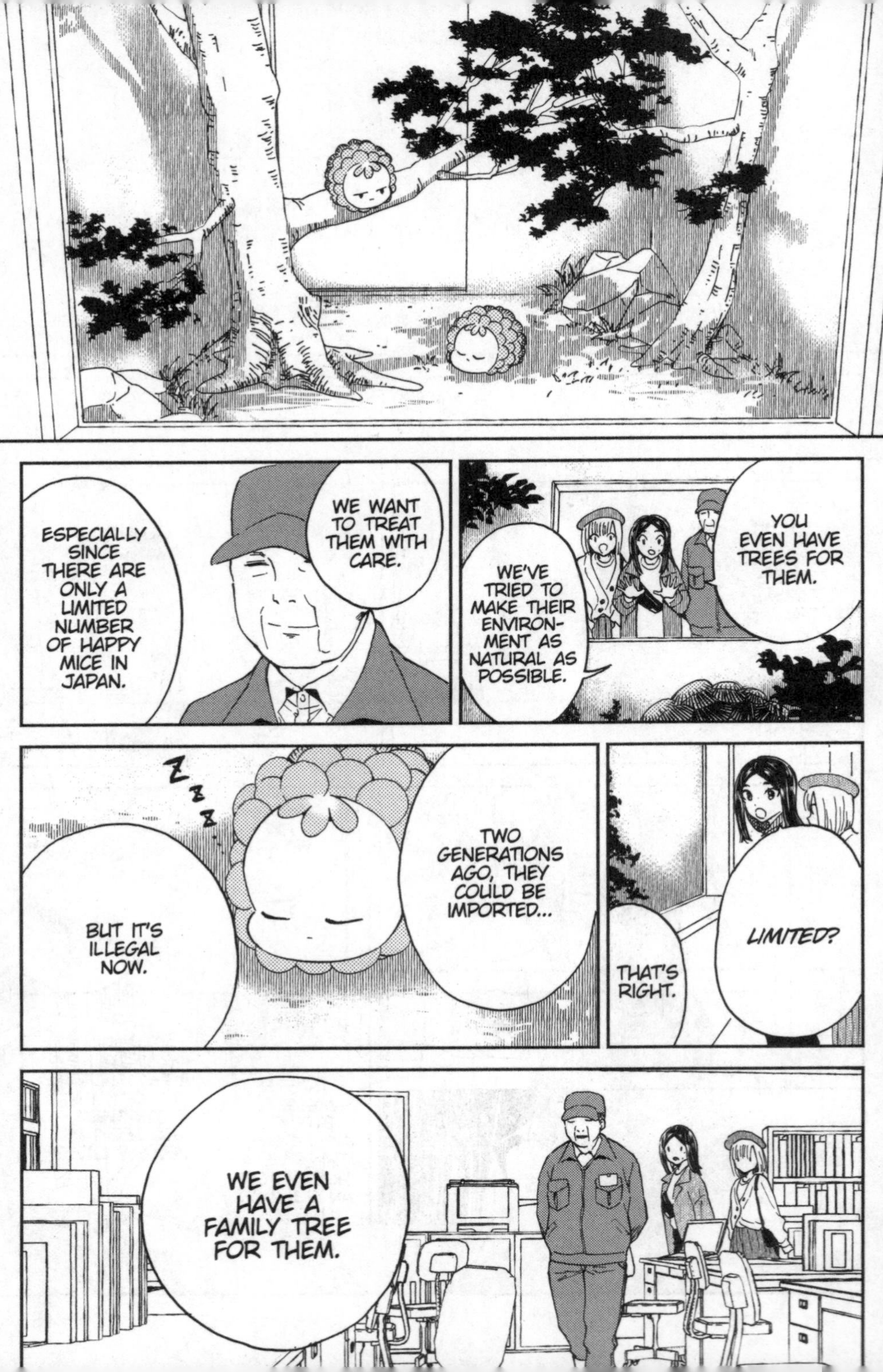
YOU EVEN HAVE TREES FOR THEM.
WE'VE TRIED TO MAKE THEIR ENVIRONMENT AS NATURAL AS POSSIBLE.
WE WANT TO TREAT THEM WITH CARE.
ESPECIALLY SINCE THERE ARE ONLY A LIMITED NUMBER OF HAPPY MICE IN JAPAN.
LIMITED?
THAT'S RIGHT.
TWO GENERATIONS AGO, THEY COULD BE IMPORTED...
BUT IT'S ILLEGAL NOW.
Z Z Z
WE EVEN HAVE A FAMILY TREE FOR THEM.

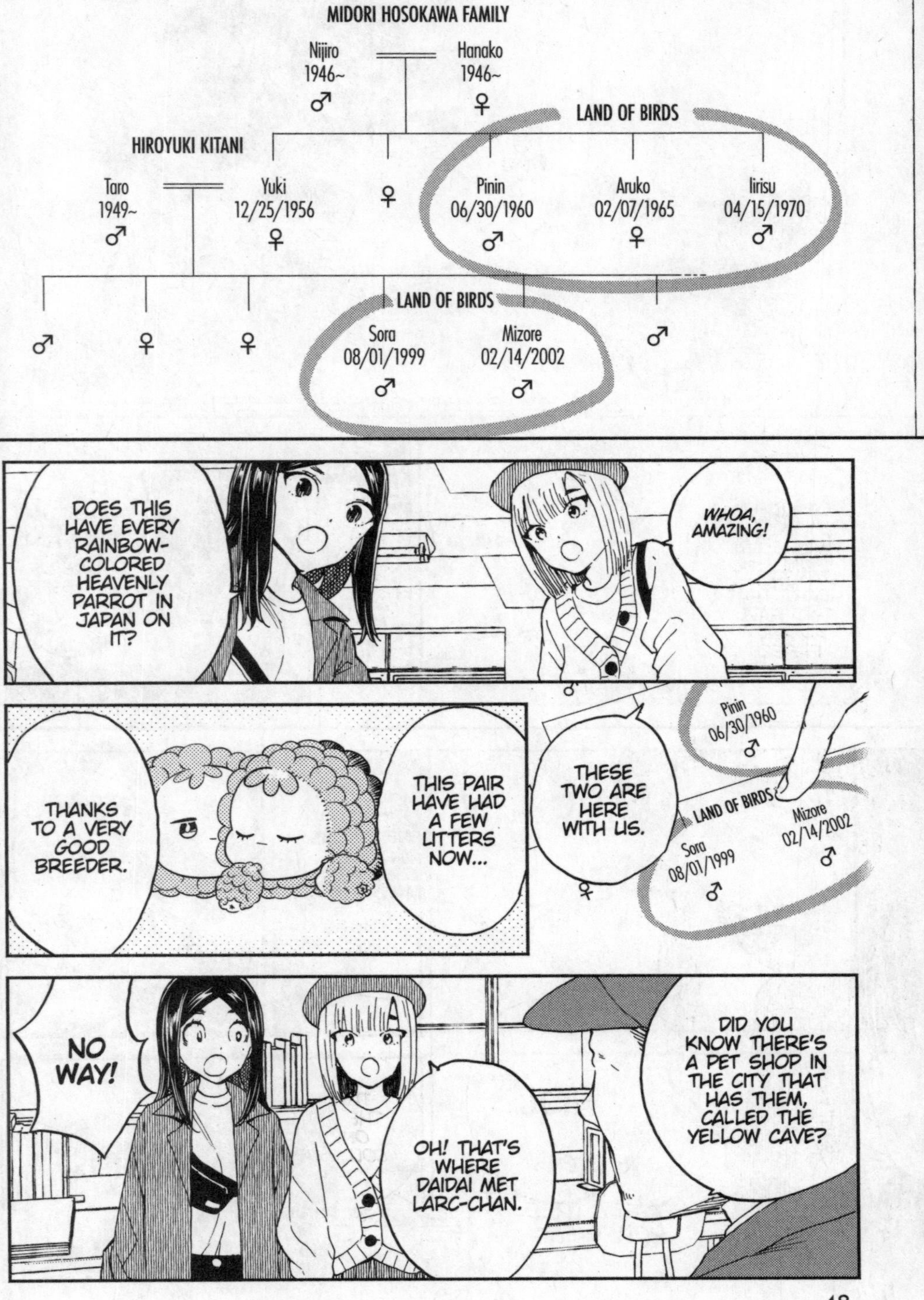

MIDORI HOSOKAWA FAMILY
Nijiro 1946~ ♂
Hanako 1946~ ♀
LAND OF BIRDS
HIROYUKI KITANI
Taro 1949~ ♂
Yuki 12/25/1956 ♀
♀
Pinin 06/30/1960 ♂
Aruko 02/07/1965 ♀
Iirisu 04/15/1970 ♂
♂
♀
♀
LAND OF BIRDS
Sora 08/01/1999 ♂
Mizore 02/14/2002 ♂
♂
WHOA, AMAZING!
DOES THIS HAVE EVERY RAINBOW-COLORED HEAVENLY PARROT IN JAPAN ON IT?
THESE TWO ARE HERE WITH US.
Pinin 06/30/1960 ♂
LAND OF BIRDS
Mizore 02/14/2002 ♂
Sora 08/01/1999 ♂
THIS PAIR HAVE HAD A FEW LITTERS NOW...
THANKS TO A VERY GOOD BREEDER.
DID YOU KNOW THERE'S A PET SHOP IN THE CITY THAT HAS THEM, CALLED THE YELLOW CAVE?
OH! THAT'S WHERE DAIDAI MET LARC-CHAN.
NO WAY!

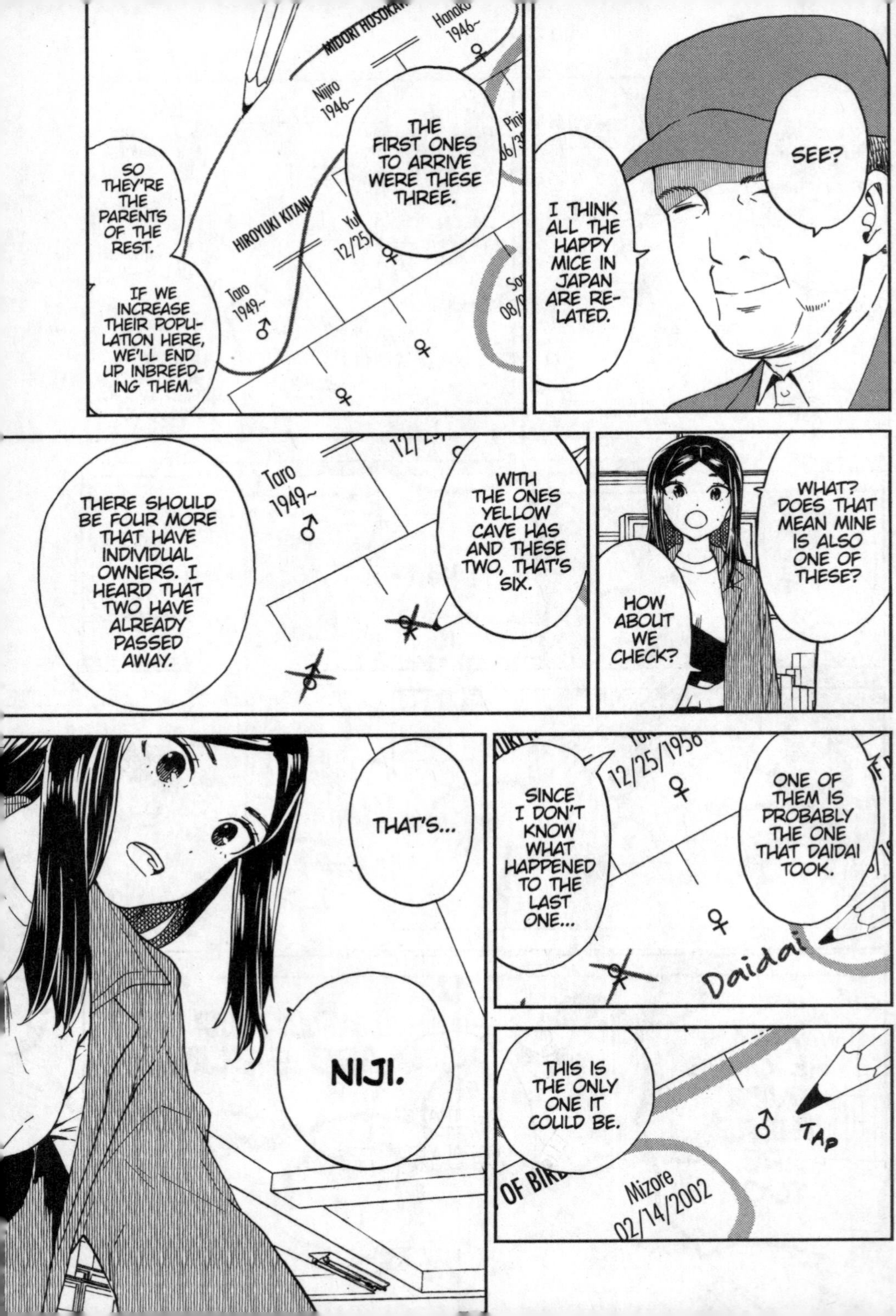
SEE?
I THINK ALL THE HAPPY MICE IN JAPAN ARE RELATED.
Hanako 1946~
MIDORI HOSOKAWA
Niijiro 1946~
HIROYUKI KITANI
Taro 1949~
THE FIRST ONES TO ARRIVE WERE THESE THREE.
SO THEY'RE THE PARENTS OF THE REST.
IF WE INCREASE THEIR POPULATION HERE, WE'LL END UP INBREEDING THEM.
WHAT? DOES THAT MEAN MINE IS ALSO ONE OF THESE?
HOW ABOUT WE CHECK?
WITH THE ONES YELLOW CAVE HAS AND THESE TWO, THAT'S SIX.
Taro 1949~
THERE SHOULD BE FOUR MORE THAT HAVE INDIVIDUAL OWNERS. I HEARD THAT TWO HAVE ALREADY PASSED AWAY.
12/25/1956
ONE OF THEM IS PROBABLY THE ONE THAT DAIDAI TOOK.
SINCE I DON'T KNOW WHAT HAPPENED TO THE LAST ONE...
Daidai
THIS IS THE ONLY ONE IT COULD BE.
TAP
Mizore 02/14/2002
THAT'S...
NIJI.

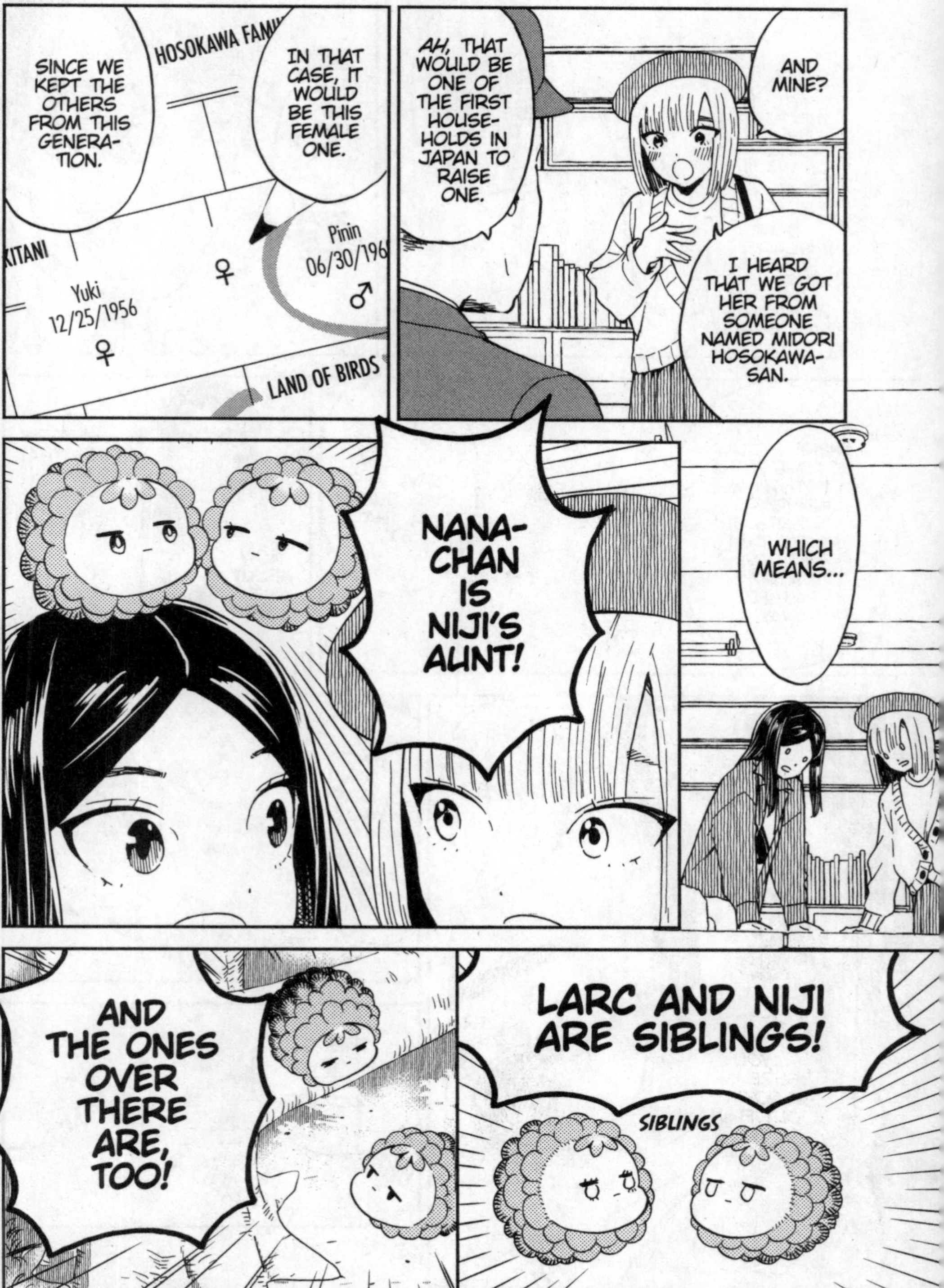
AND MINE?
I HEARD THAT WE GOT HER FROM SOMEONE NAMED MIDORI HOSOKAWA-SAN.
AH, THAT WOULD BE ONE OF THE FIRST HOUSEHOLDS IN JAPAN TO RAISE ONE.
IN THAT CASE, IT WOULD BE THIS FEMALE ONE.
SINCE WE KEPT THE OTHERS FROM THIS GENERATION.
HOSOKAWA FAMI
KITANI
Pinin
06/30/196
♂
♀
Yuki
12/25/1956
♀
LAND OF BIRDS
WHICH MEANS...
NANA-CHAN IS NIJI'S AUNT!
LARC AND NIJI ARE SIBLINGS!
SIBLINGS
AND THE ONES OVER THERE ARE, TOO!

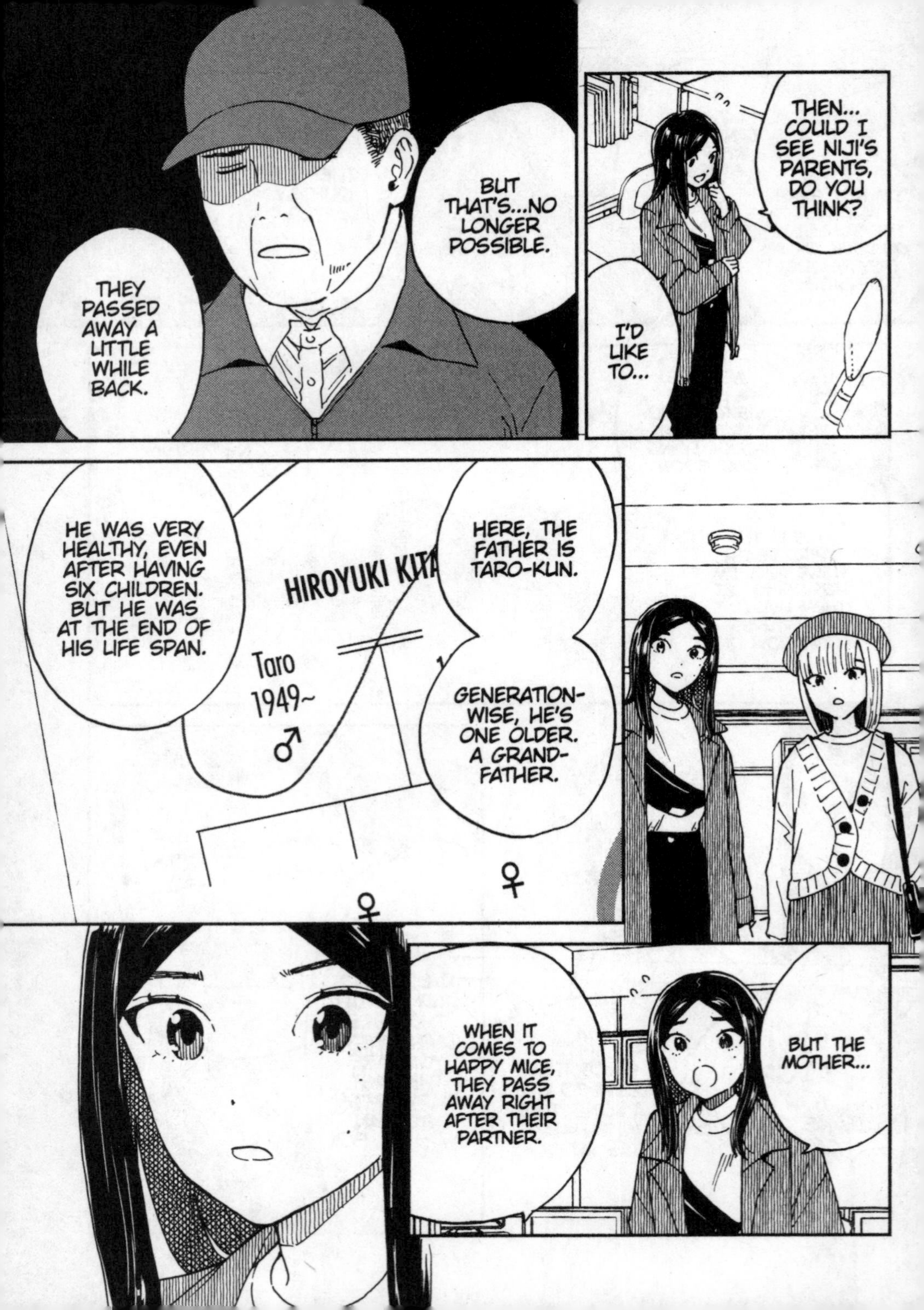
THEN... COULD I SEE NIJI'S PARENTS, DO YOU THINK?
I'D LIKE TO...
BUT THAT'S...NO LONGER POSSIBLE.
THEY PASSED AWAY A LITTLE WHILE BACK.
HERE, THE FATHER IS TARO-KUN.
GENERATION-WISE, HE'S ONE OLDER. A GRAND-FATHER.
HIROYUKI KITA
Taro
1949~
♂
♀
♀
HE WAS VERY HEALTHY, EVEN AFTER HAVING SIX CHILDREN. BUT HE WAS AT THE END OF HIS LIFE SPAN.
BUT THE MOTHER...
WHEN IT COMES TO HAPPY MICE, THEY PASS AWAY RIGHT AFTER THEIR PARTNER.

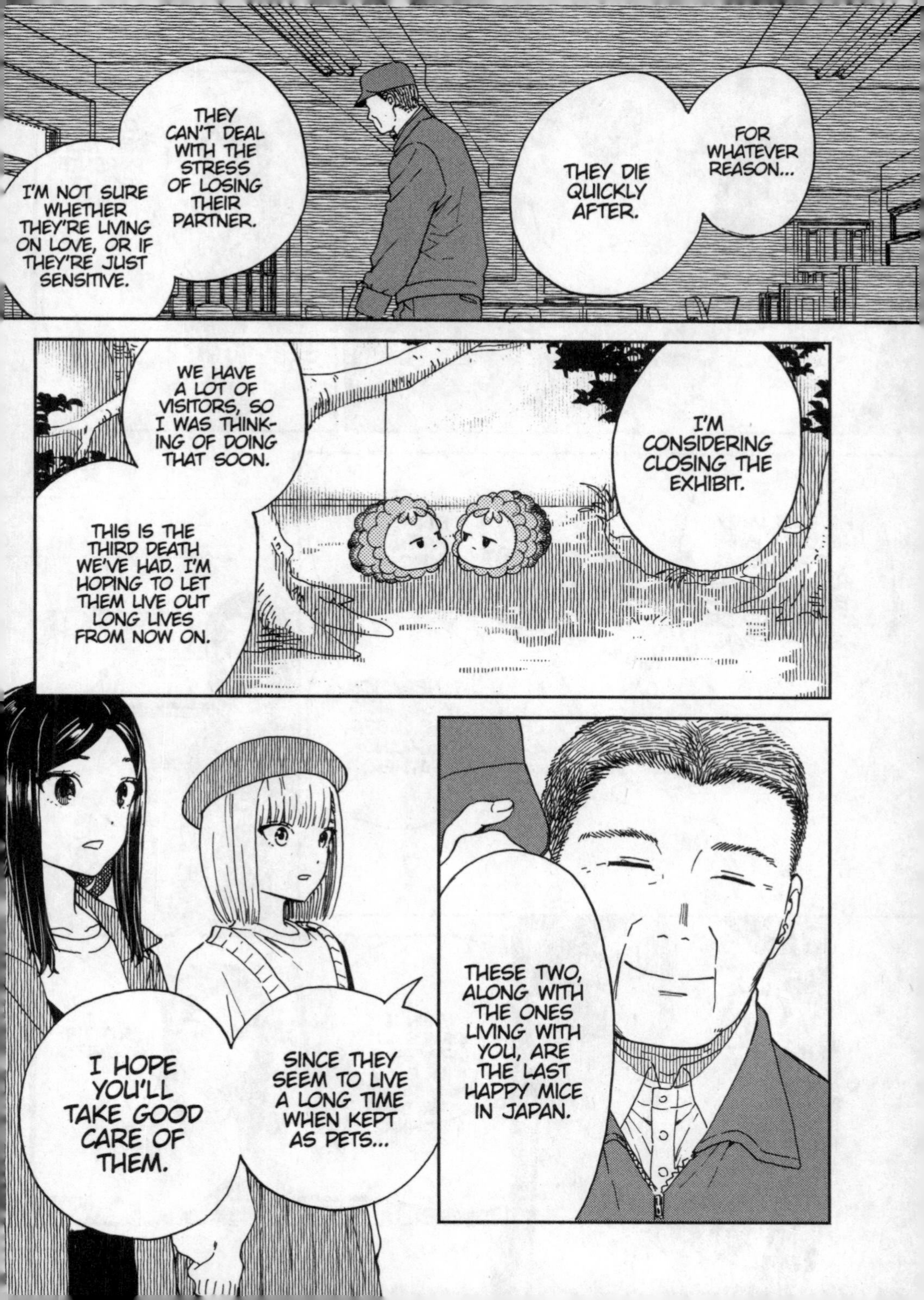
FOR WHATEVER REASON...
THEY DIE QUICKLY AFTER.
THEY CAN'T DEAL WITH THE STRESS OF LOSING THEIR PARTNER.
I'M NOT SURE WHETHER THEY'RE LIVING ON LOVE, OR IF THEY'RE JUST SENSITIVE.
I'M CONSIDERING CLOSING THE EXHIBIT.
WE HAVE A LOT OF VISITORS, SO I WAS THINKING OF DOING THAT SOON.
THIS IS THE THIRD DEATH WE'VE HAD. I'M HOPING TO LET THEM LIVE OUT LONG LIVES FROM NOW ON.
THESE TWO, ALONG WITH THE ONES LIVING WITH YOU, ARE THE LAST HAPPY MICE IN JAPAN.
SINCE THEY SEEM TO LIVE A LONG TIME WHEN KEPT AS PETS...
I HOPE YOU'LL TAKE GOOD CARE OF THEM.

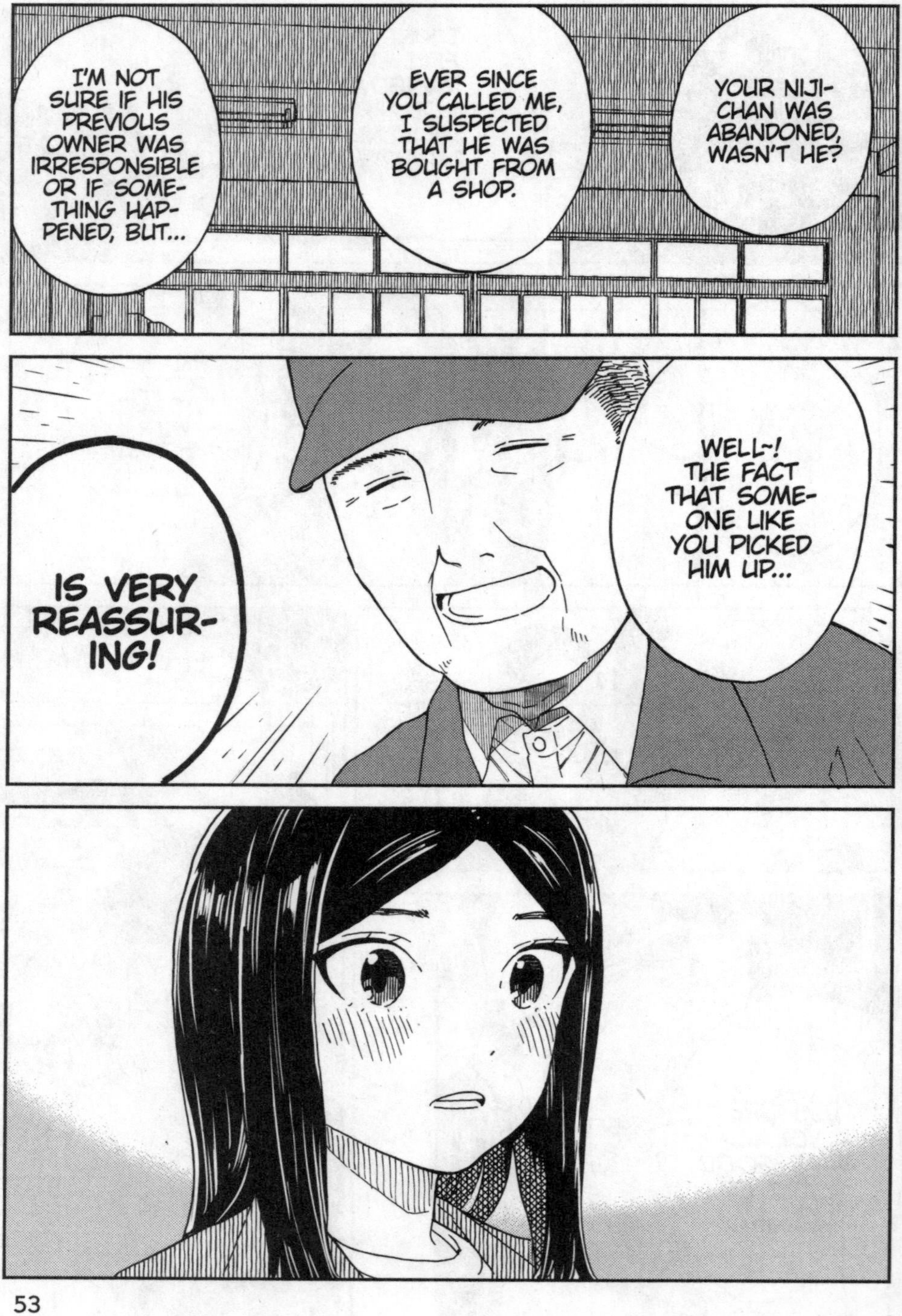
YOUR NIJI-CHAN WAS ABANDONED, WASN'T HE?
EVER SINCE YOU CALLED ME, I SUSPECTED THAT HE WAS BOUGHT FROM A SHOP.
I'M NOT SURE IF HIS PREVIOUS OWNER WAS IRRESPONSIBLE OR IF SOMETHING HAPPENED, BUT...
WELL~! THE FACT THAT SOMEONE LIKE YOU PICKED HIM UP...
IS VERY REASSURING!

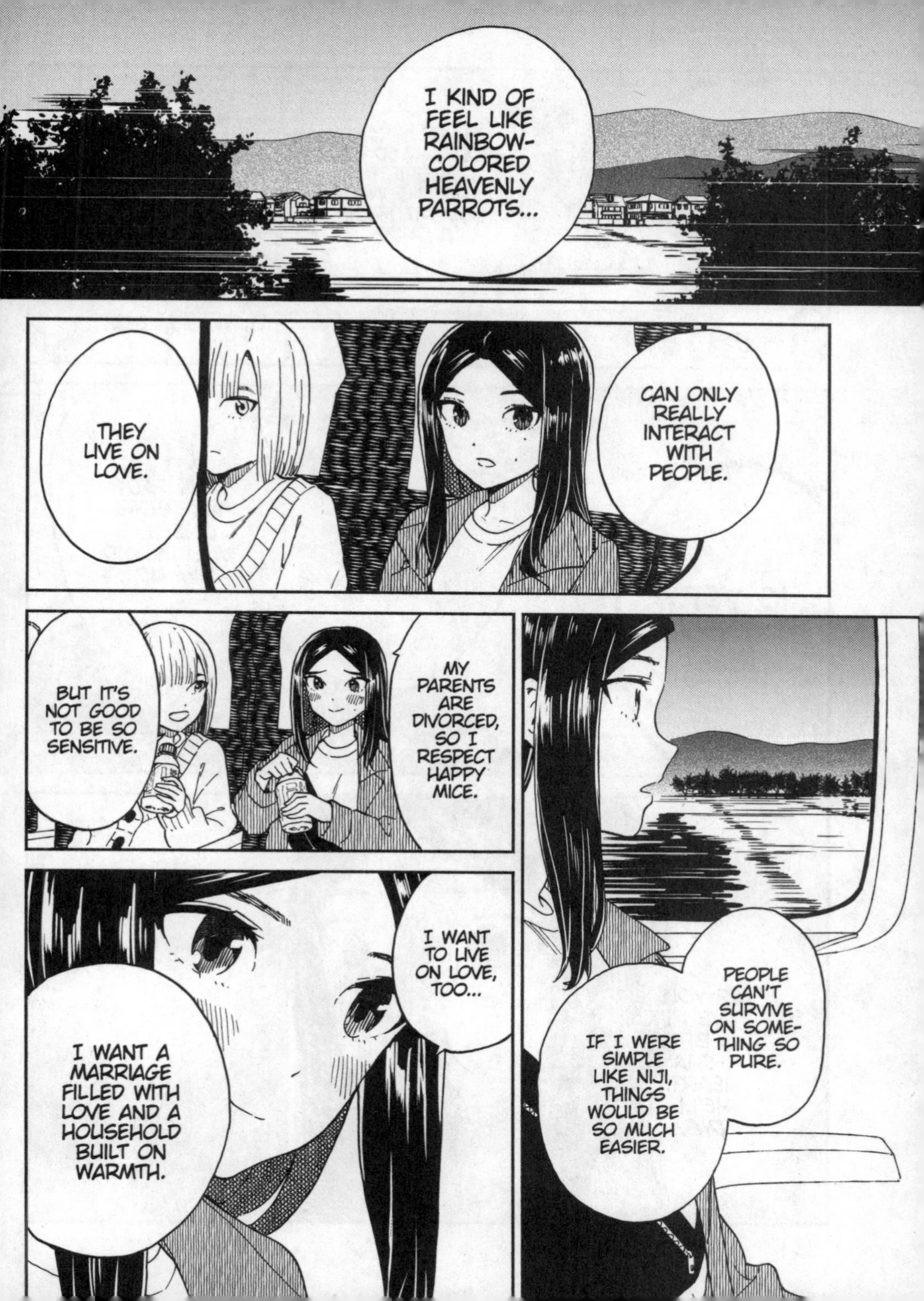
I KIND OF FEEL LIKE RAINBOW-COLORED HEAVENLY PARROTS...
CAN ONLY REALLY INTERACT WITH PEOPLE.
THEY LIVE ON LOVE.
PEOPLE CAN'T SURVIVE ON SOMETHING SO PURE.
IF I WERE SIMPLE LIKE NIJI, THINGS WOULD BE SO MUCH EASIER.
MY PARENTS ARE DIVORCED, SO I RESPECT HAPPY MICE.
BUT IT'S NOT GOOD TO BE SO SENSITIVE.
I WANT TO LIVE ON LOVE, TOO...
I WANT A MARRIAGE FILLED WITH LOVE AND A HOUSEHOLD BUILT ON WARMTH.

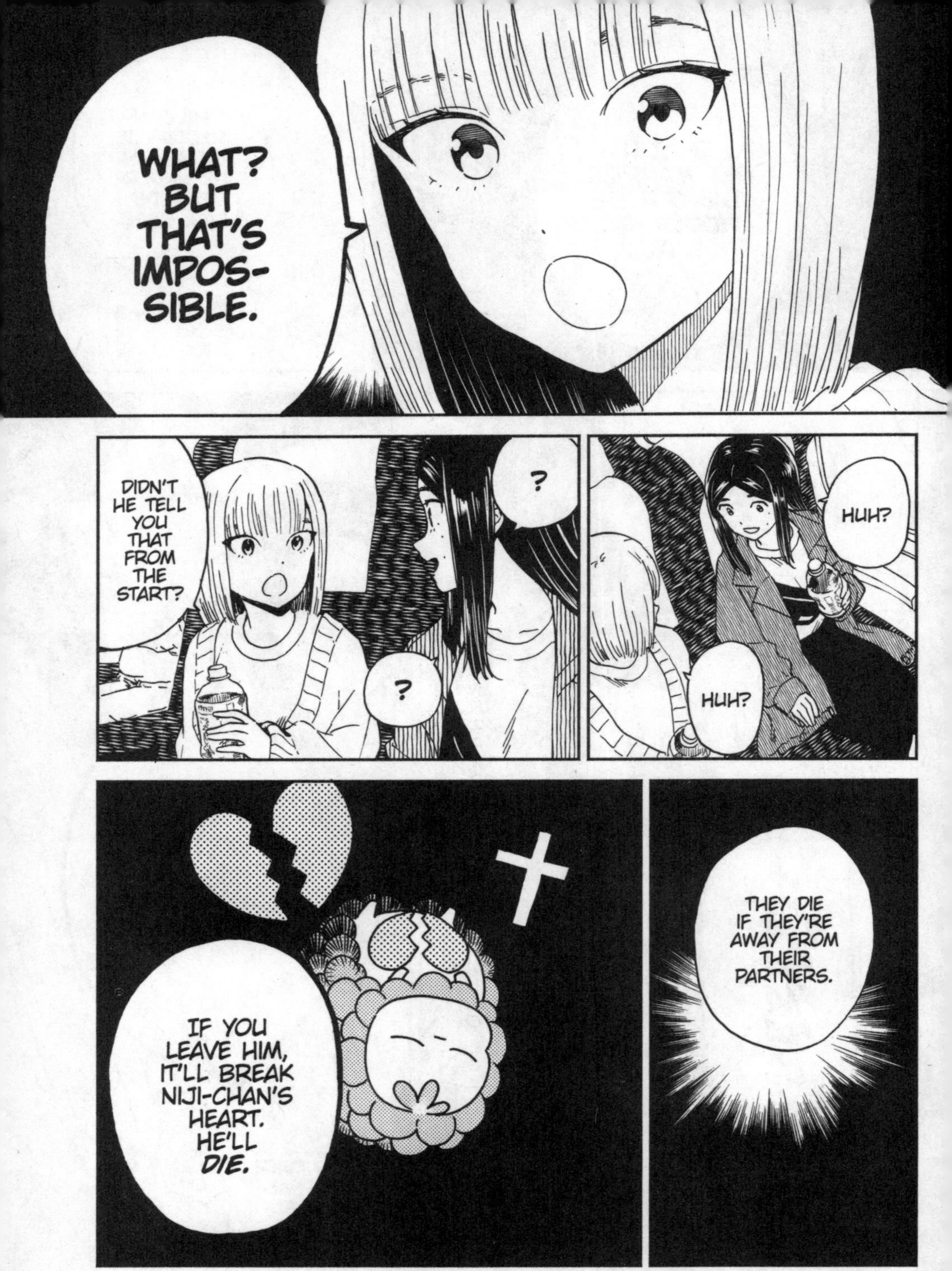
WHAT? BUT THAT'S IMPOS-SIBLE.
HUH?
HUH?
?
DIDN'T HE TELL YOU THAT FROM THE START?
?
THEY DIE IF THEY'RE AWAY FROM THEIR PARTNERS.
IF YOU LEAVE HIM, IT'LL BREAK NIJI-CHAN'S HEART. HE'LL *DIE.*

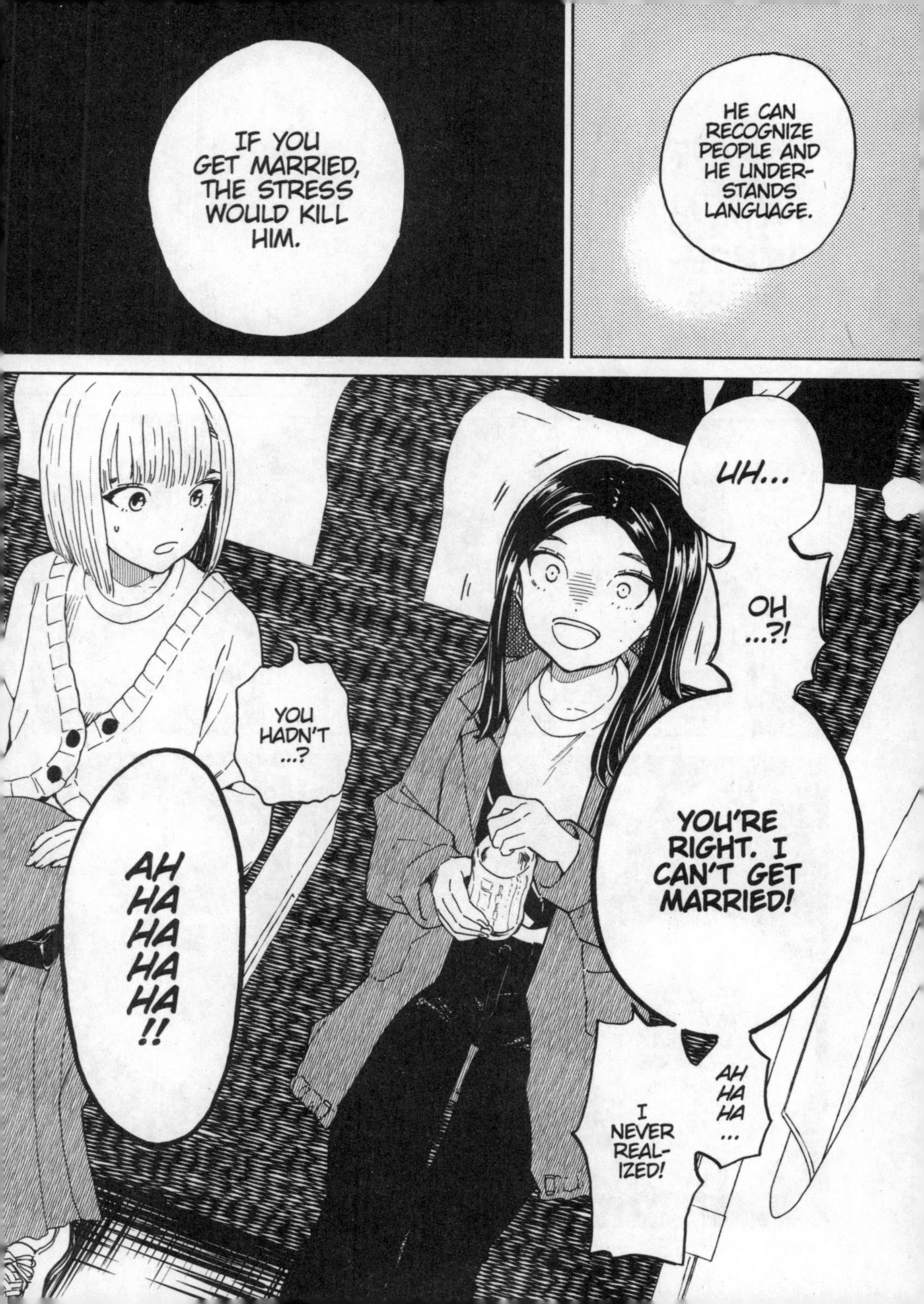
HE CAN RECOGNIZE PEOPLE AND HE UNDER-STANDS LANGUAGE.
IF YOU GET MARRIED, THE STRESS WOULD KILL HIM.
UH...
OH ...?!
YOU'RE RIGHT. I CAN'T GET MARRIED!
AH HA HA ...
I NEVER REAL-IZED!
YOU HADN'T ...?
AH HA HA HA HA HA!!

Rainbow and Black

Story & Art by **Eri Takenashi**

NOW LOADING...

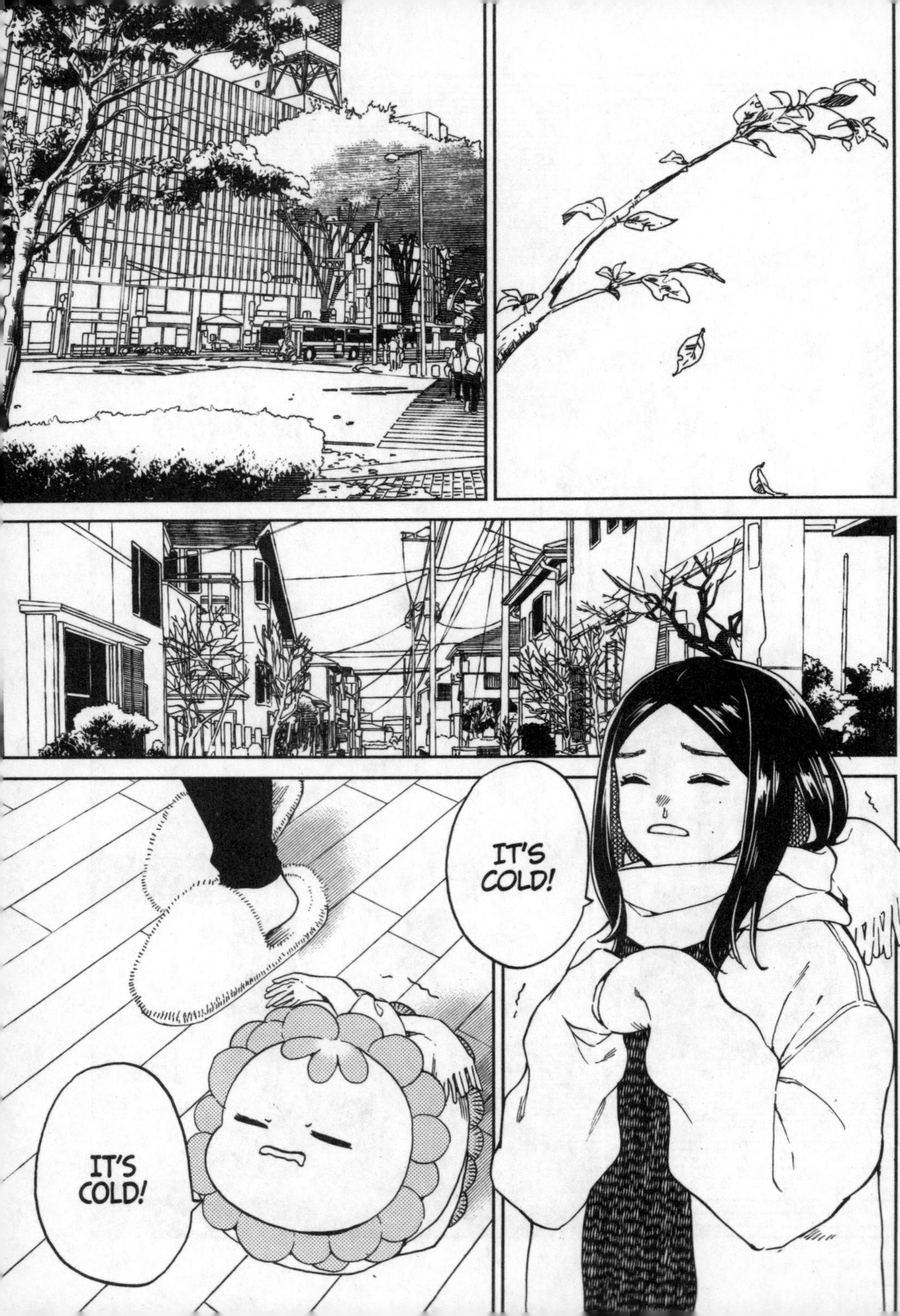
IT'S COLD!
IT'S COLD!

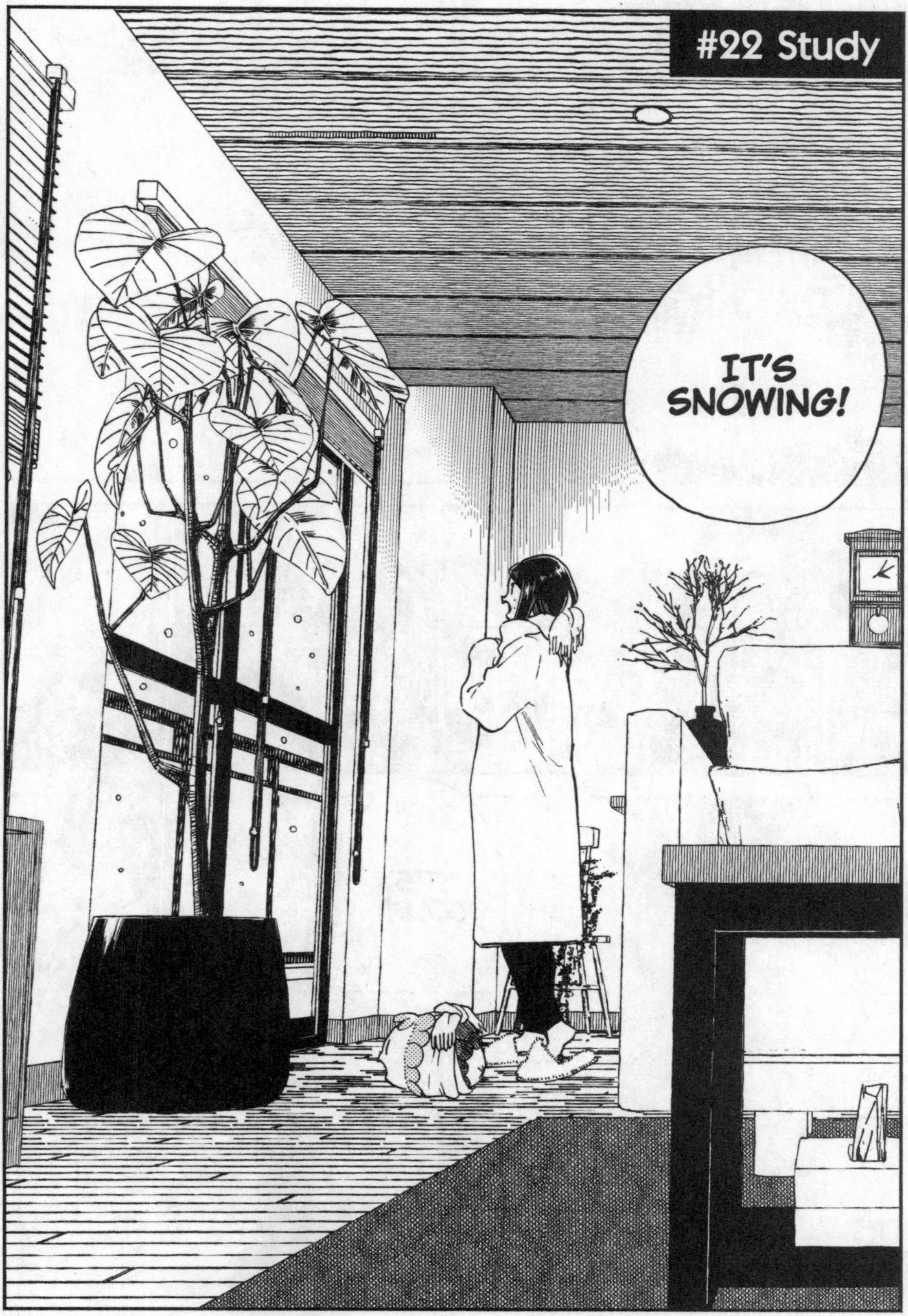
#22 Study
IT'S SNOWING!

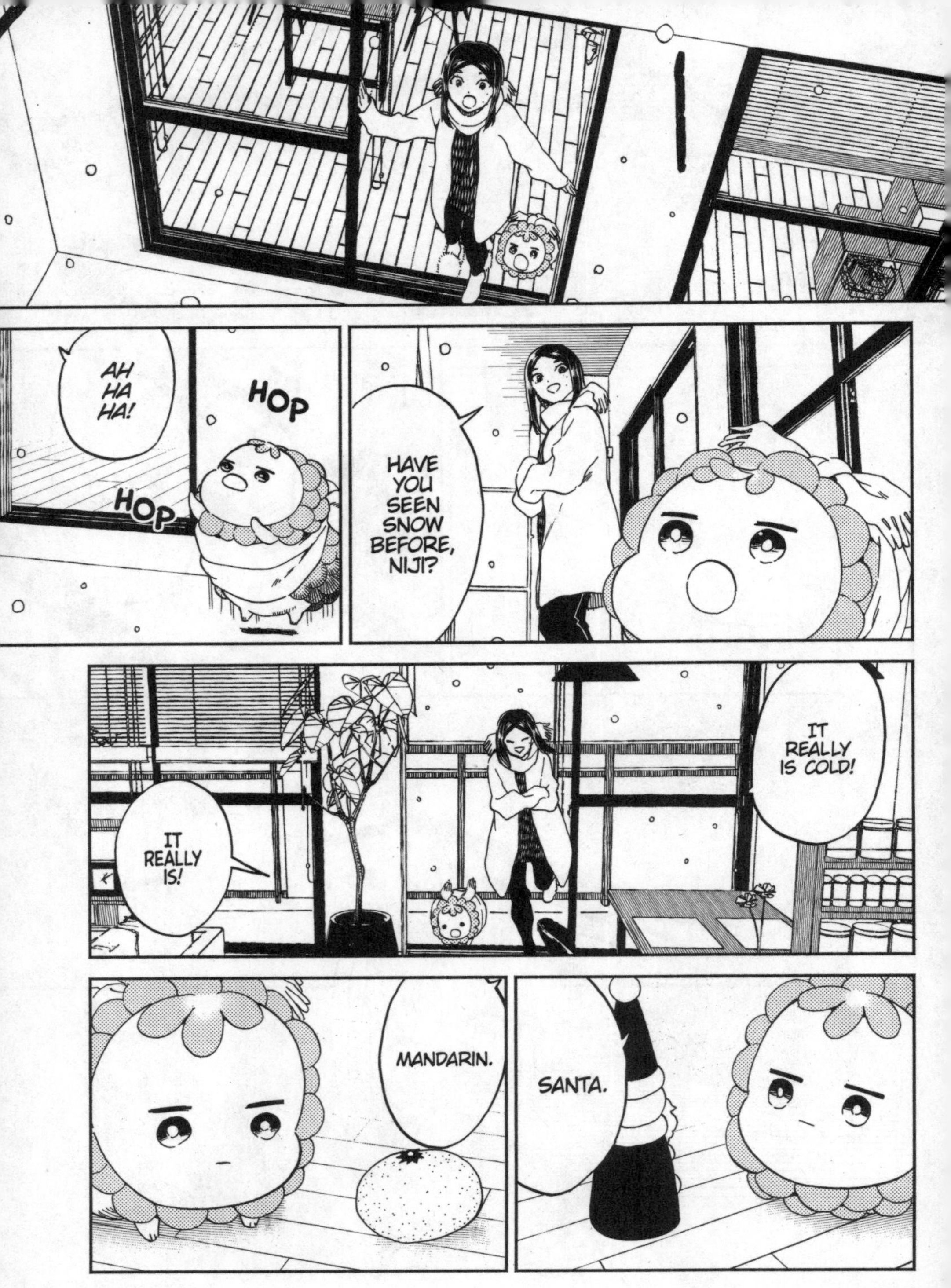
HAVE YOU SEEN SNOW BEFORE, NIJI?
AH HA HA!
HOP
HOP
IT REALLY IS COLD!
IT REALLY IS!
SANTA.
MANDARIN.

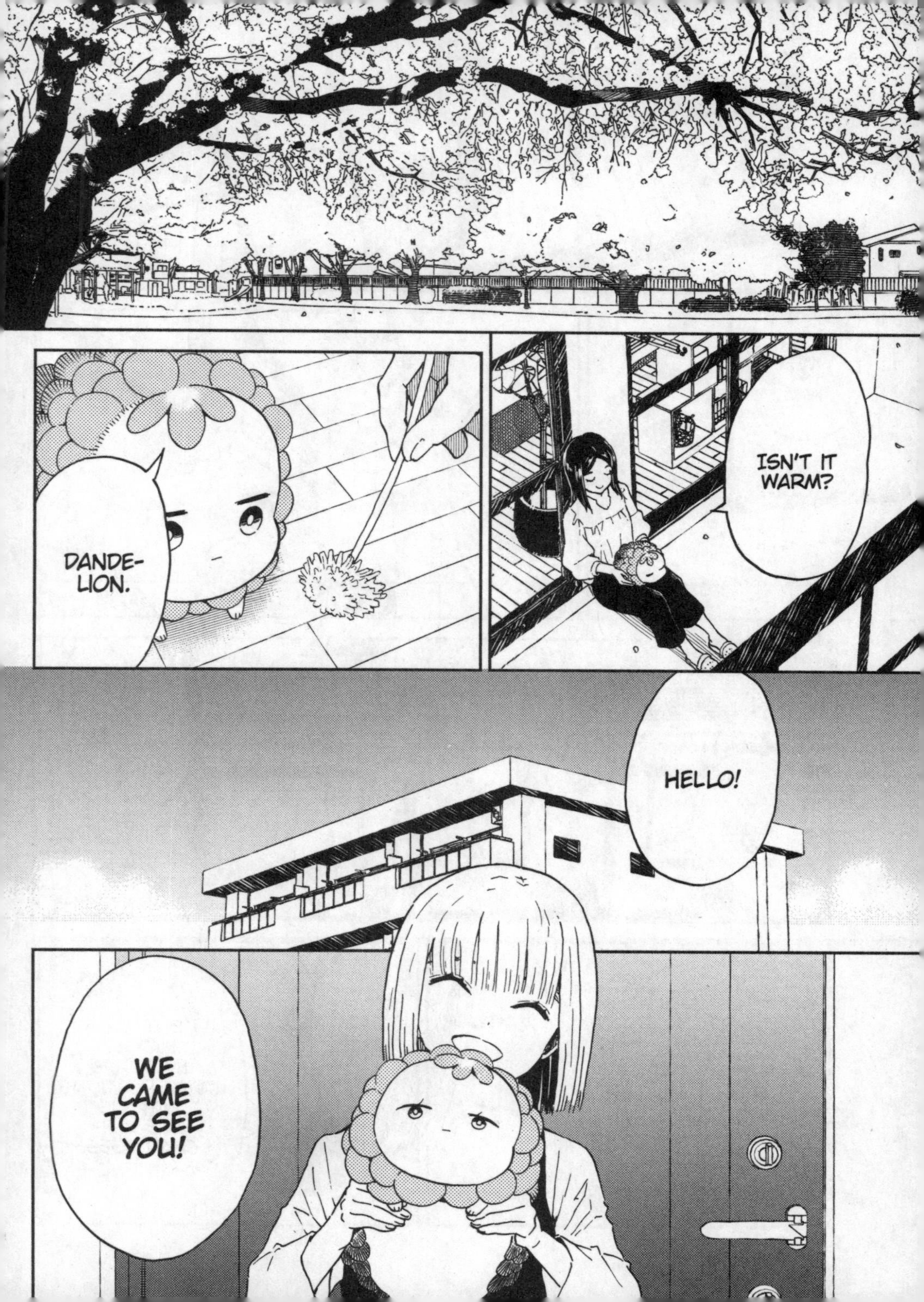
ISN'T IT WARM?
DANDE-LION.
HELLO!
WE CAME TO SEE YOU!

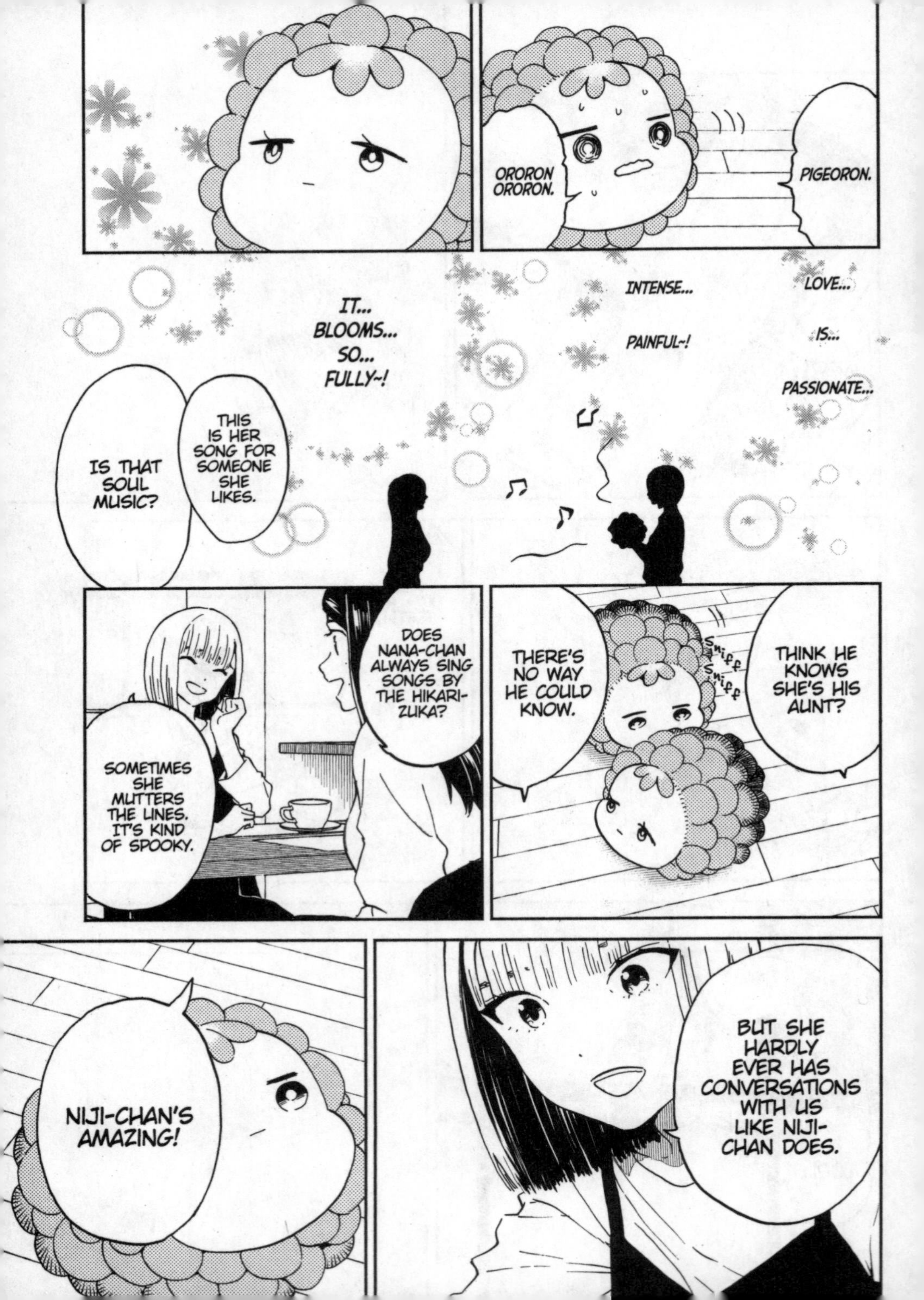
PIGEORON.
ORORON ORORON.
LOVE... IS... PASSIONATE...
INTENSE... PAINFUL~!
IT... BLOOMS... SO... FULLY~!
THIS IS HER SONG FOR SOMEONE SHE LIKES.
IS THAT SOUL MUSIC?
THINK HE KNOWS SHE'S HIS AUNT?
Sniff Sniff
THERE'S NO WAY HE COULD KNOW.
DOES NANA-CHAN ALWAYS SING SONGS BY THE HIKARI-ZUKA?
SOMETIMES SHE MUTTERS THE LINES. IT'S KIND OF SPOOKY.
BUT SHE HARDLY EVER HAS CONVERSATIONS WITH US LIKE NIJI-CHAN DOES.
NIJI-CHAN'S AMAZING!

IT'S HOOOT!

HOOOT!

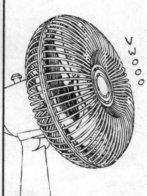

VWOOO

ICE.

WATER BATH.

WATER.

FINALLY.

IT'S FINALLY COOLING DOWN.

COOL.

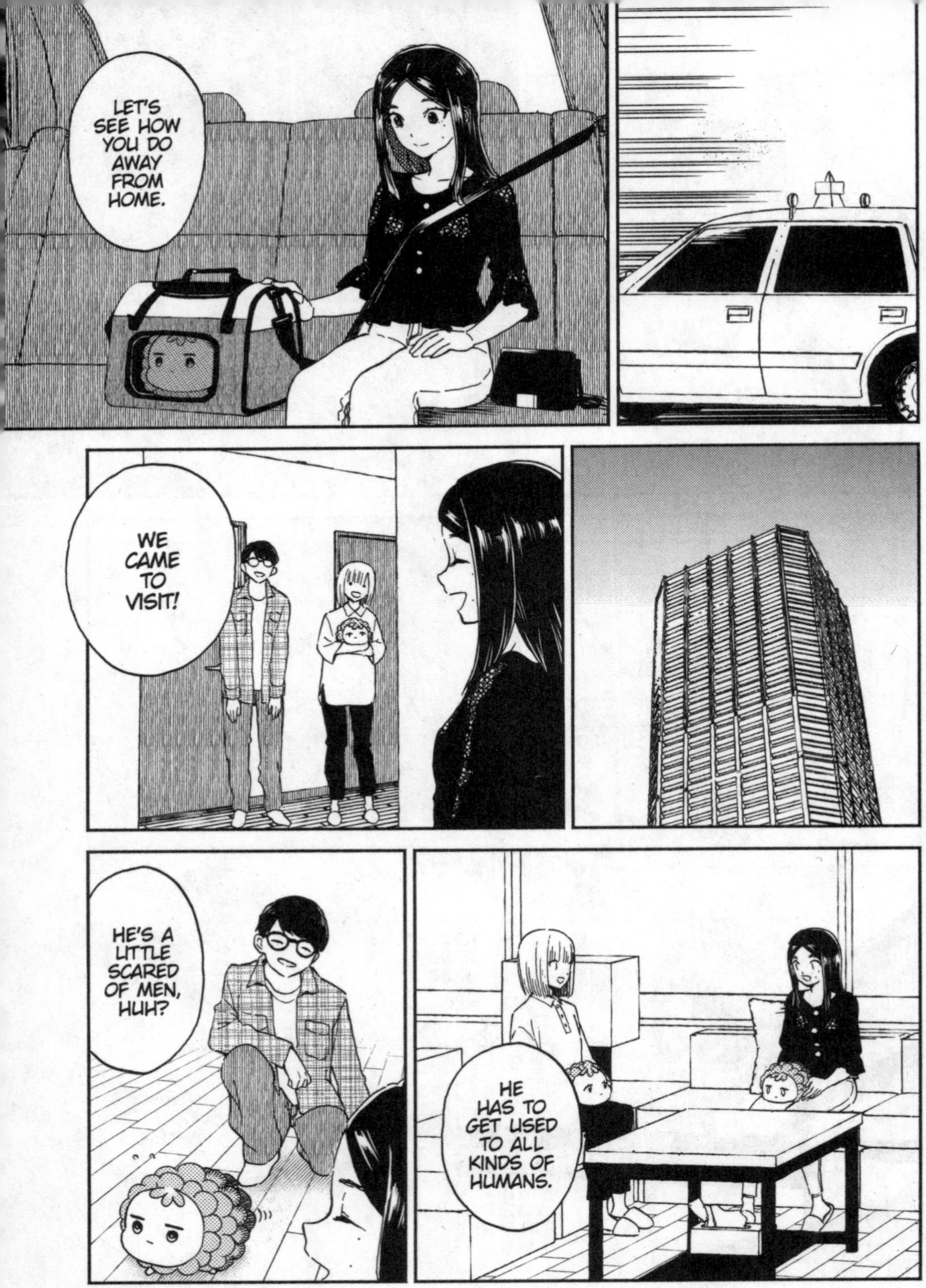
LET'S SEE HOW YOU DO AWAY FROM HOME.
WE CAME TO VISIT!
HE HAS TO GET USED TO ALL KINDS OF HUMANS.
HE'S A LITTLE SCARED OF MEN, HUH?

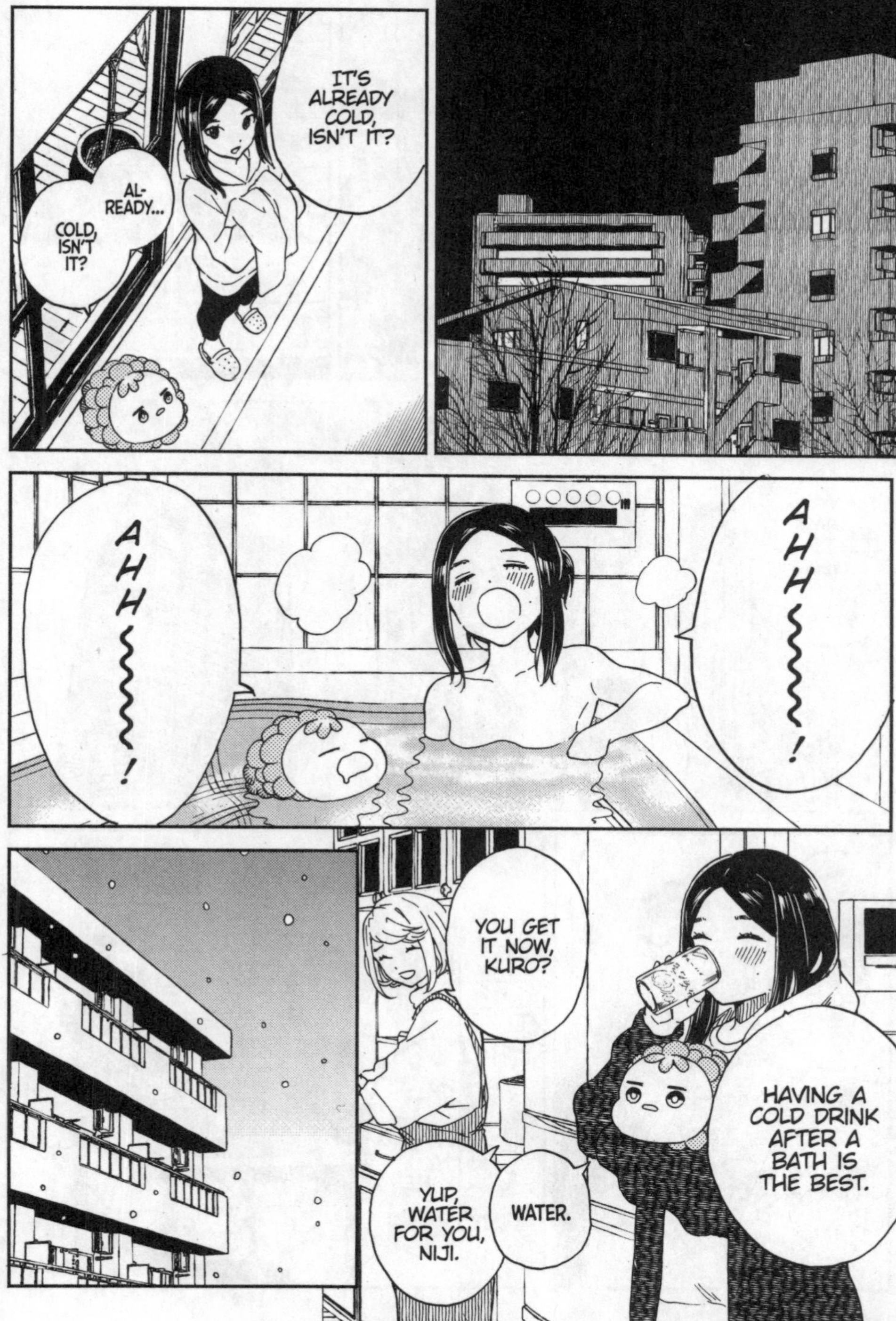
IT'S ALREADY COLD, ISN'T IT?
AL-READY... COLD, ISN'T IT?
AHH~!
AHH~!
HAVING A COLD DRINK AFTER A BATH IS THE BEST.
YOU GET IT NOW, KURO?
WATER.
YUP, WATER FOR YOU, NIJI.

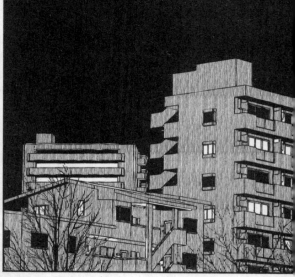

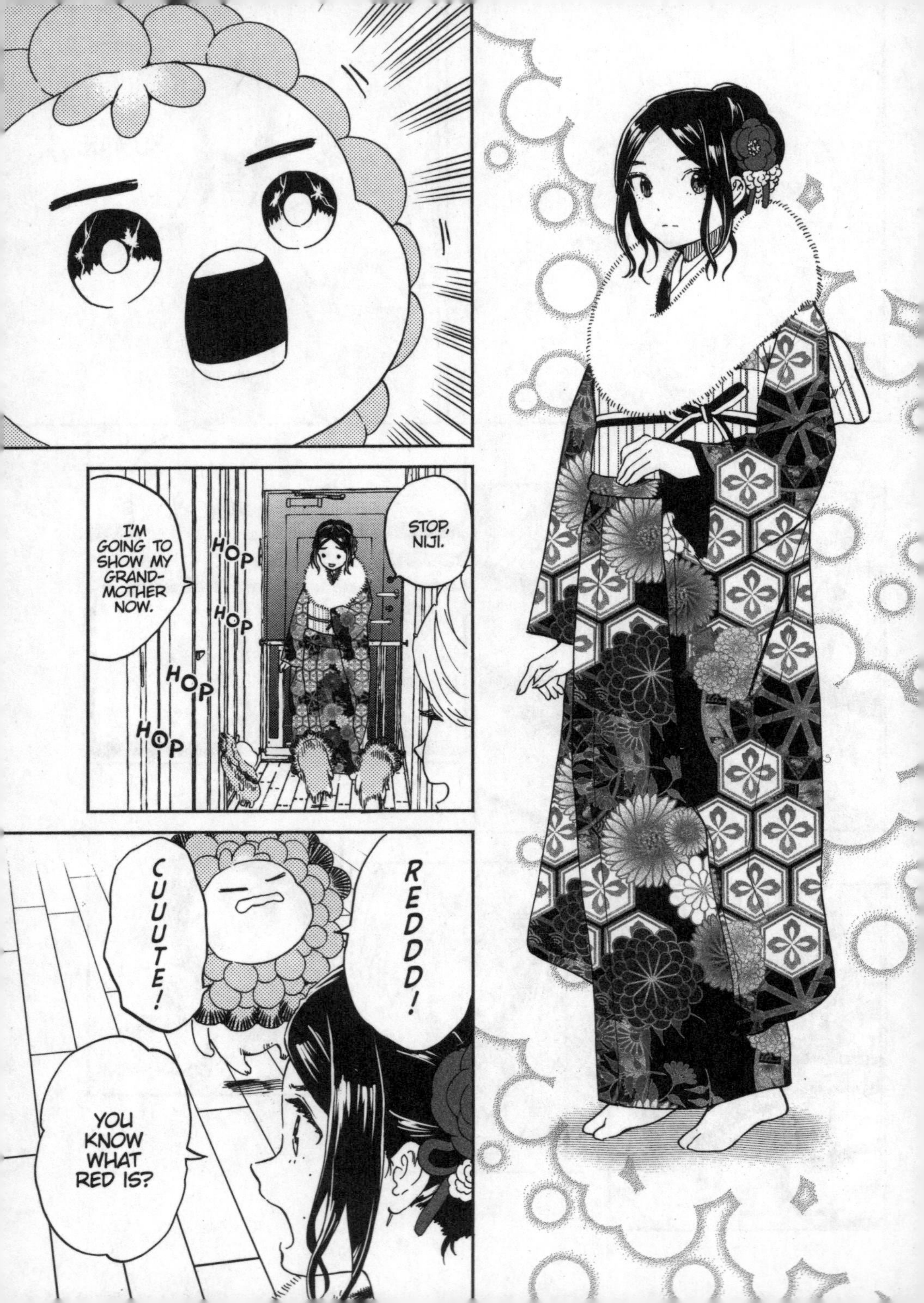
STOP, NIJI.
I'M GOING TO SHOW MY GRAND-MOTHER NOW.
HOP
HOP
HOP
HOP
REDDDD!
CUUUTE!
YOU KNOW WHAT RED IS?

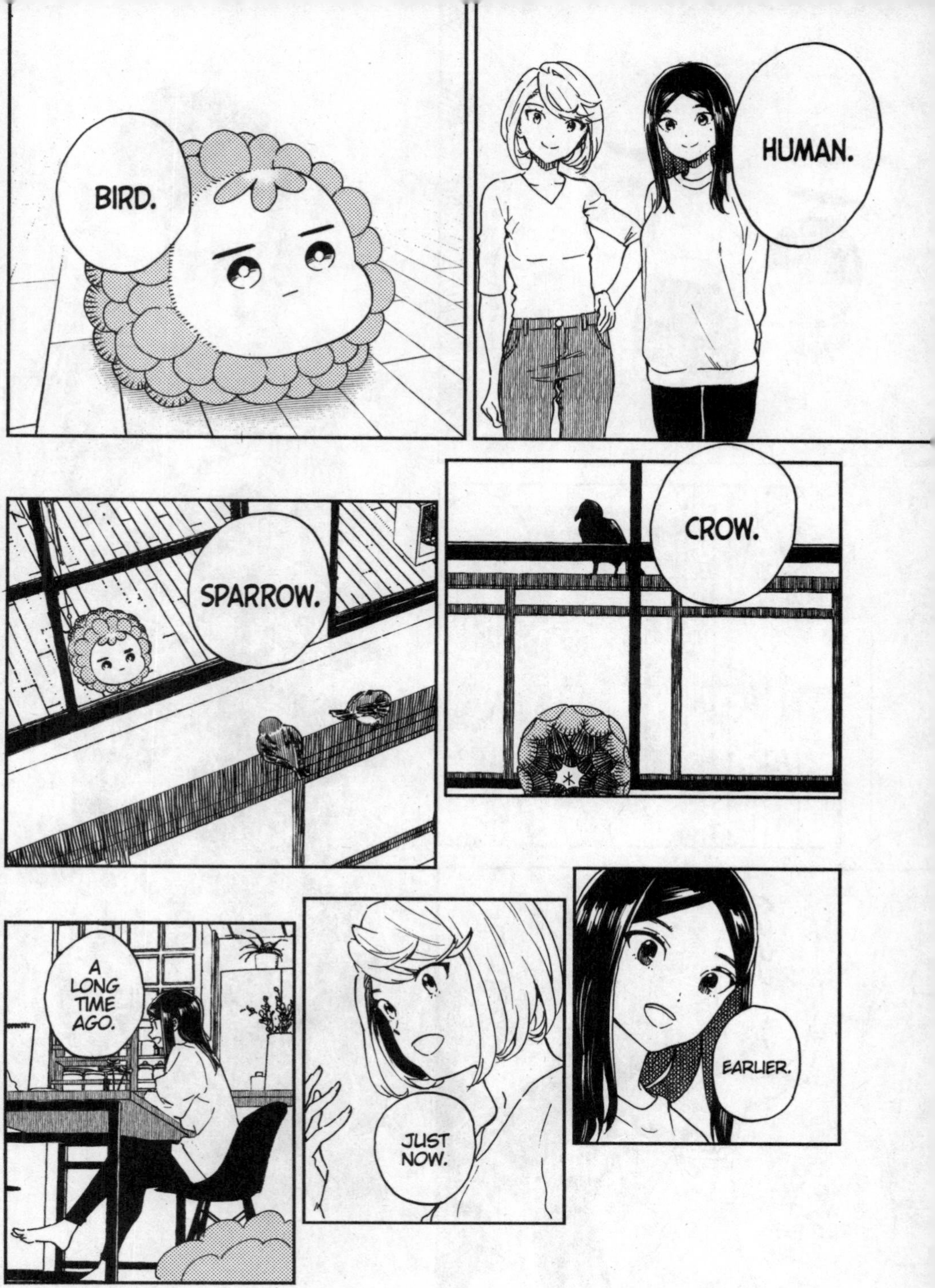
HUMAN.
BIRD.
CROW.
SPARROW.
EARLIER.
JUST NOW.
A LONG TIME AGO.

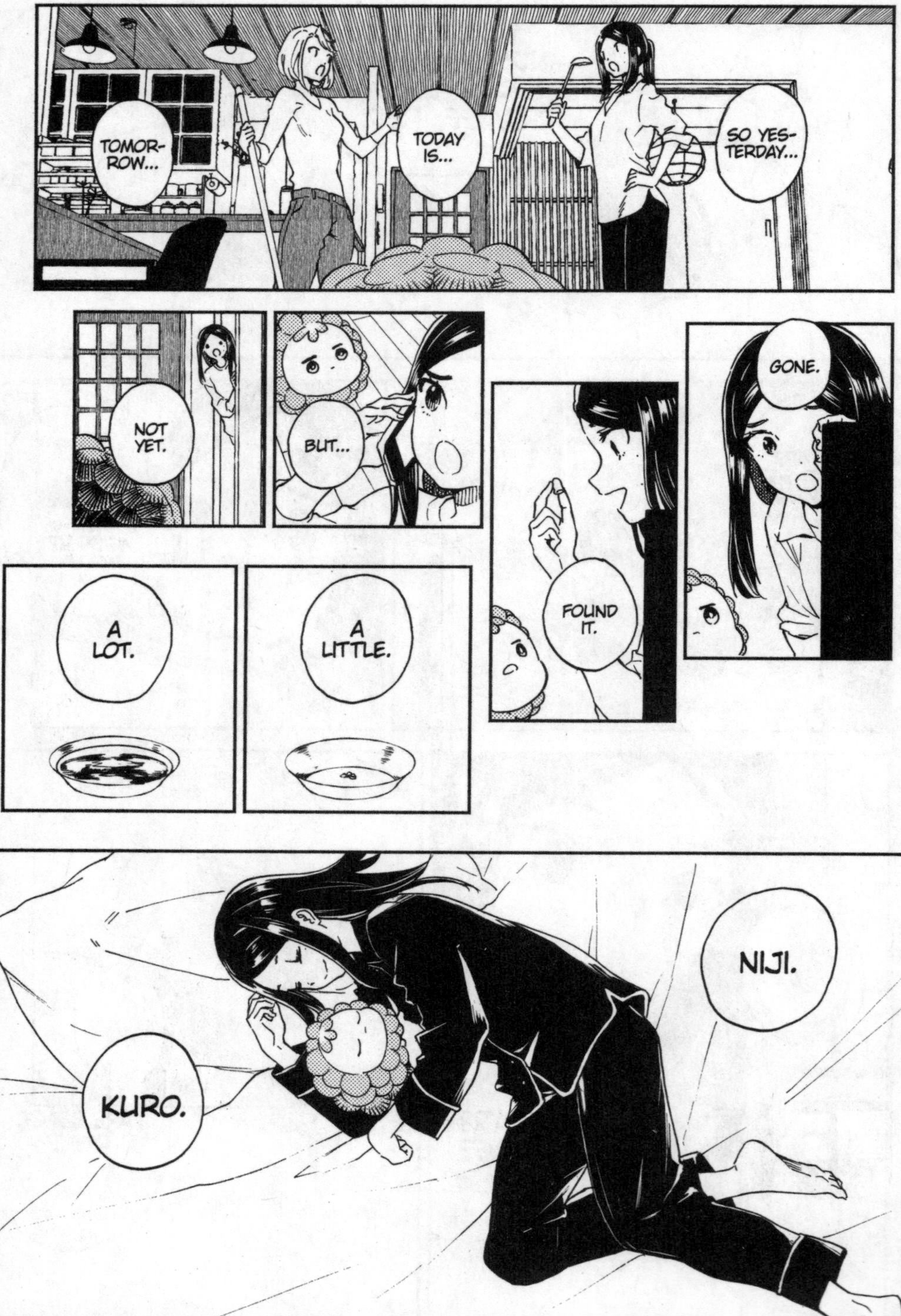
SO YES-
TERDAY...
TODAY
IS...
TOMOR-
ROW...
GONE.
FOUND
IT.
BUT...
NOT
YET.
A
LITTLE.
A
LOT.
NIJI.
KURO.

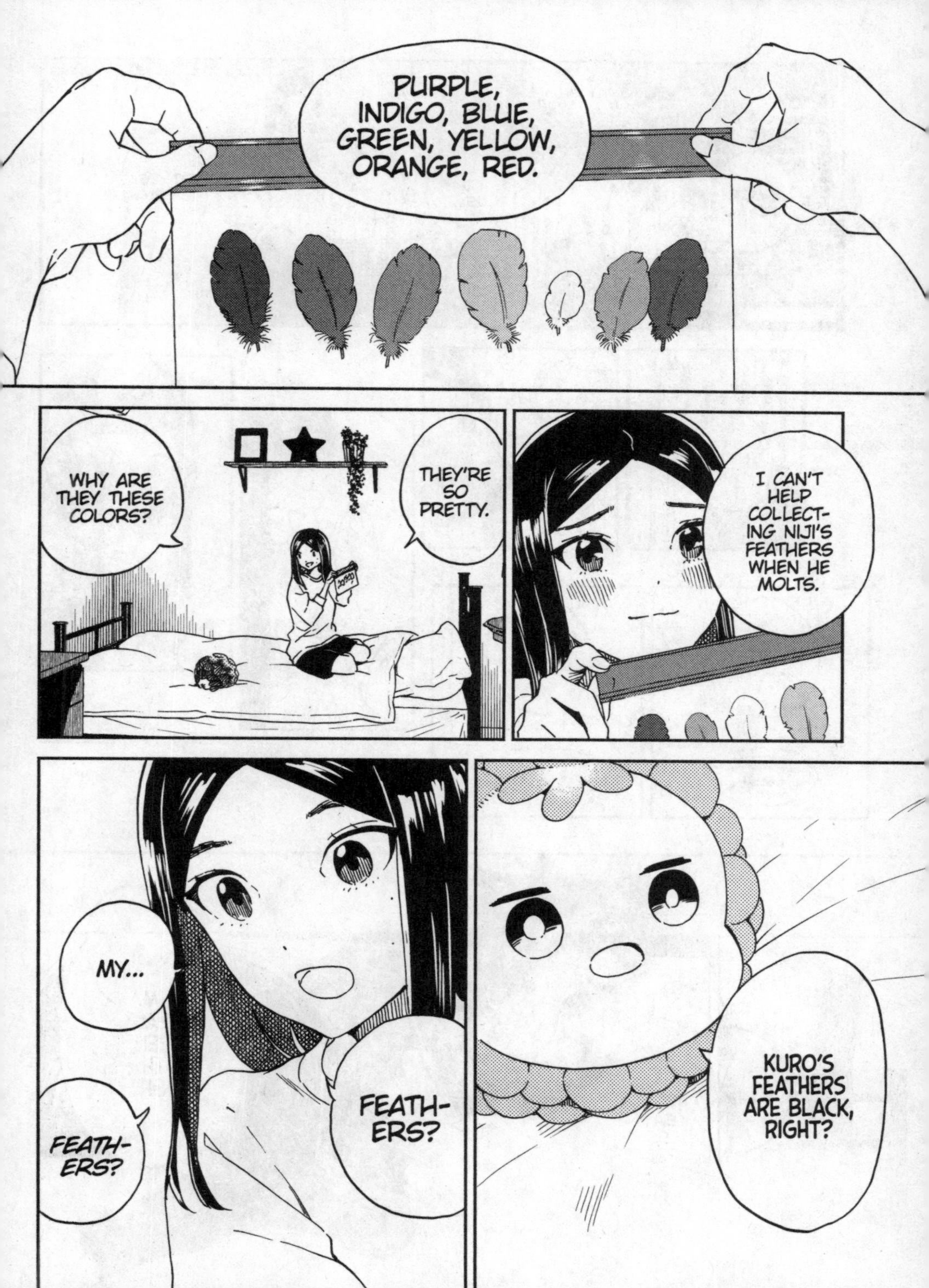
PURPLE, INDIGO, BLUE, GREEN, YELLOW, ORANGE, RED.
I CAN'T HELP COLLECT-ING NIJI'S FEATHERS WHEN HE MOLTS.
THEY'RE SO PRETTY.
WHY ARE THEY THESE COLORS?
KURO'S FEATHERS ARE BLACK, RIGHT?
MY...
FEATH-ERS?
FEATH-ERS?

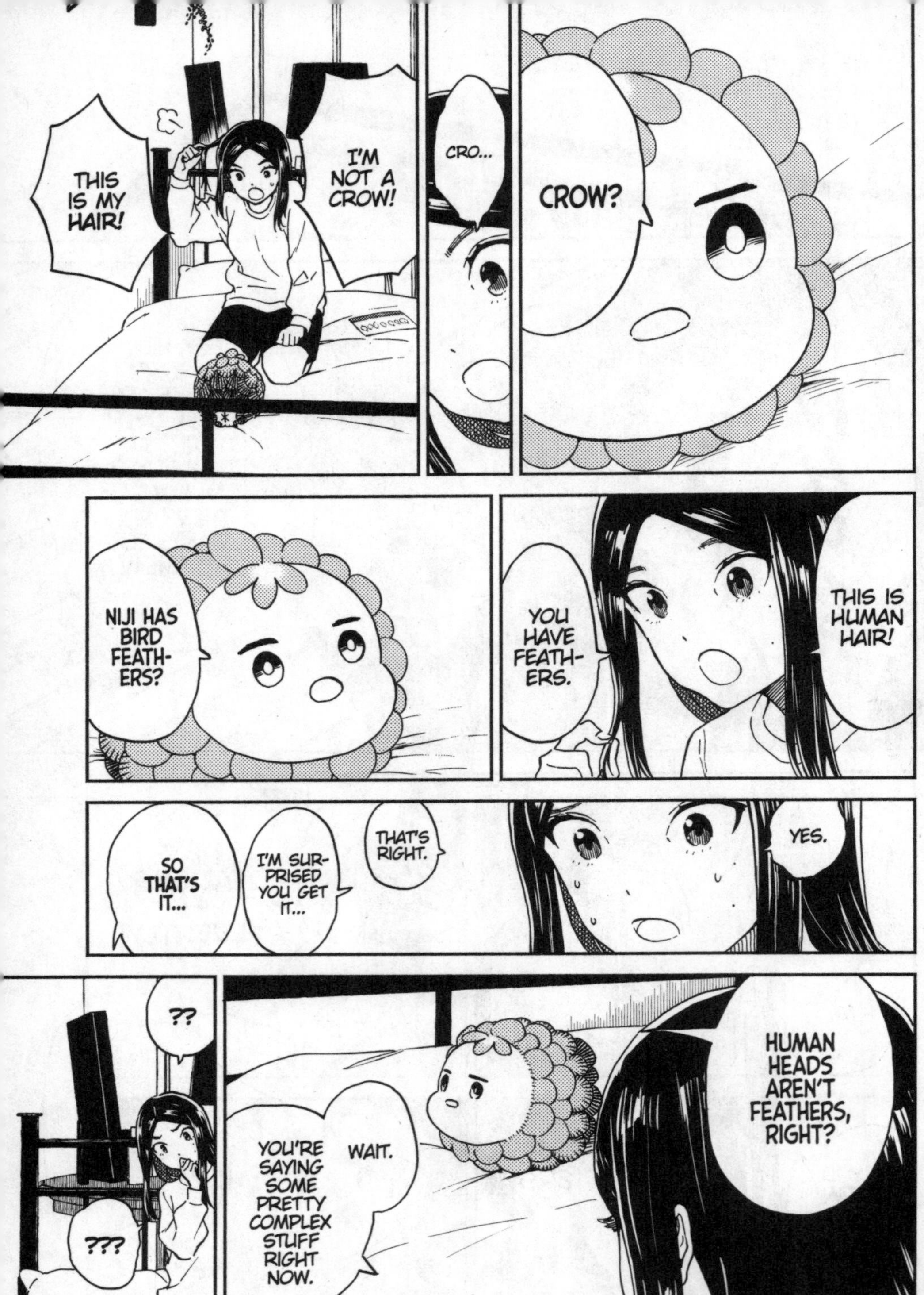
CROW?
CRO...
I'M NOT A CROW!
THIS IS MY HAIR!
THIS IS HUMAN HAIR!
YOU HAVE FEATHERS.
NIJI HAS BIRD FEATHERS?
YES.
THAT'S RIGHT.
I'M SURPRISED YOU GET IT...
SO THAT'S IT...
HUMAN HEADS AREN'T FEATHERS, RIGHT?
WAIT.
YOU'RE SAYING SOME PRETTY COMPLEX STUFF RIGHT NOW.
??
???

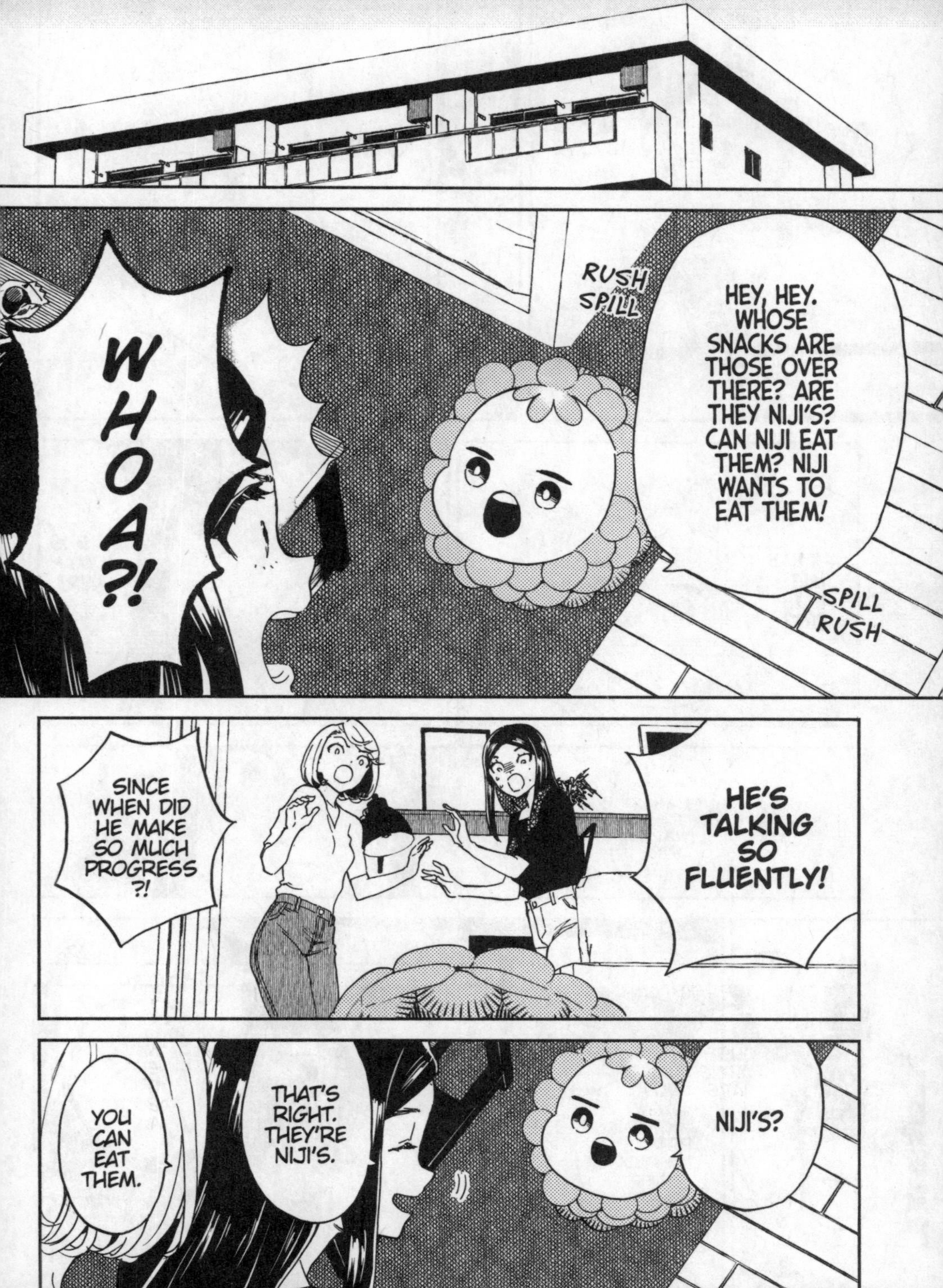
HEY, HEY. WHOSE SNACKS ARE THOSE OVER THERE? ARE THEY NIJI'S? CAN NIJI EAT THEM? NIJI WANTS TO EAT THEM!
RUSH SPILL
SPILL RUSH
WHOA?!
HE'S TALKING SO FLUENTLY!
SINCE WHEN DID HE MAKE SO MUCH PROGRESS?!
NIJI'S?
THAT'S RIGHT. THEY'RE NIJI'S.
YOU CAN EAT THEM.

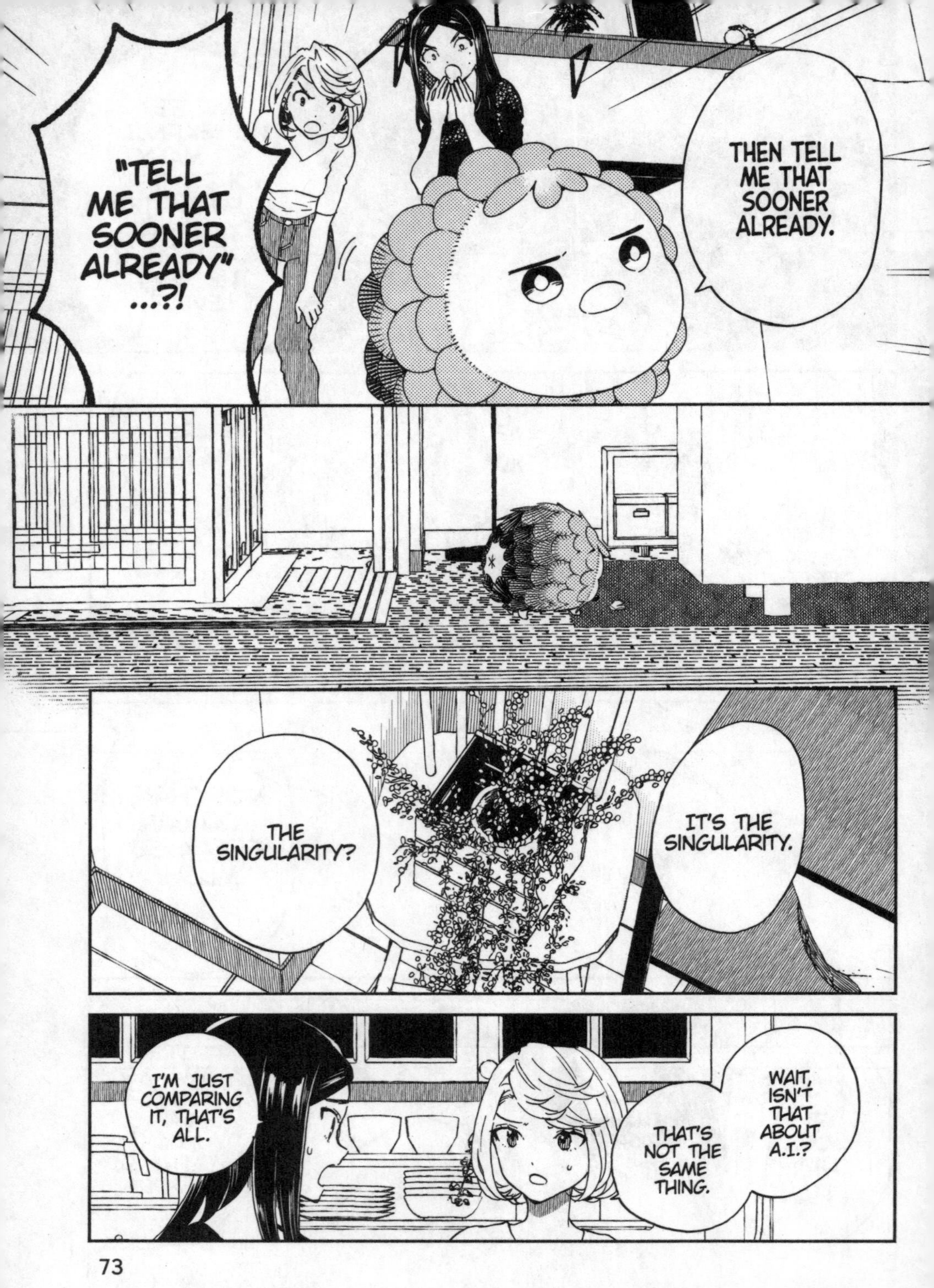
THEN TELL ME THAT SOONER ALREADY.
"TELL ME THAT SOONER ALREADY" ...?!
IT'S THE SINGULARITY.
THE SINGULARITY?
WAIT, ISN'T THAT ABOUT A.I.?
THAT'S NOT THE SAME THING.
I'M JUST COMPARING IT, THAT'S ALL.

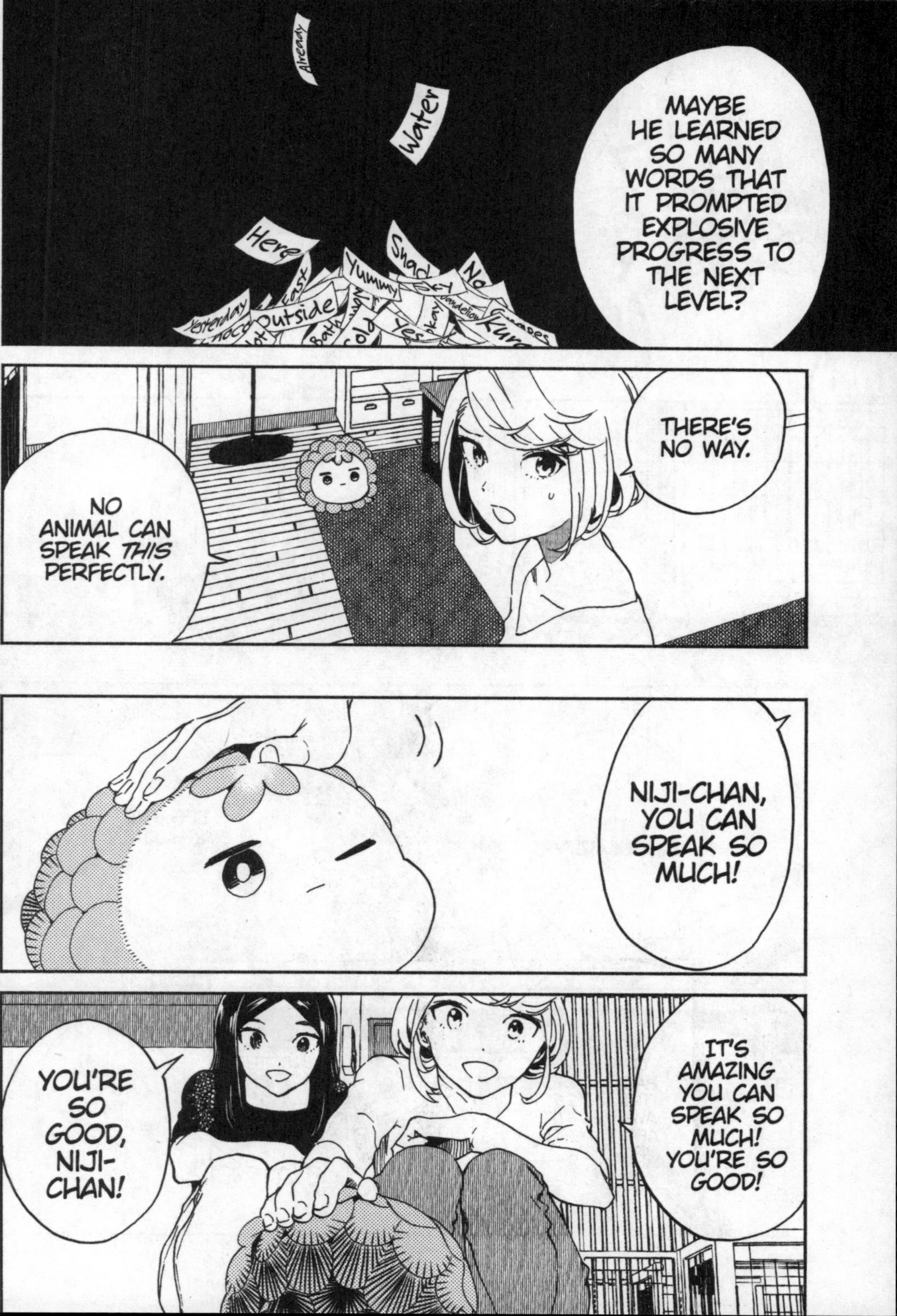
Already
Water
Here
Yummy
Easy
Yesterday
Outside
Cold
Yes
Dandelion
MAYBE HE LEARNED SO MANY WORDS THAT IT PROMPTED EXPLOSIVE PROGRESS TO THE NEXT LEVEL?
THERE'S NO WAY.
NO ANIMAL CAN SPEAK *THIS* PERFECTLY.
NIJI-CHAN, YOU CAN SPEAK SO MUCH!
IT'S AMAZING YOU CAN SPEAK SO MUCH! YOU'RE SO GOOD!
YOU'RE SO GOOD, NIJI-CHAN!

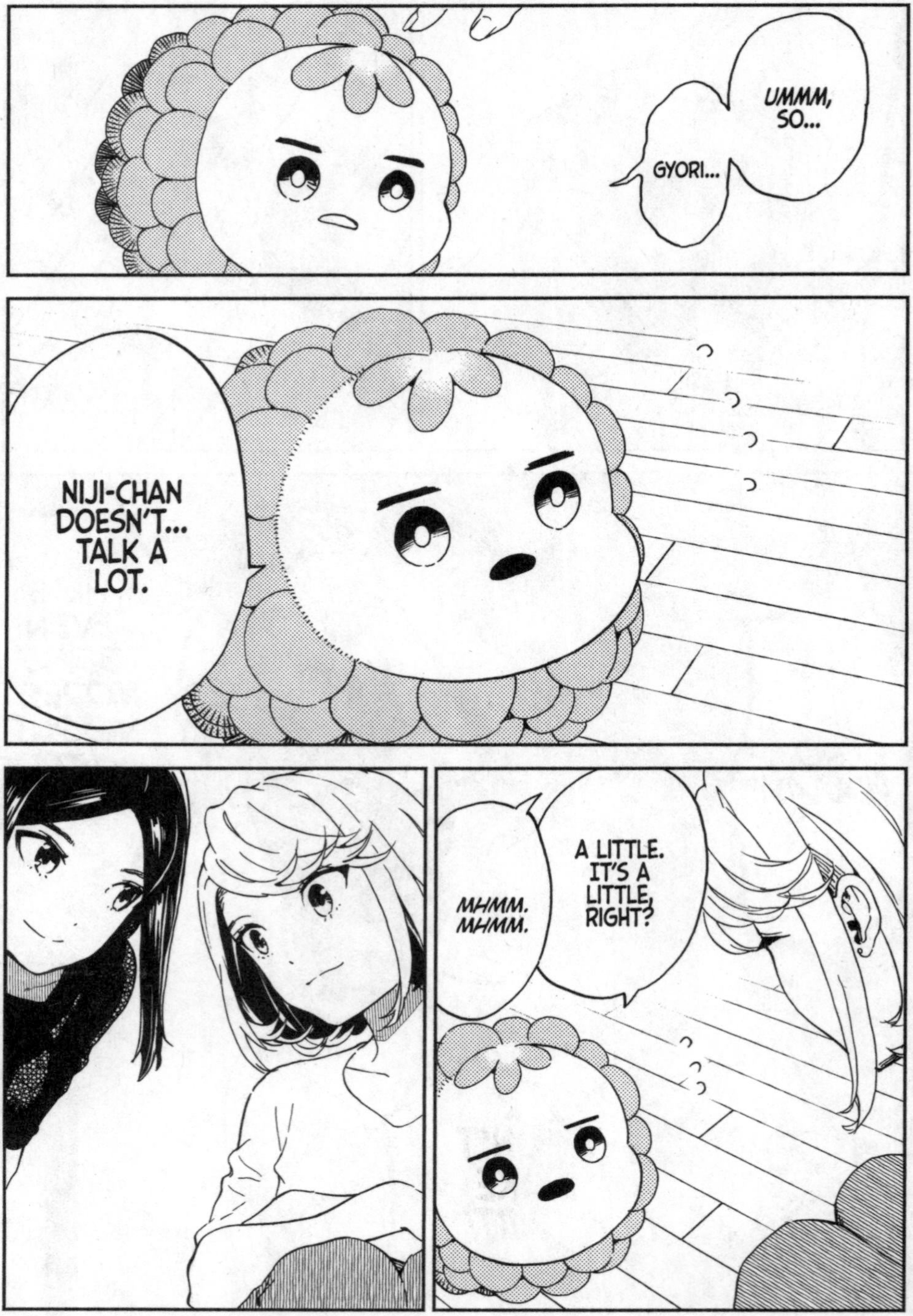
UMMM, SO...
GYORI...
NIJI-CHAN DOESN'T... TALK A LOT.
A LITTLE. IT'S A LITTLE, RIGHT?
MHMM. MHMM.

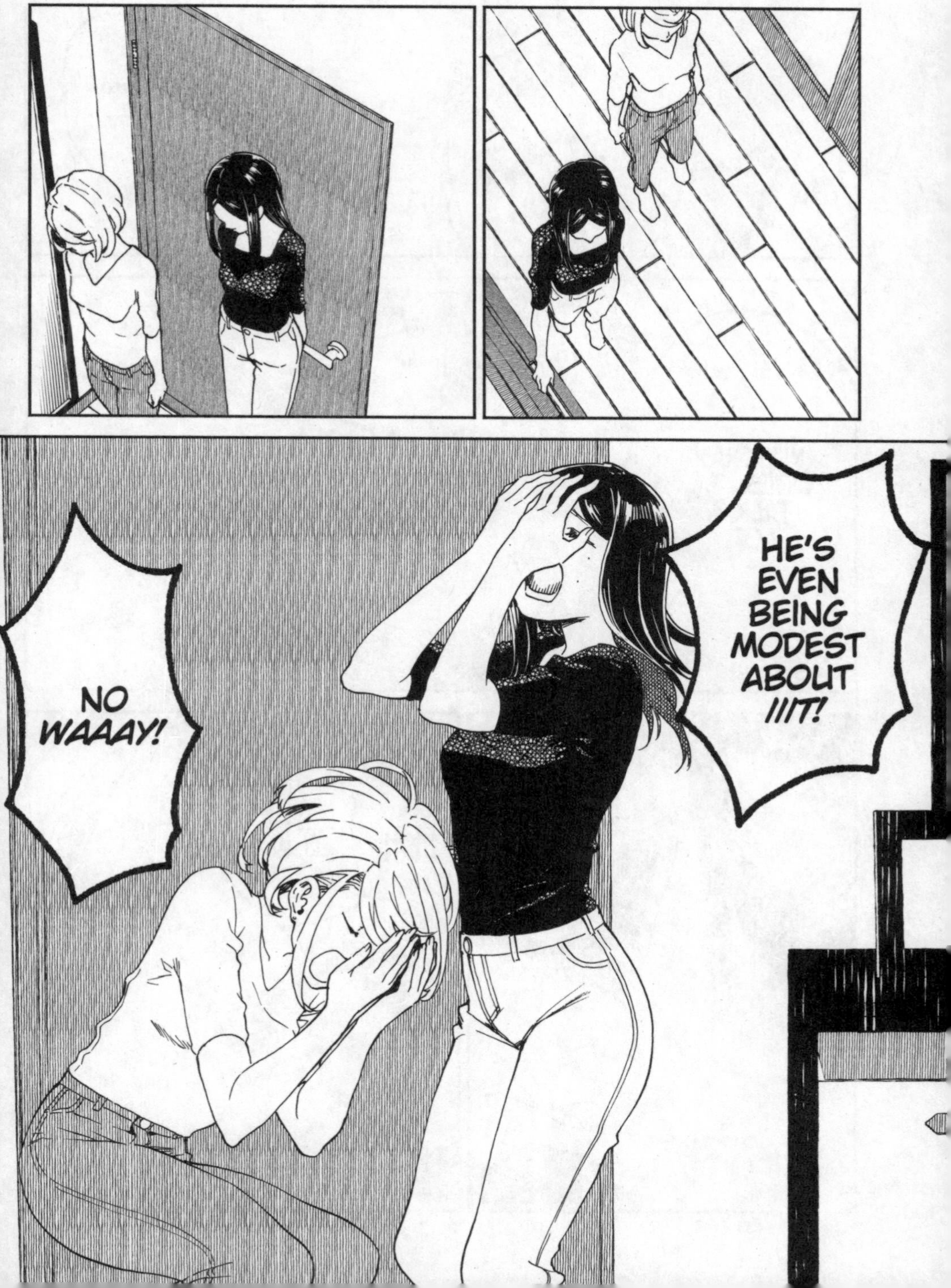
HE'S EVEN BEING MODEST ABOUT IIIT!
NO WAAAY!

Rainbow and Black

Story & Art by **Eri Takenashi**

NOW LOADING...

#23 Growing

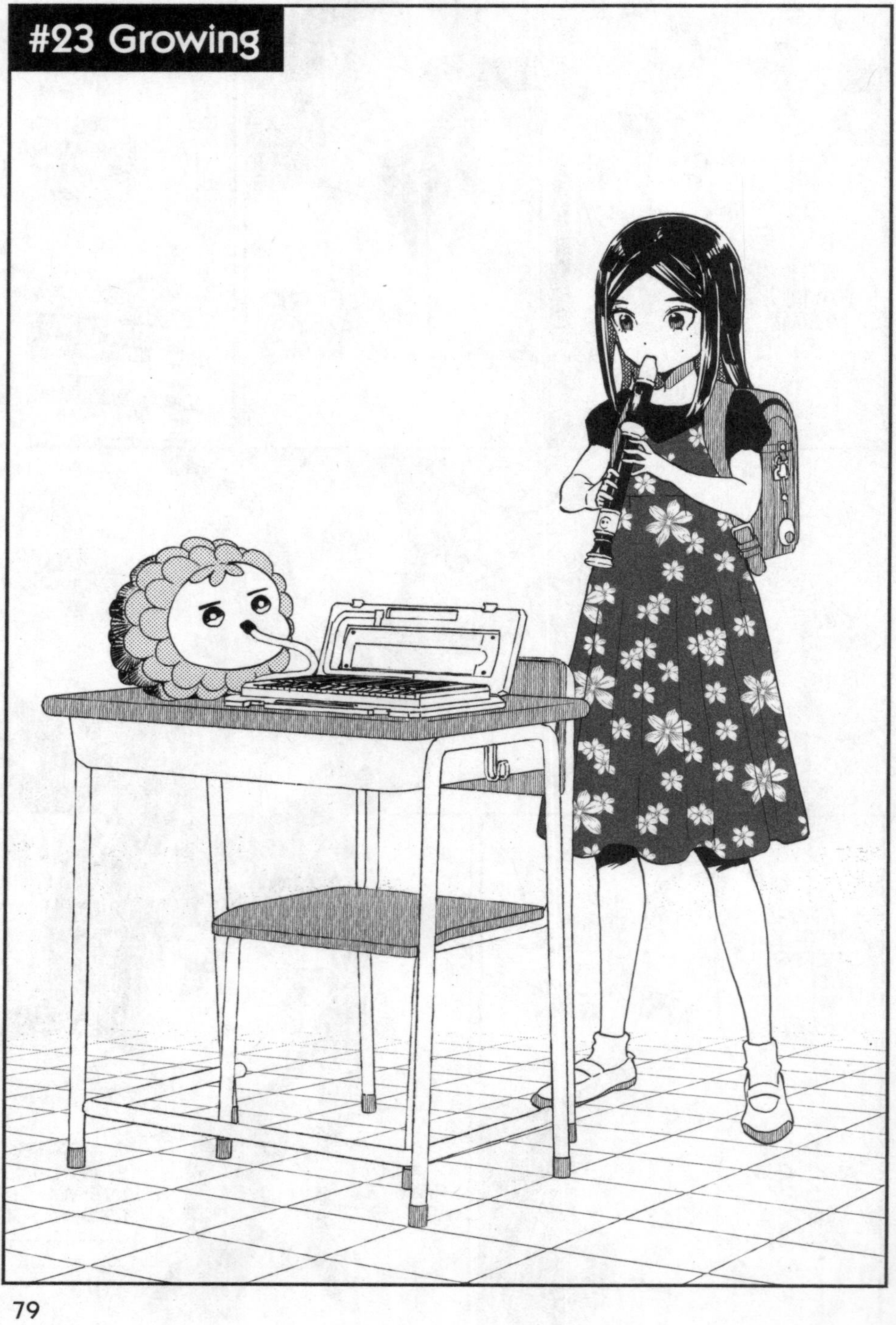

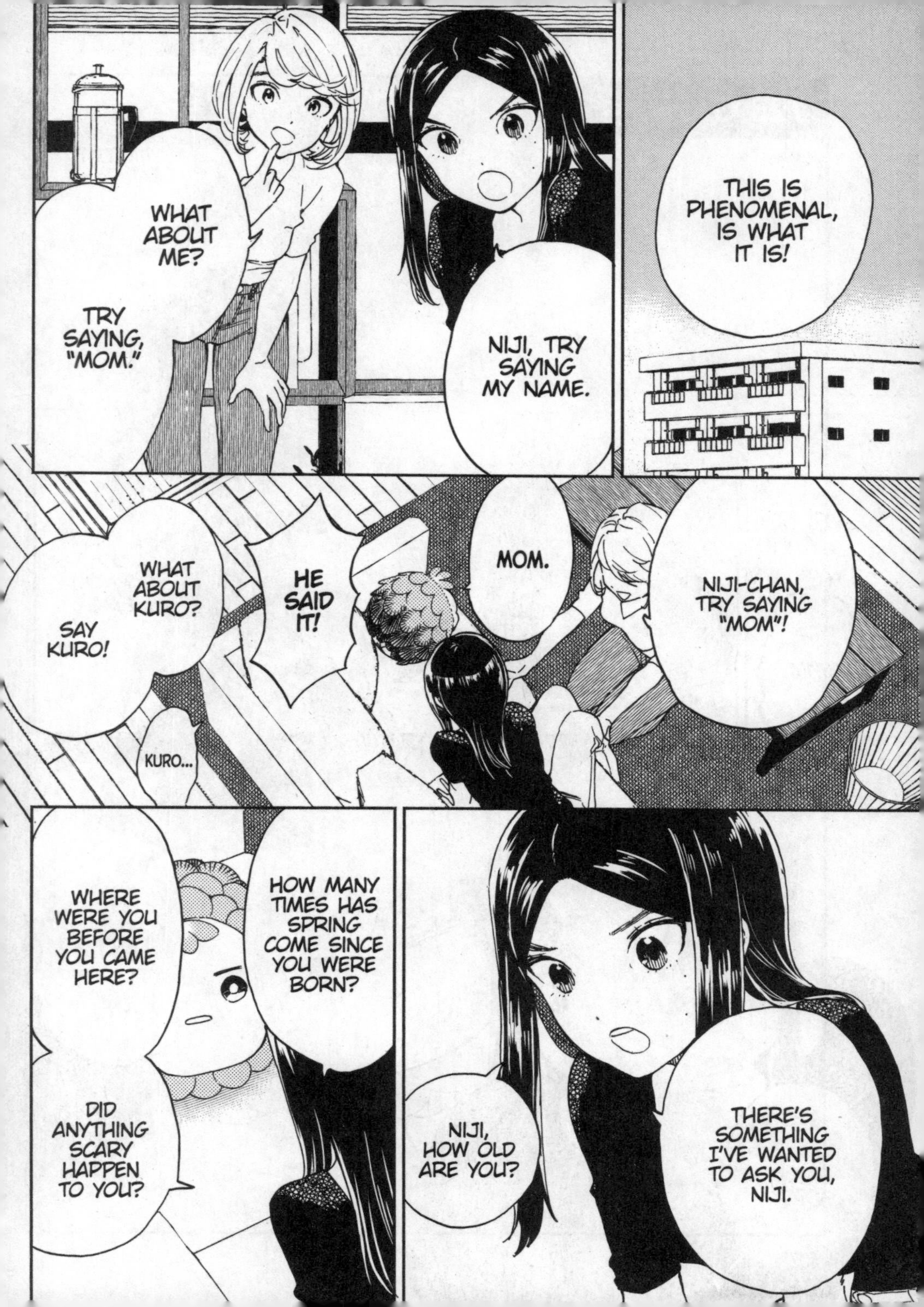
THIS IS PHENOMENAL, IS WHAT IT IS!
NIJI, TRY SAYING MY NAME.
WHAT ABOUT ME?
TRY SAYING, "MOM."
NIJI-CHAN, TRY SAYING "MOM"!
MOM.
HE SAID IT!
WHAT ABOUT KURO?
SAY KURO!
KURO...
THERE'S SOMETHING I'VE WANTED TO ASK YOU, NIJI.
NIJI, HOW OLD ARE YOU?
HOW MANY TIMES HAS SPRING COME SINCE YOU WERE BORN?
WHERE WERE YOU BEFORE YOU CAME HERE?
DID ANYTHING SCARY HAPPEN TO YOU?

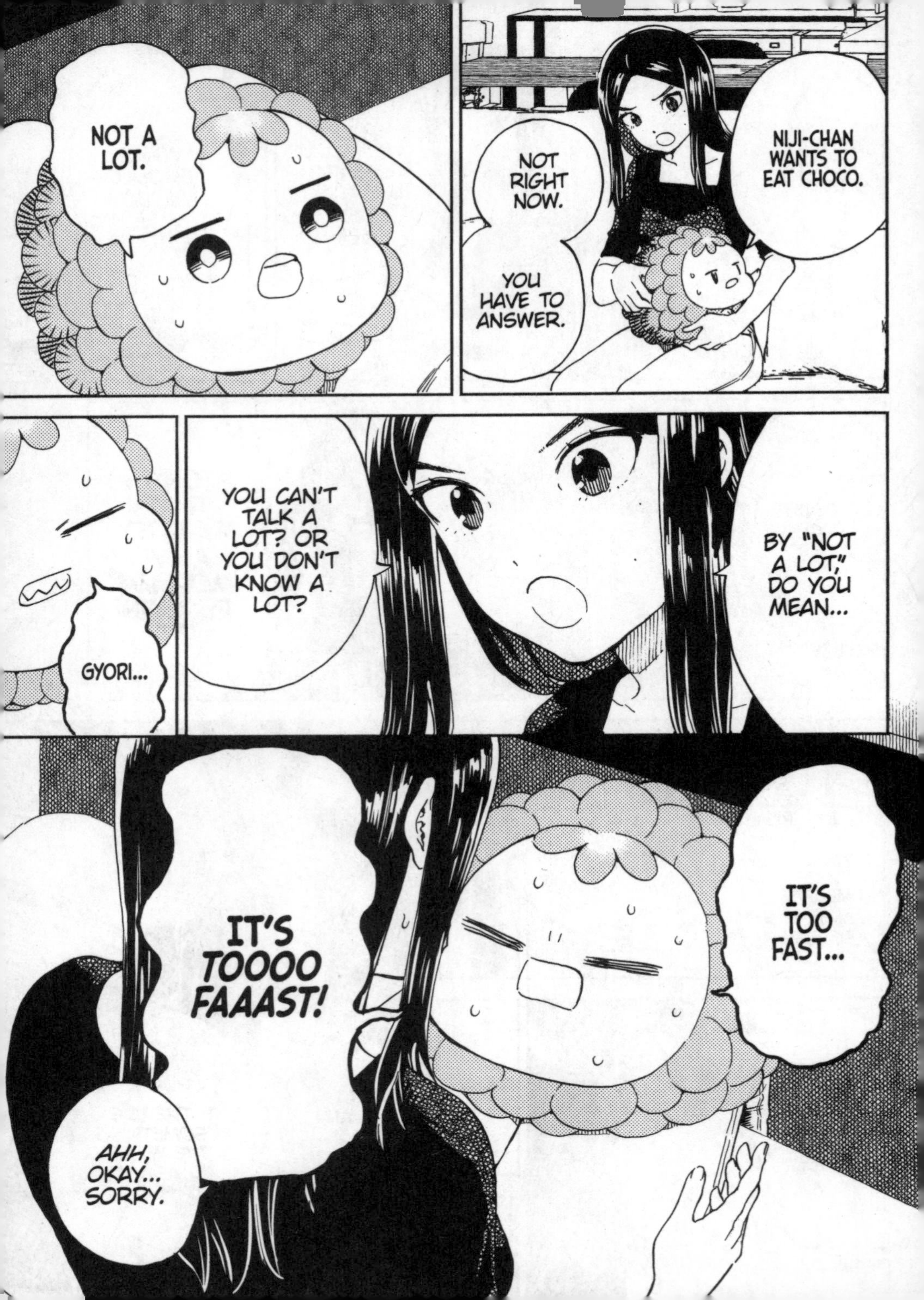
NIJI-CHAN WANTS TO EAT CHOCO.
NOT RIGHT NOW.
YOU HAVE TO ANSWER.
NOT A LOT.
BY "NOT A LOT," DO YOU MEAN...
YOU CAN'T TALK A LOT? OR YOU DON'T KNOW A LOT?
GYORI...
IT'S TOO FAST...
IT'S TOOOO FAAAST!
AHH, OKAY... SORRY.

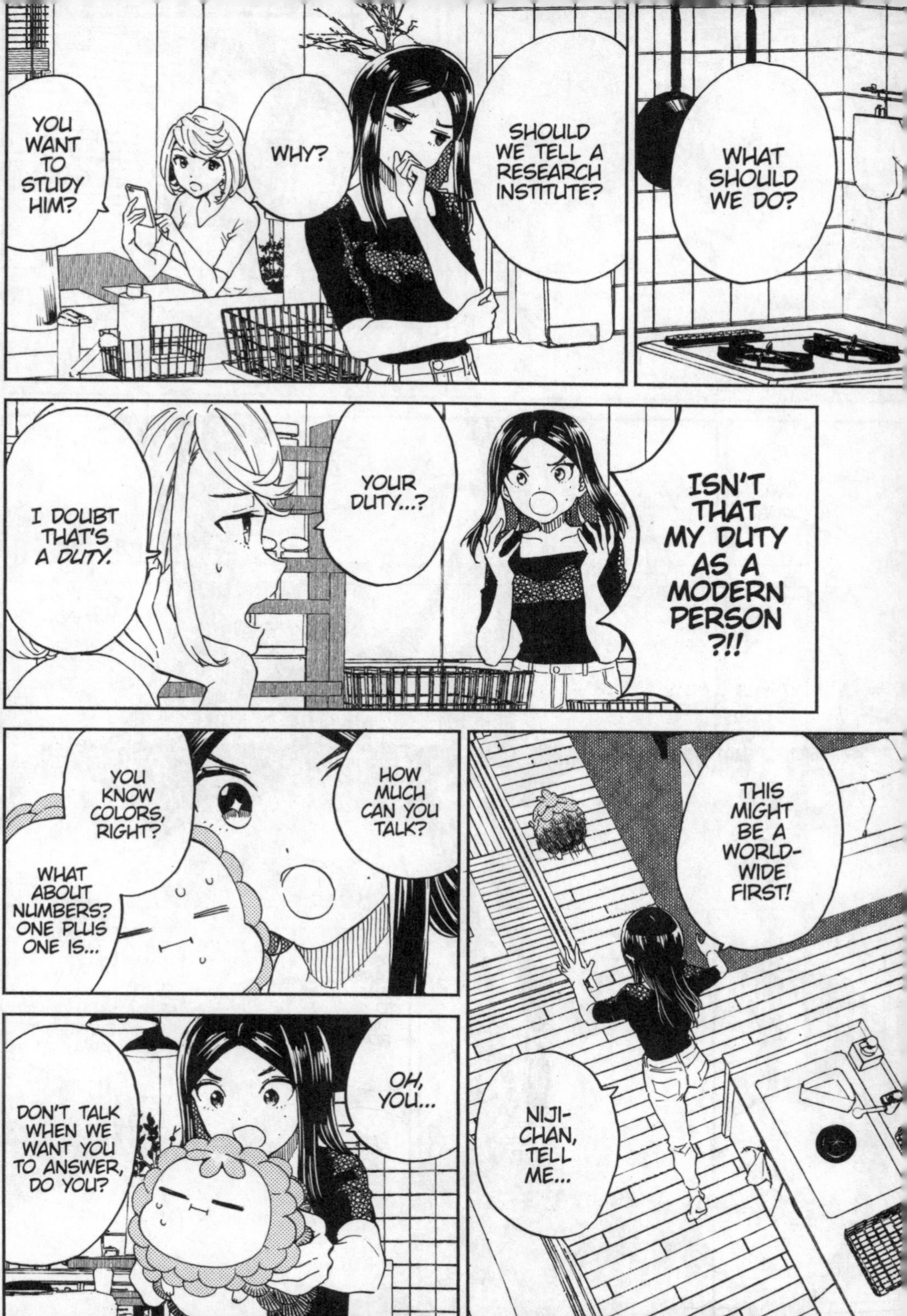
WHAT SHOULD WE DO?
SHOULD WE TELL A RESEARCH INSTITUTE?
WHY?
YOU WANT TO STUDY HIM?
ISN'T THAT MY DUTY AS A MODERN PERSON?!!
YOUR DUTY...?
I DOUBT THAT'S A *DUTY*.
THIS MIGHT BE A WORLD-WIDE FIRST!
NIJI-CHAN, TELL ME...
HOW MUCH CAN YOU TALK?
YOU KNOW COLORS, RIGHT?
WHAT ABOUT NUMBERS? ONE PLUS ONE IS...
OH, YOU...
DON'T TALK WHEN WE WANT YOU TO ANSWER, DO YOU?

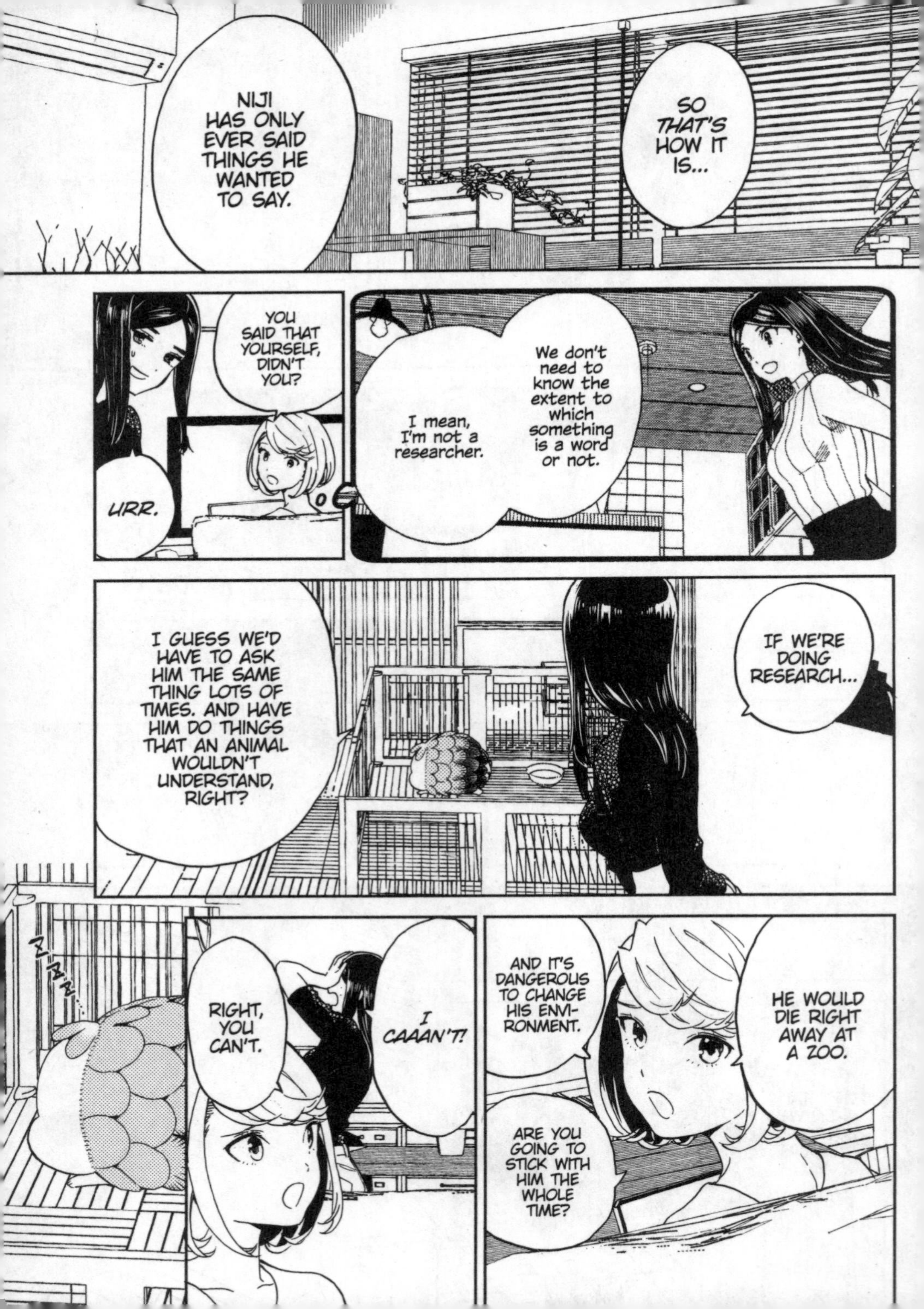
SO THAT'S HOW IT IS...
NIJI HAS ONLY EVER SAID THINGS HE WANTED TO SAY.
We don't need to know the extent to which something is a word or not.
I mean, I'm not a researcher.
YOU SAID THAT YOURSELF, DIDN'T YOU?
URR.
IF WE'RE DOING RESEARCH...
I GUESS WE'D HAVE TO ASK HIM THE SAME THING LOTS OF TIMES. AND HAVE HIM DO THINGS THAT AN ANIMAL WOULDN'T UNDERSTAND, RIGHT?
HE WOULD DIE RIGHT AWAY AT A ZOO.
AND IT'S DANGEROUS TO CHANGE HIS ENVI-RONMENT.
ARE YOU GOING TO STICK WITH HIM THE WHOLE TIME?
I CAAAN'T!
RIGHT, YOU CAN'T.
ZZZ

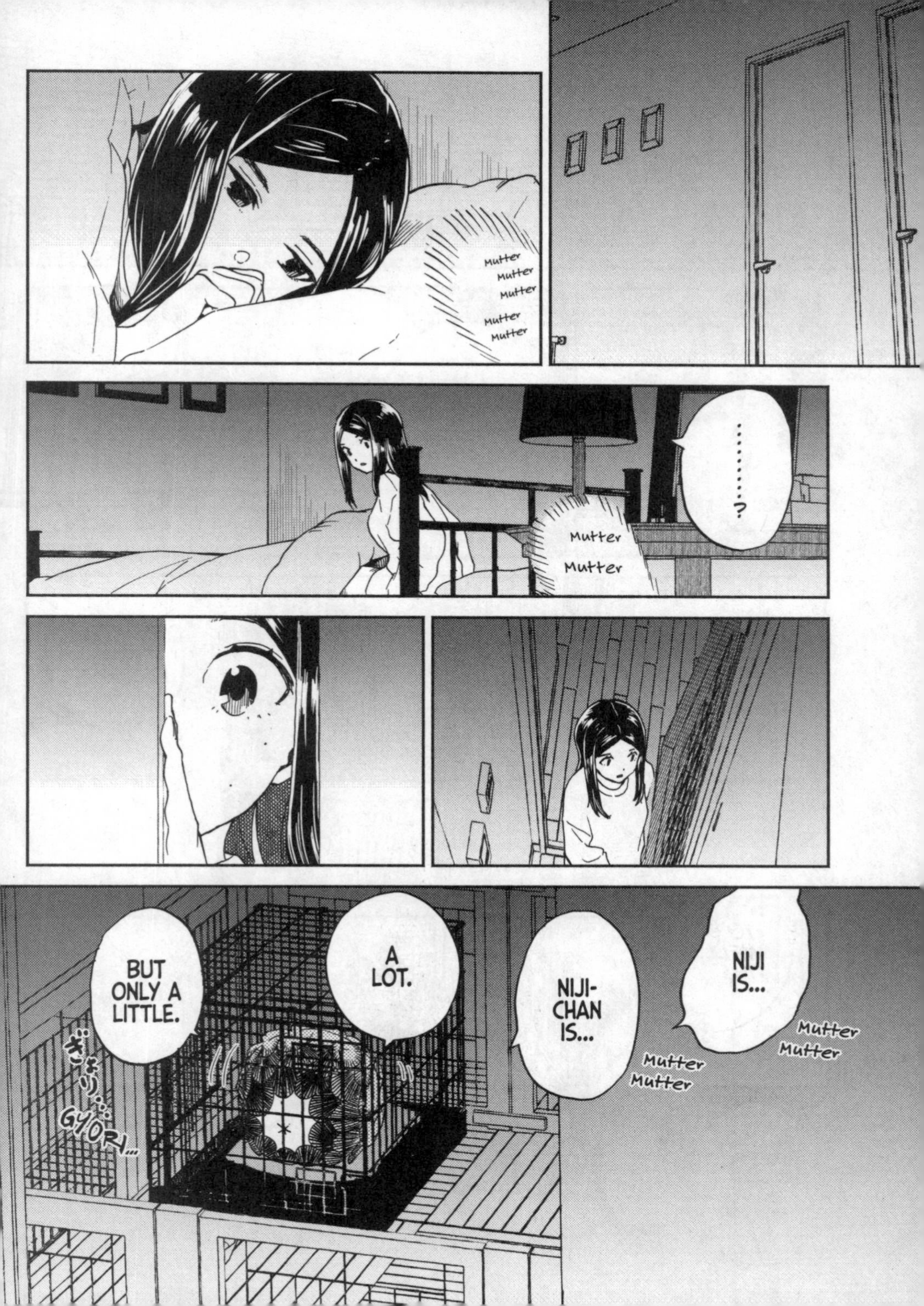
Mutter
Mutter
Mutter
Mutter
Mutter
......?
Mutter
Mutter
Mutter
Mutter
NIJI IS...
Mutter
Mutter
NIJI-CHAN IS...
A LOT.
BUT ONLY A LITTLE.
ぎょり…
GYORI...

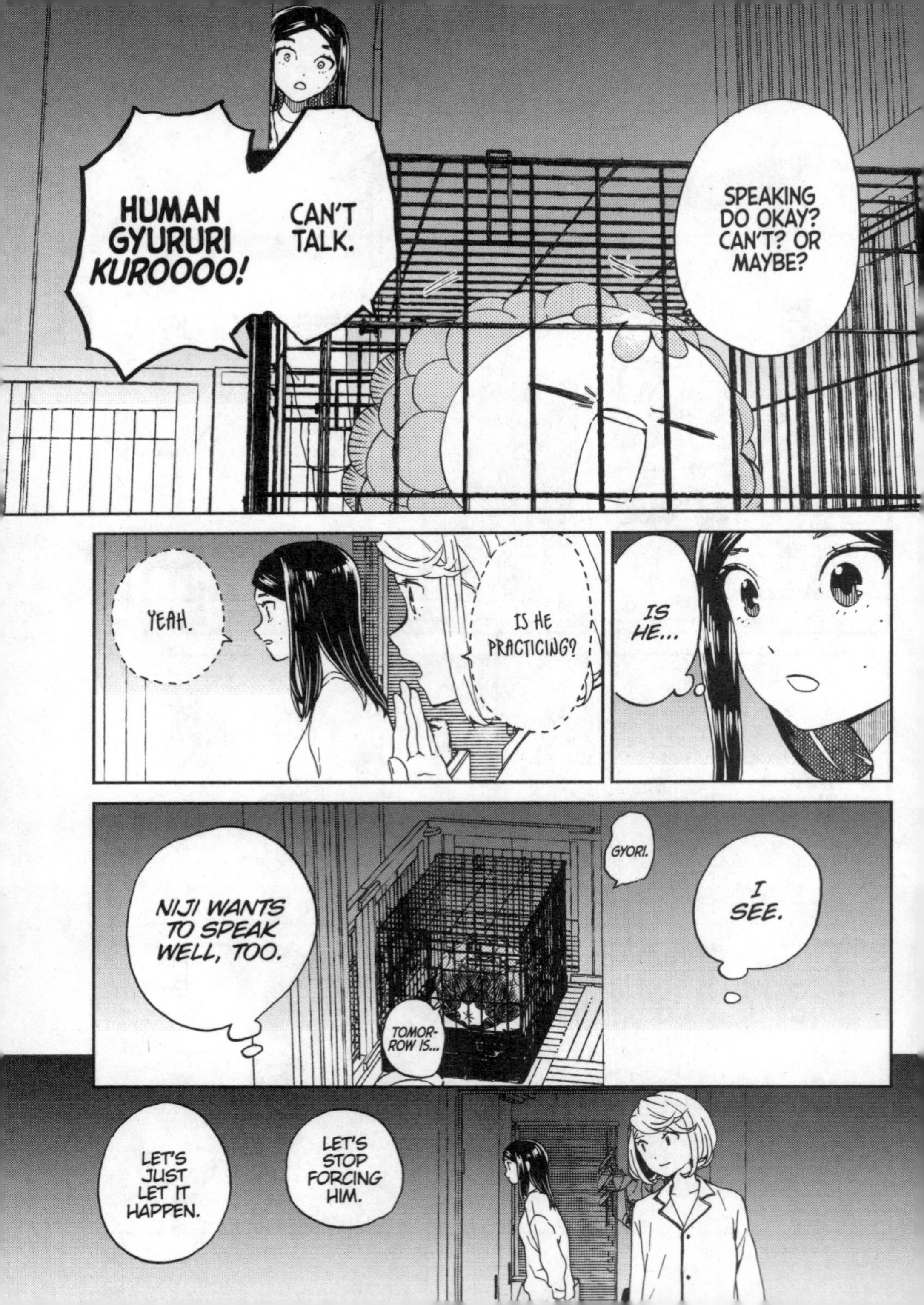
SPEAKING DO OKAY? CAN'T? OR MAYBE?
CAN'T TALK.
HUMAN GYURURI KUROOOO!
IS HE...
IS HE PRACTICING?
YEAH.
I SEE.
GYORI.
NIJI WANTS TO SPEAK WELL, TOO.
TOMOR-ROW IS...
LET'S STOP FORCING HIM.
LET'S JUST LET IT HAPPEN.

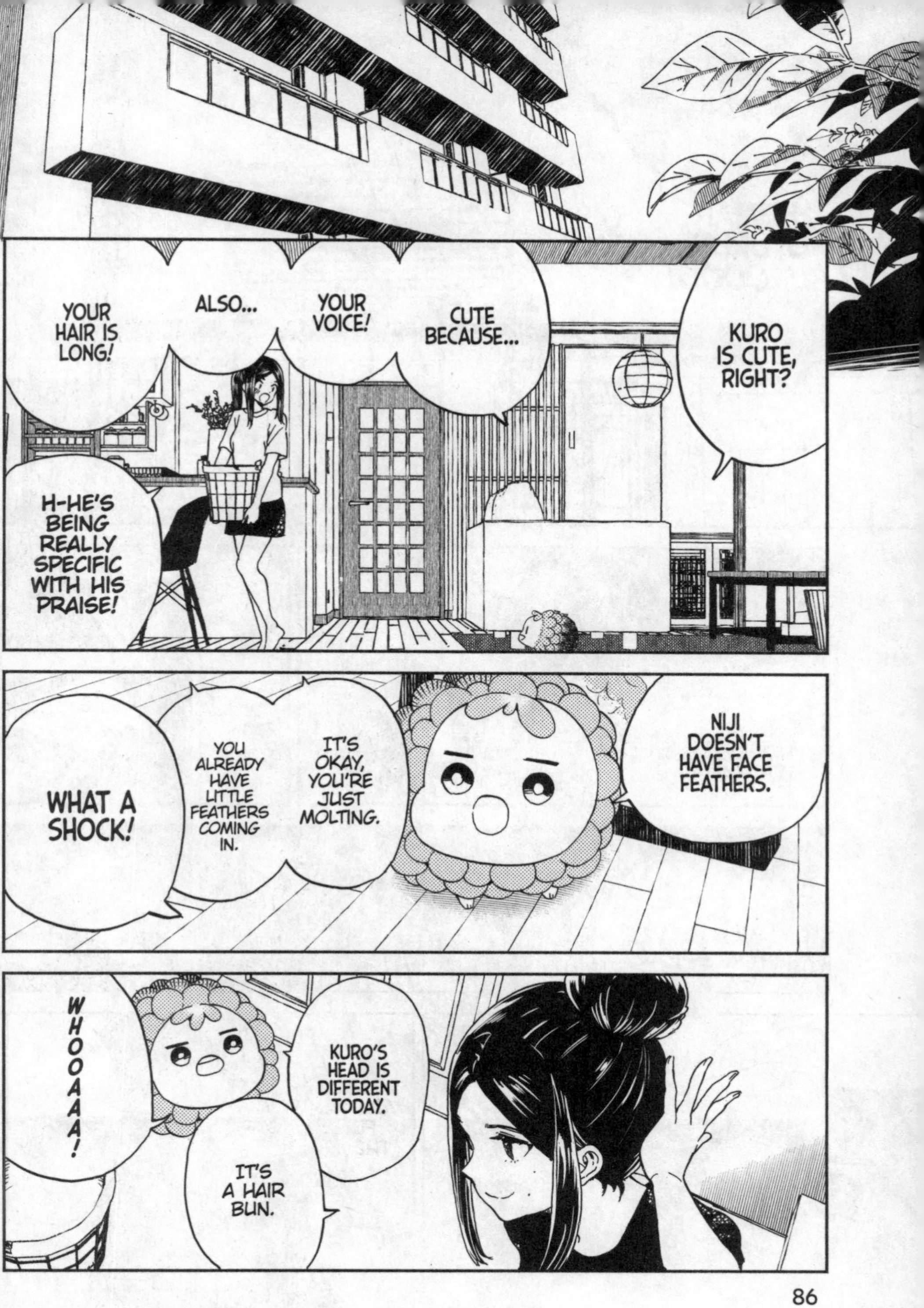
KURO IS CUTE, RIGHT?
CUTE BECAUSE...
YOUR VOICE!
ALSO...
YOUR HAIR IS LONG!
H-HE'S BEING REALLY SPECIFIC WITH HIS PRAISE!
NIJI DOESN'T HAVE FACE FEATHERS.
IT'S OKAY, YOU'RE JUST MOLTING.
YOU ALREADY HAVE LITTLE FEATHERS COMING IN.
WHAT A SHOCK!
KURO'S HEAD IS DIFFERENT TODAY.
IT'S A HAIR BUN.
WHOOAAA!

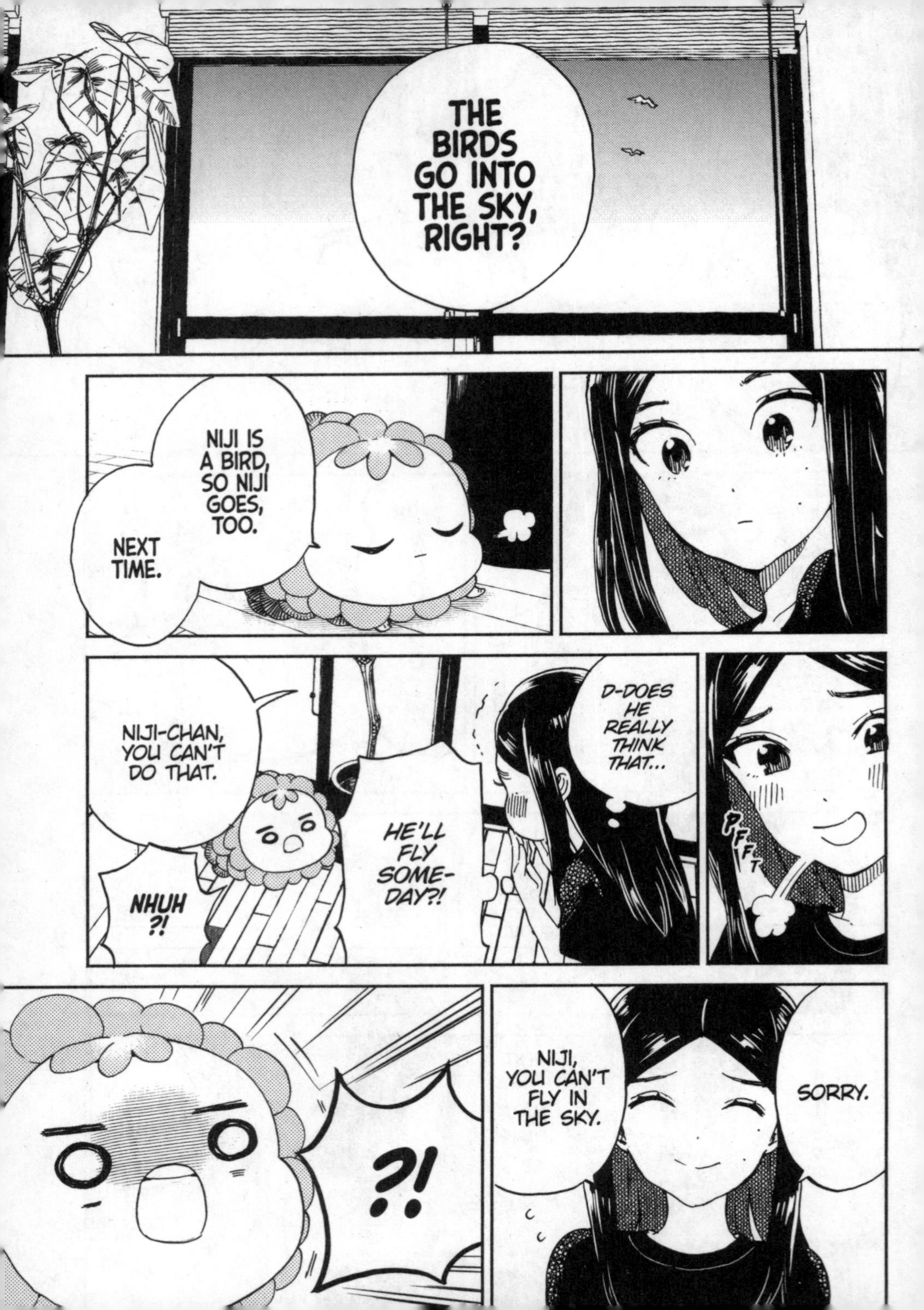
THE BIRDS GO INTO THE SKY, RIGHT?
NIJI IS A BIRD, SO NIJI GOES, TOO.
NEXT TIME.
PFFFT
D-DOES HE REALLY THINK THAT...
HE'LL FLY SOME-DAY?!
NIJI-CHAN, YOU CAN'T DO THAT.
NHUH ?!
NIJI, YOU CAN'T FLY IN THE SKY.
SORRY.
?!

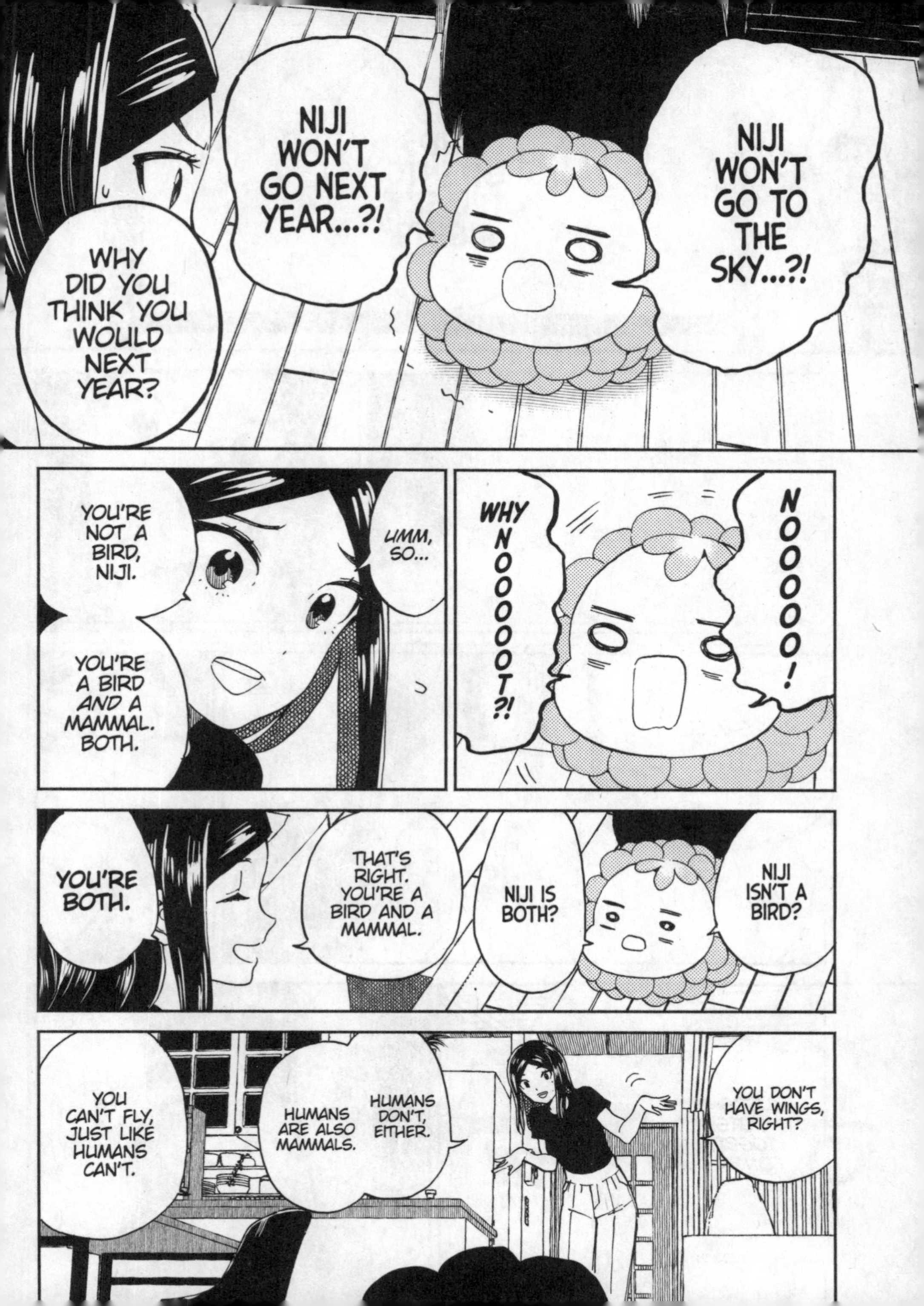
NIJI WON'T GO TO THE SKY...?!
NIJI WON'T GO NEXT YEAR...?!
WHY DID YOU THINK YOU WOULD NEXT YEAR?
NOOOOOO!
WHY NOOOOOOT?!
UMM, SO...
YOU'RE NOT A BIRD, NIJI.
YOU'RE A BIRD AND A MAMMAL. BOTH.
NIJI ISN'T A BIRD?
NIJI IS BOTH?
THAT'S RIGHT. YOU'RE A BIRD AND A MAMMAL.
YOU'RE BOTH.
YOU DON'T HAVE WINGS, RIGHT?
HUMANS DON'T, EITHER.
HUMANS ARE ALSO MAMMALS.
YOU CAN'T FLY, JUST LIKE HUMANS CAN'T.

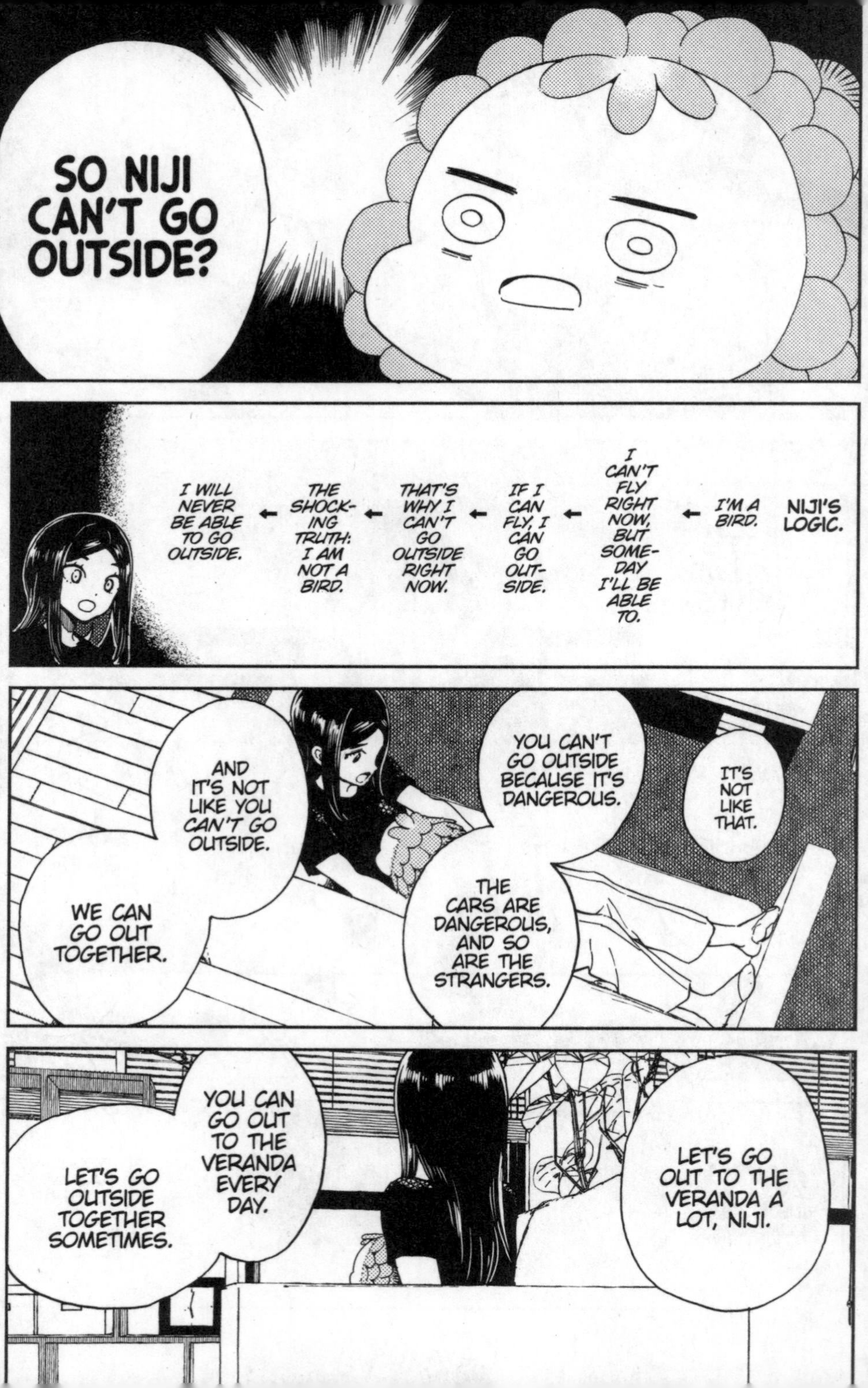
SO NIJI CAN'T GO OUTSIDE?
NIJI'S LOGIC.
I'M A BIRD.
←
I CAN'T FLY RIGHT NOW, BUT SOMEDAY I'LL BE ABLE TO.
←
IF I CAN FLY, I CAN GO OUTSIDE.
←
THAT'S WHY I CAN'T GO OUTSIDE RIGHT NOW.
←
THE SHOCKING TRUTH: I AM NOT A BIRD.
←
I WILL NEVER BE ABLE TO GO OUTSIDE.
IT'S NOT LIKE THAT.
YOU CAN'T GO OUTSIDE BECAUSE IT'S DANGEROUS.
THE CARS ARE DANGEROUS, AND SO ARE THE STRANGERS.
AND IT'S NOT LIKE YOU CAN'T GO OUTSIDE.
WE CAN GO OUT TOGETHER.
LET'S GO OUT TO THE VERANDA A LOT, NIJI.
YOU CAN GO OUT TO THE VERANDA EVERY DAY.
LET'S GO OUTSIDE TOGETHER SOMETIMES.

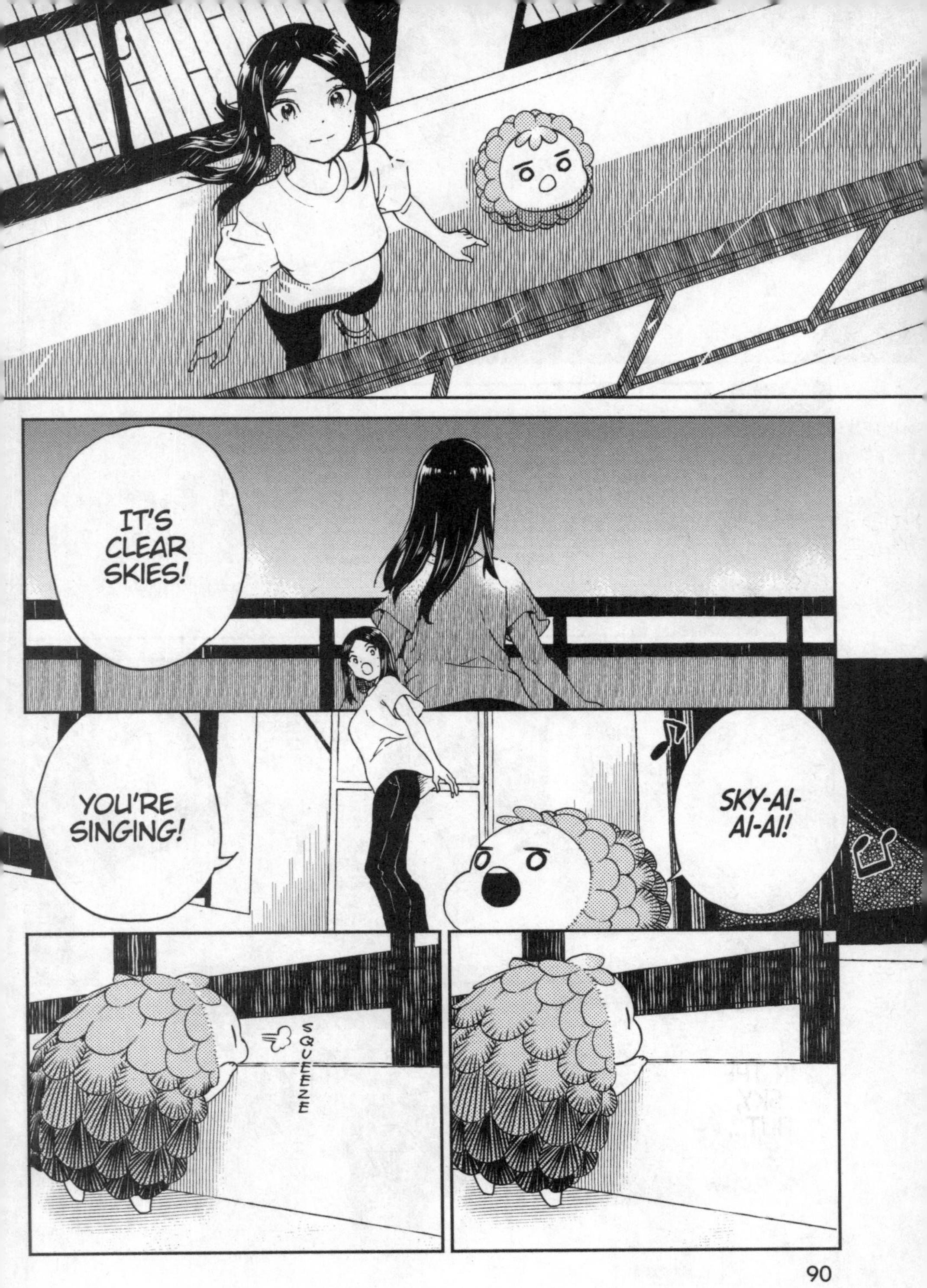
IT'S CLEAR SKIES!
SKY-AI-AI-AI!
YOU'RE SINGING!
SQUEEZE

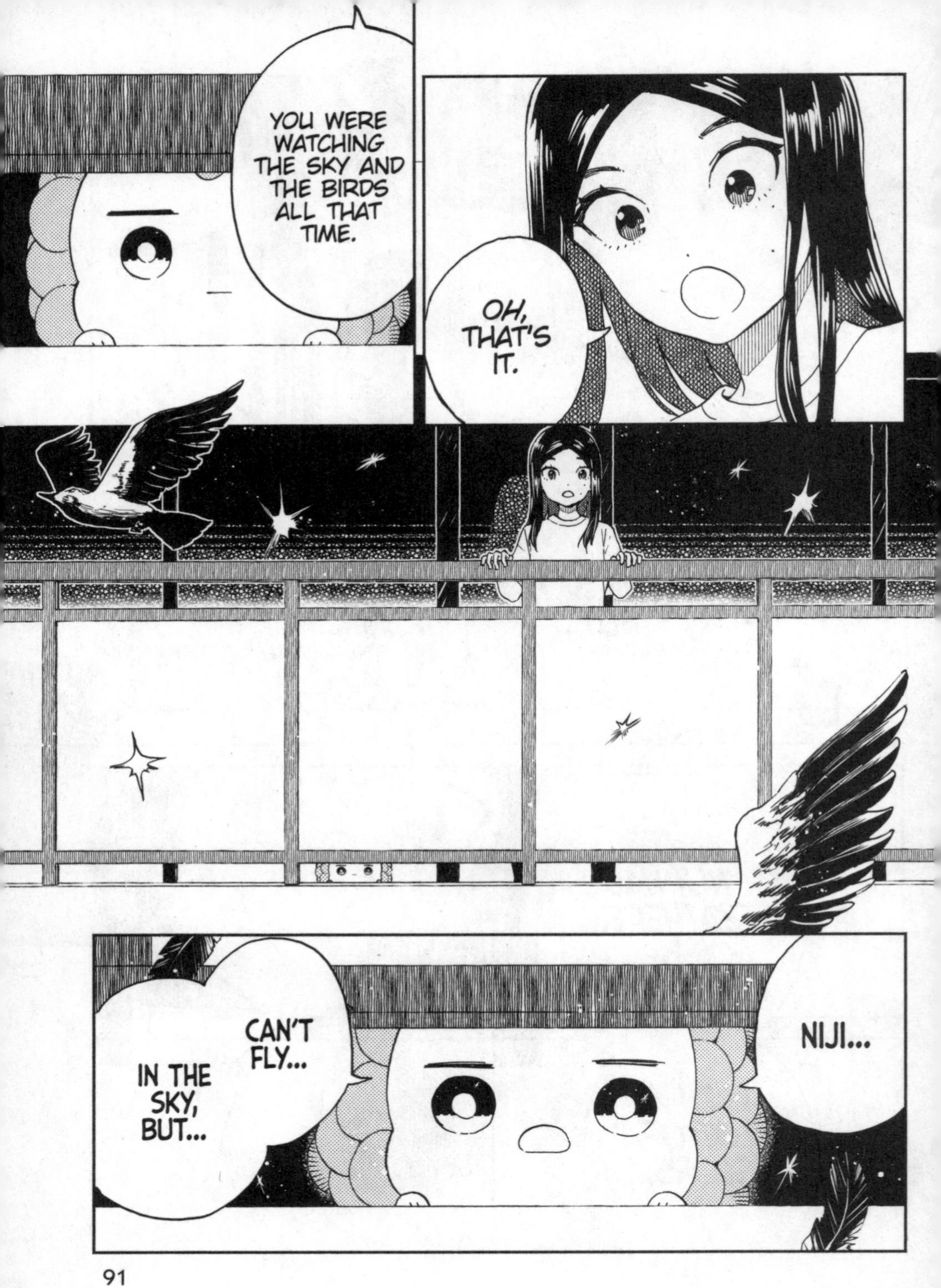
OH, THAT'S IT.
YOU WERE WATCHING THE SKY AND THE BIRDS ALL THAT TIME.
NIJI...
CAN'T FLY...
IN THE SKY, BUT...

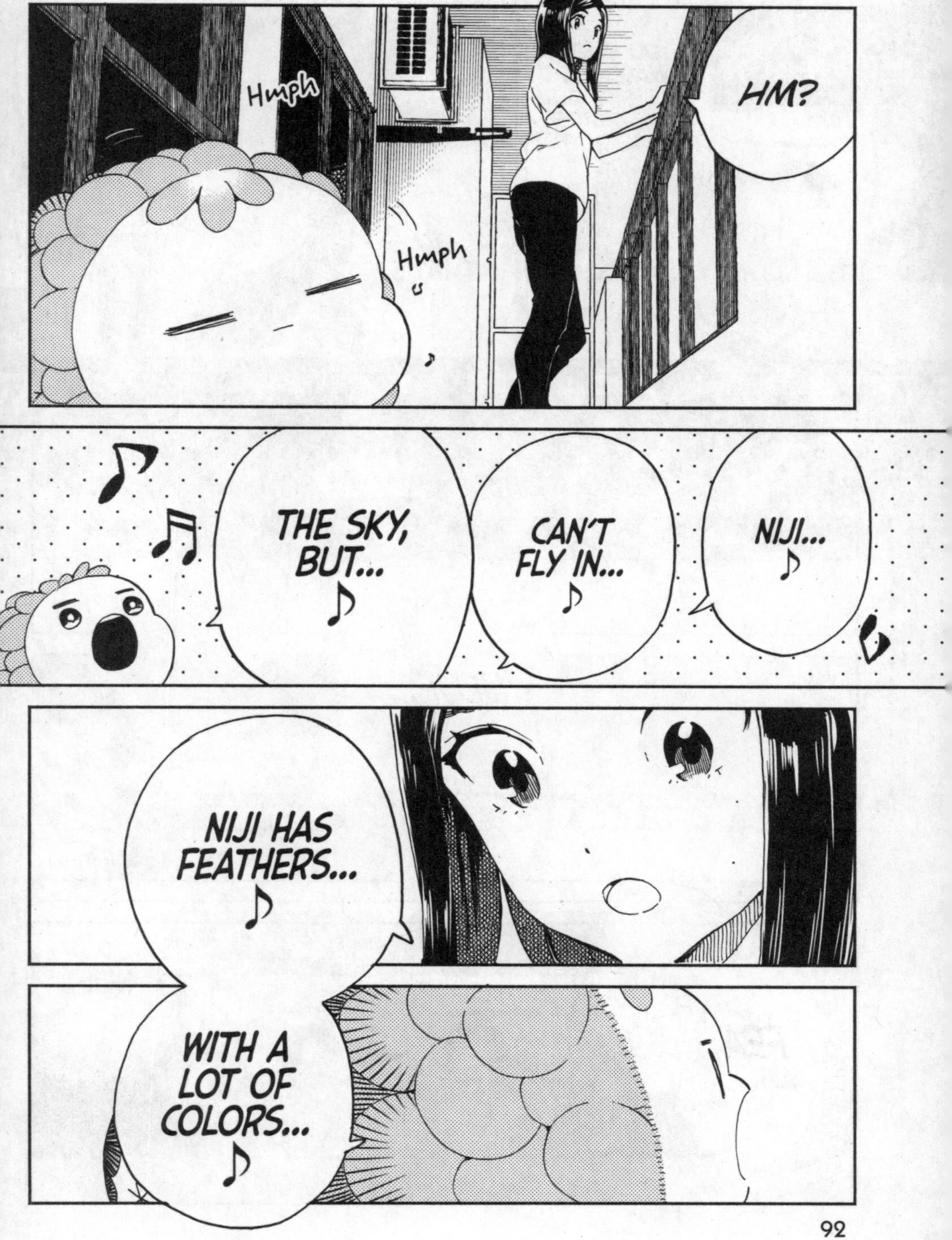
HM?
Hmph
Hmph
NIJI... ♪
CAN'T FLY IN... ♪
THE SKY, BUT... ♪
NIJI HAS FEATHERS... ♪
WITH A LOT OF COLORS... ♪

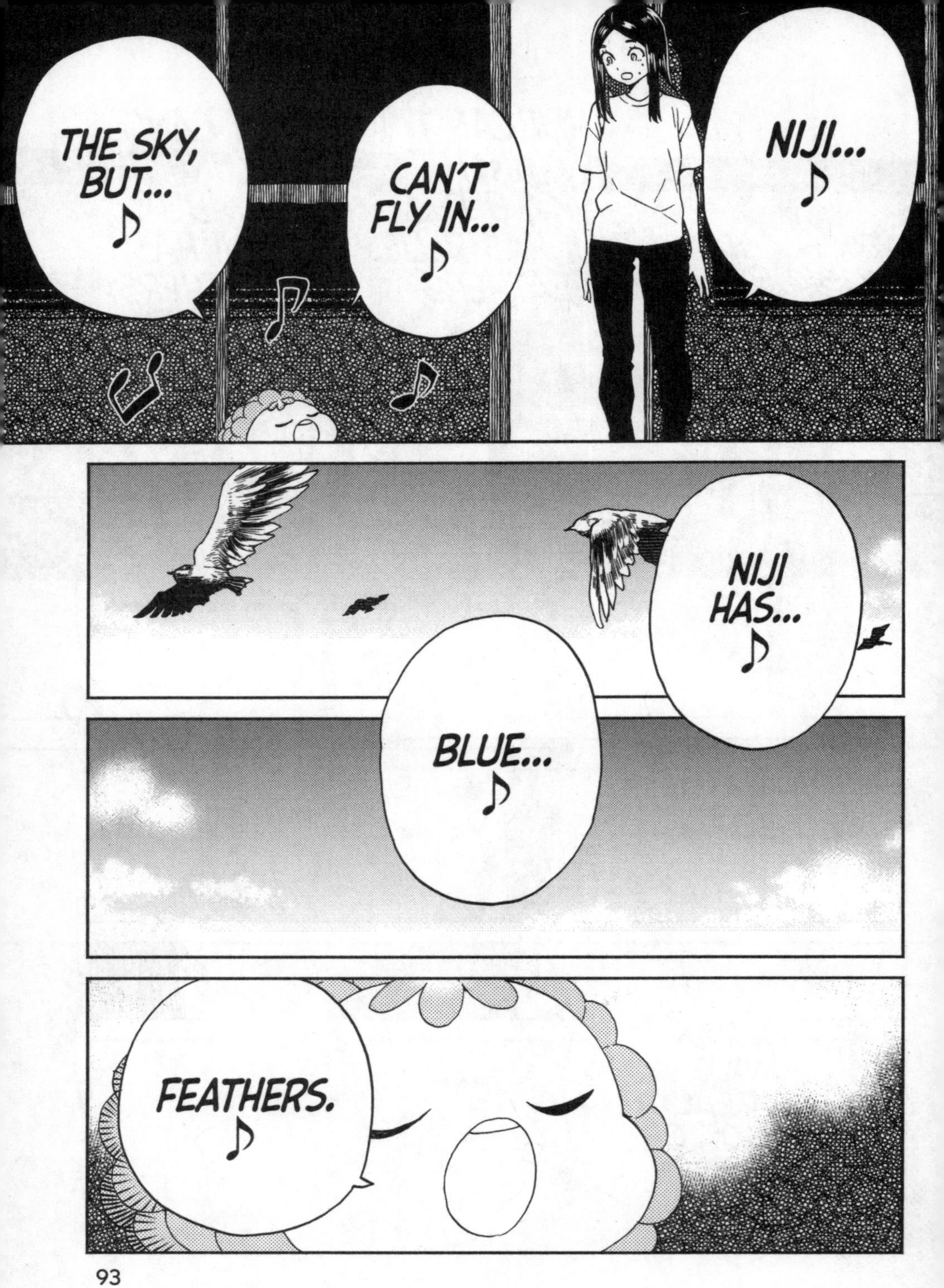
NIJI... ♪
CAN'T FLY IN... ♪
THE SKY, BUT... ♪
NIJI HAS... ♪
BLUE... ♪
FEATHERS. ♪

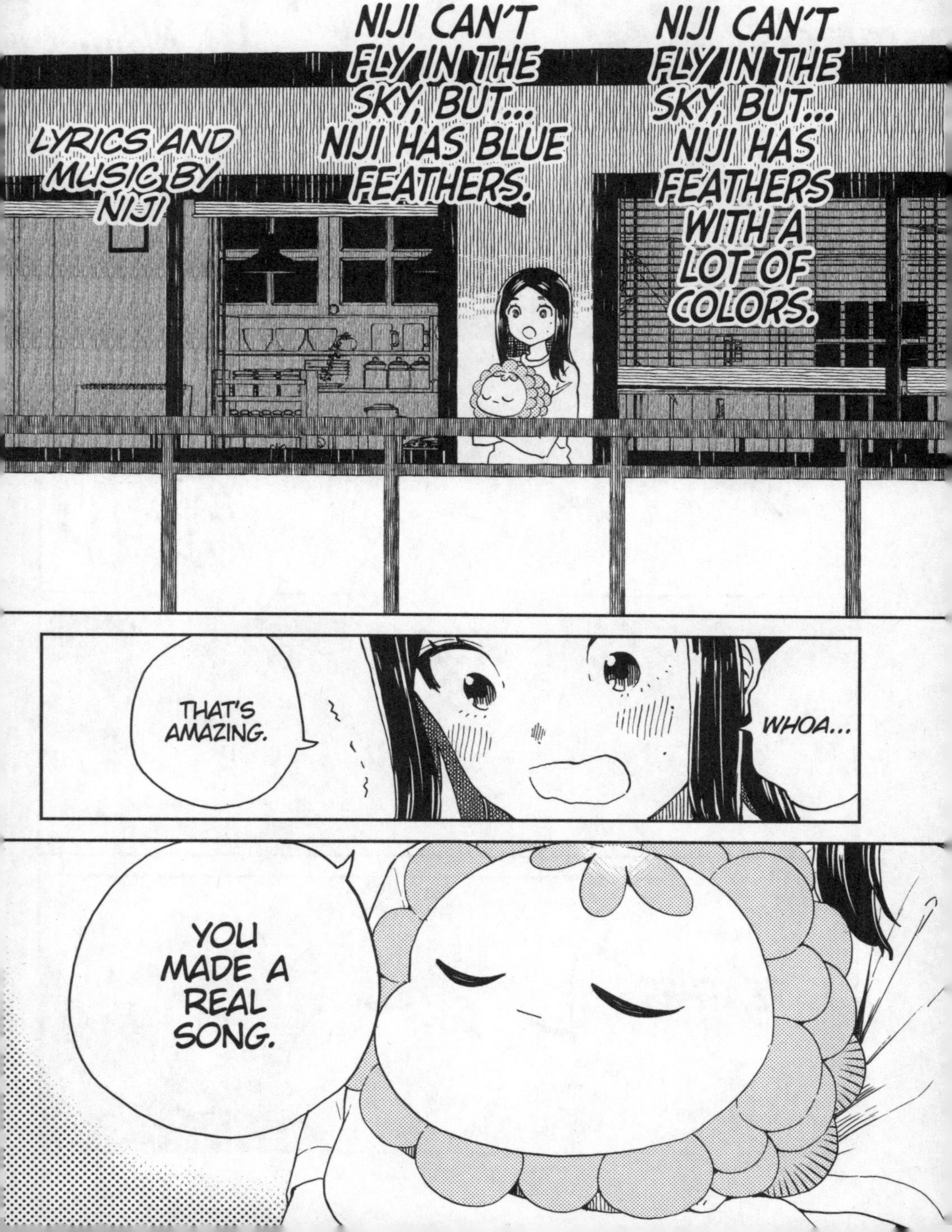
NIJI CAN'T FLY IN THE SKY, BUT... NIJI HAS FEATHERS WITH A LOT OF COLORS.
NIJI CAN'T FLY IN THE SKY, BUT... NIJI HAS BLUE FEATHERS.
LYRICS AND MUSIC BY NIJI
WHOA...
THAT'S AMAZING.
YOU MADE A REAL SONG.

Rainbow and Black

Story & Art by Eri Takenashi

NOW LOADING...

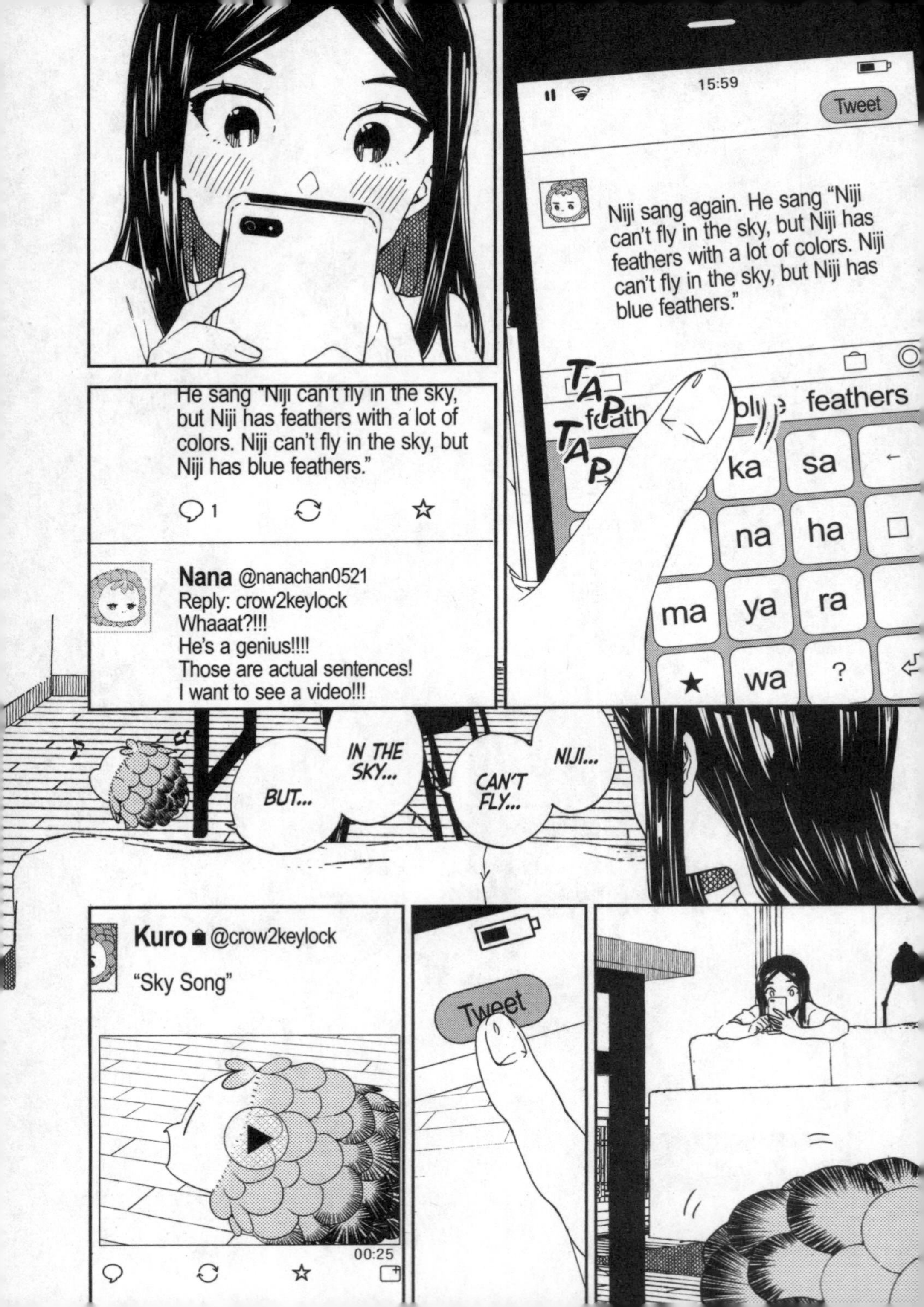
15:59
Tweet
Niji sang again. He sang "Niji can't fly in the sky, but Niji has feathers with a lot of colors. Niji can't fly in the sky, but Niji has blue feathers."
TAP TAP
feath
blue
feathers
ka sa
na ha
ma ya ra
wa ?
He sang "Niji can't fly in the sky, but Niji has feathers with a lot of colors. Niji can't fly in the sky, but Niji has blue feathers."
1
Nana @nanachan0521
Reply: crow2keylock
Whaaat?!!!
He's a genius!!!!
Those are actual sentences!
I want to see a video!!!
NIJI...
CAN'T FLY...
IN THE SKY...
BUT...
Tweet
Kuro @crow2keylock
"Sky Song"
00:25

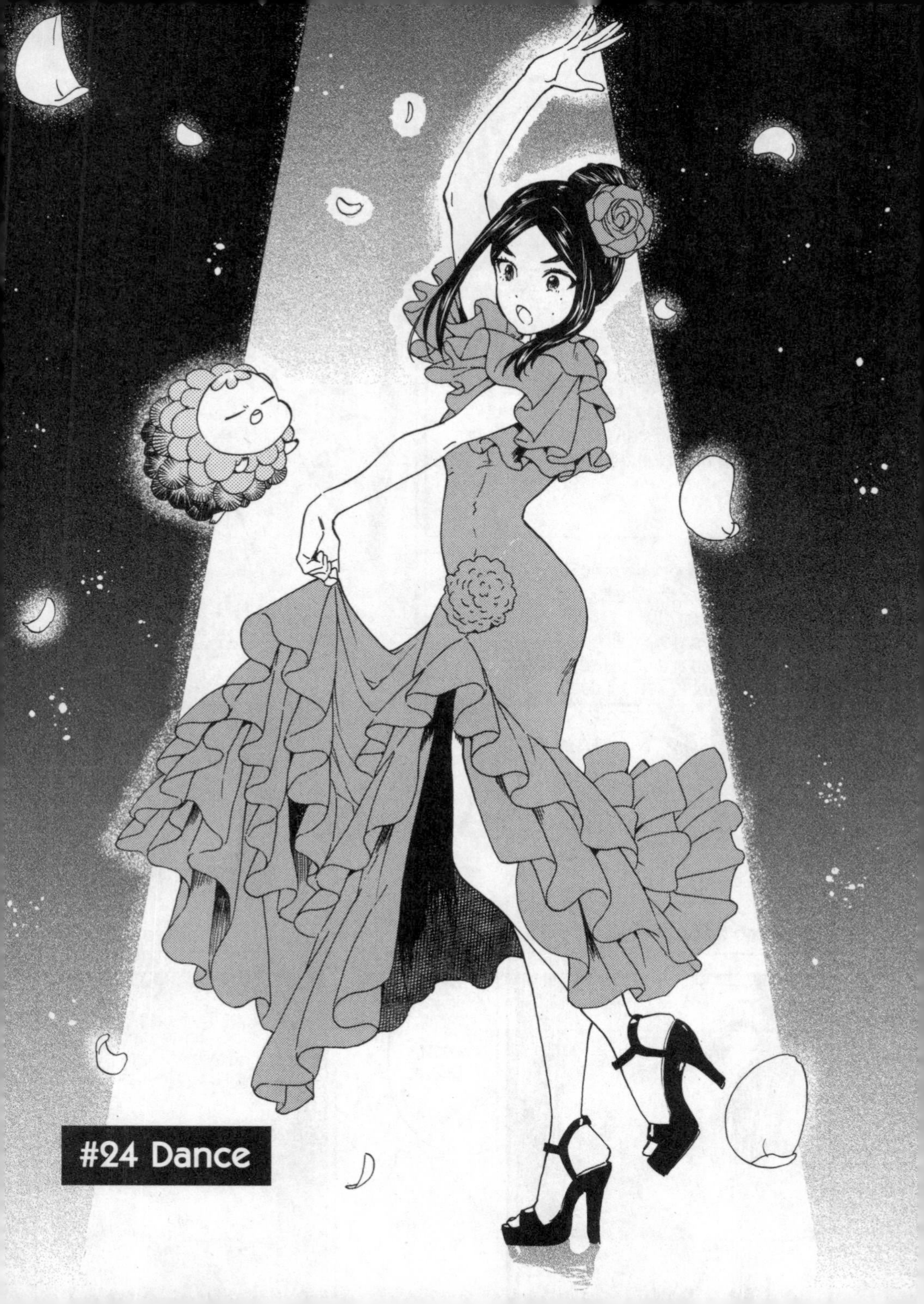
#24 Dance

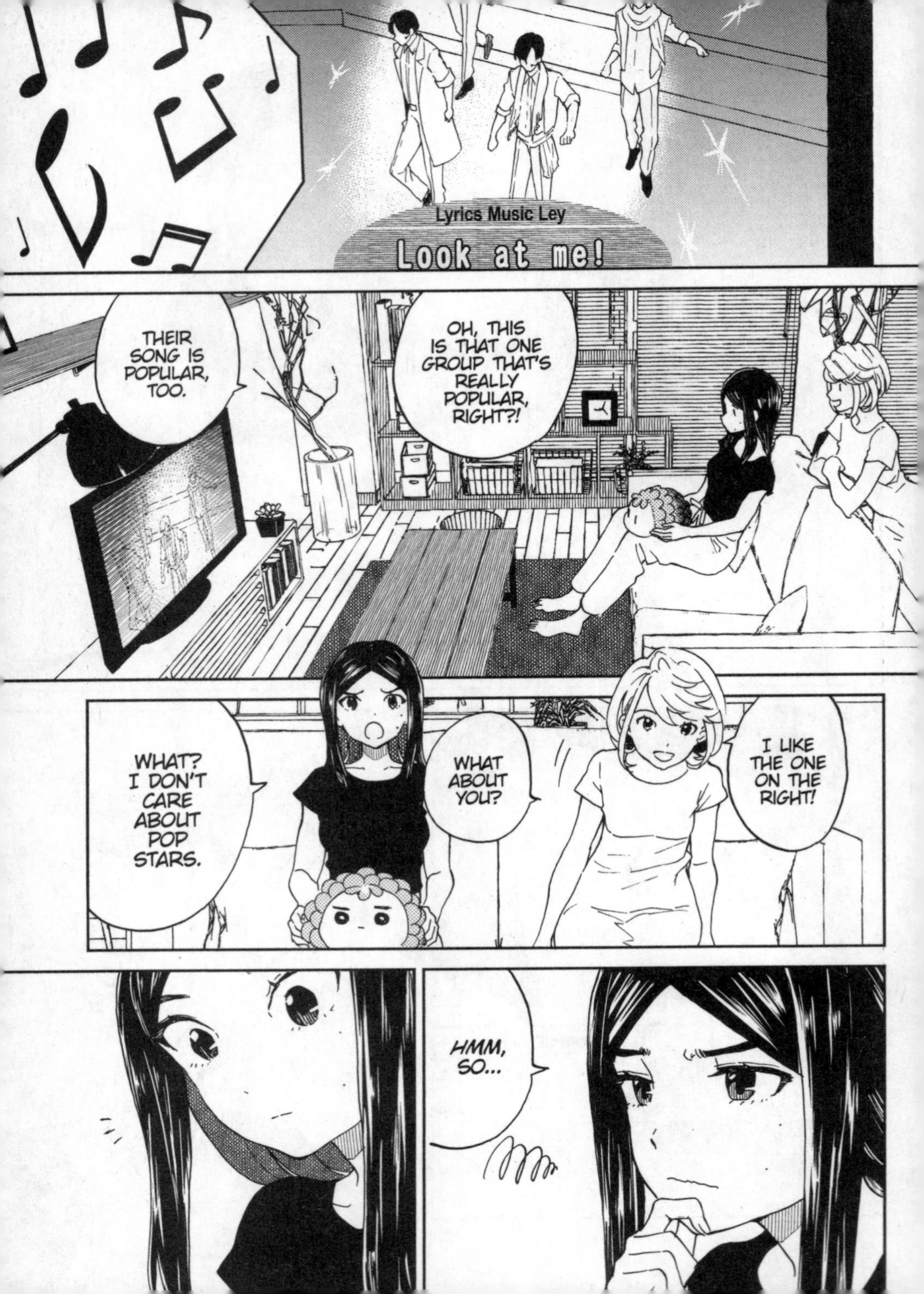
Lyrics Music Ley
Look at me!
OH, THIS IS THAT ONE GROUP THAT'S REALLY POPULAR, RIGHT?!
THEIR SONG IS POPULAR, TOO.
I LIKE THE ONE ON THE RIGHT!
WHAT ABOUT YOU?
WHAT? I DON'T CARE ABOUT POP STARS.
HMM, SO...

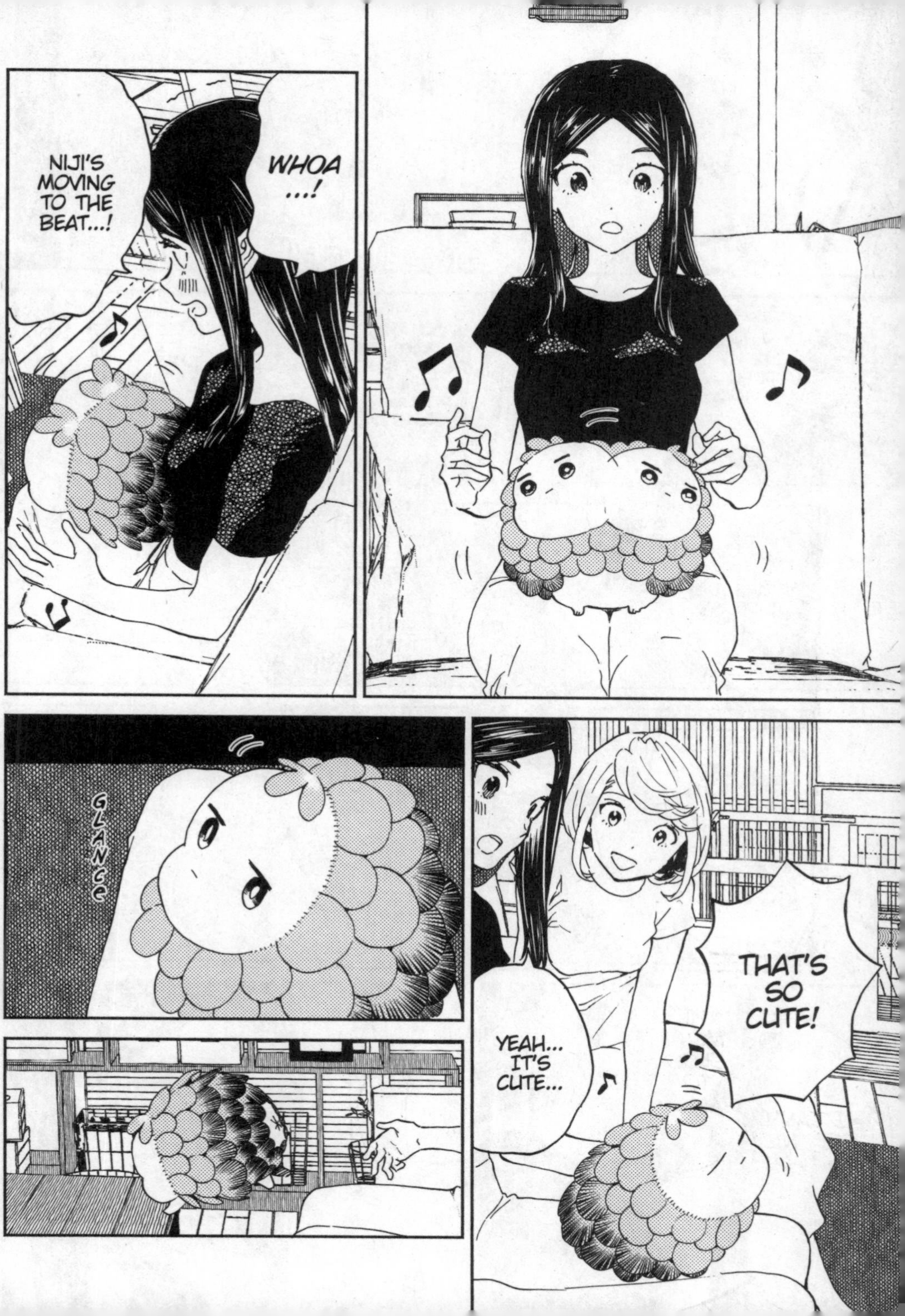
WHOA ...!
NIJI'S MOVING TO THE BEAT...!
THAT'S SO CUTE!
YEAH... IT'S CUTE...
GLANCE

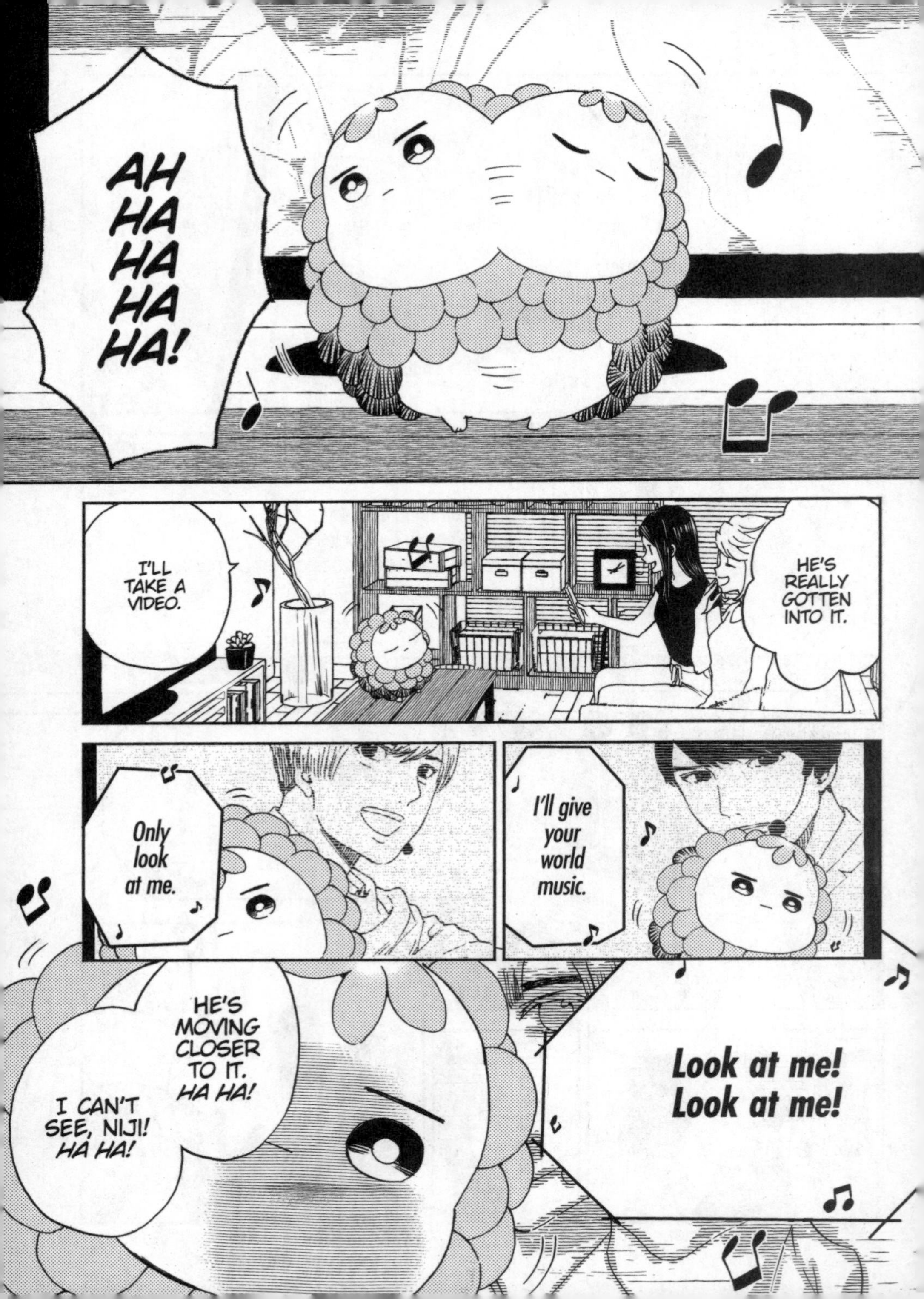
AH HA HA HA HA HA!
HE'S REALLY GOTTEN INTO IT.
I'LL TAKE A VIDEO.
I'll give your world music.
Only look at me.
Look at me! Look at me!
HE'S MOVING CLOSER TO IT. HA HA!
I CAN'T SEE, NIJI! HA HA!

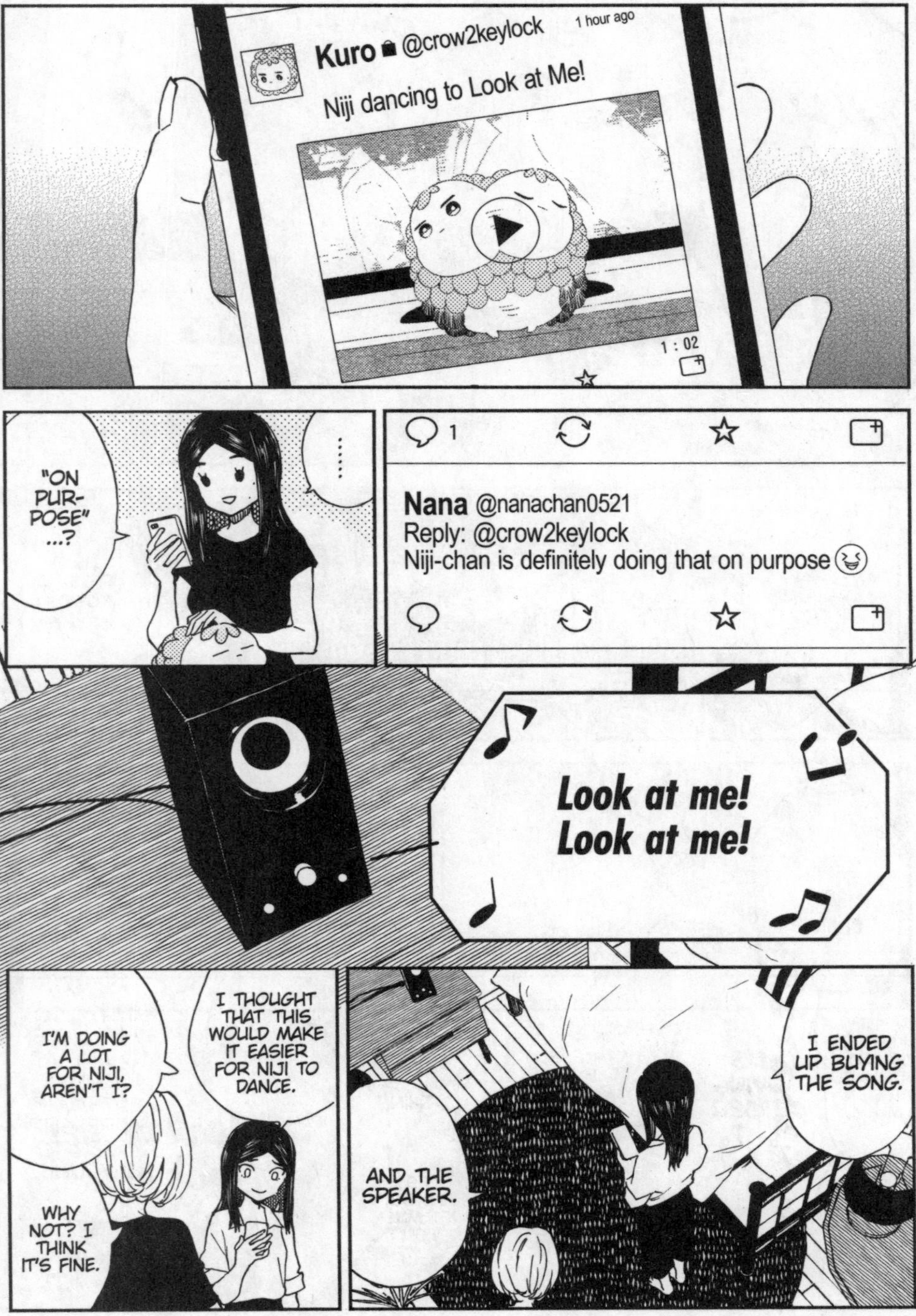
Kuro @crow2keylock
1 hour ago
Niji dancing to Look at Me!
1 : 02
1
Nana @nanachan0521
Reply: @crow2keylock
Niji-chan is definitely doing that on purpose
......
"ON PURPOSE" ...?
Look at me!
Look at me!
I ENDED UP BUYING THE SONG.
AND THE SPEAKER.
I THOUGHT THAT THIS WOULD MAKE IT EASIER FOR NIJI TO DANCE.
I'M DOING A LOT FOR NIJI, AREN'T I?
WHY NOT? I THINK IT'S FINE.

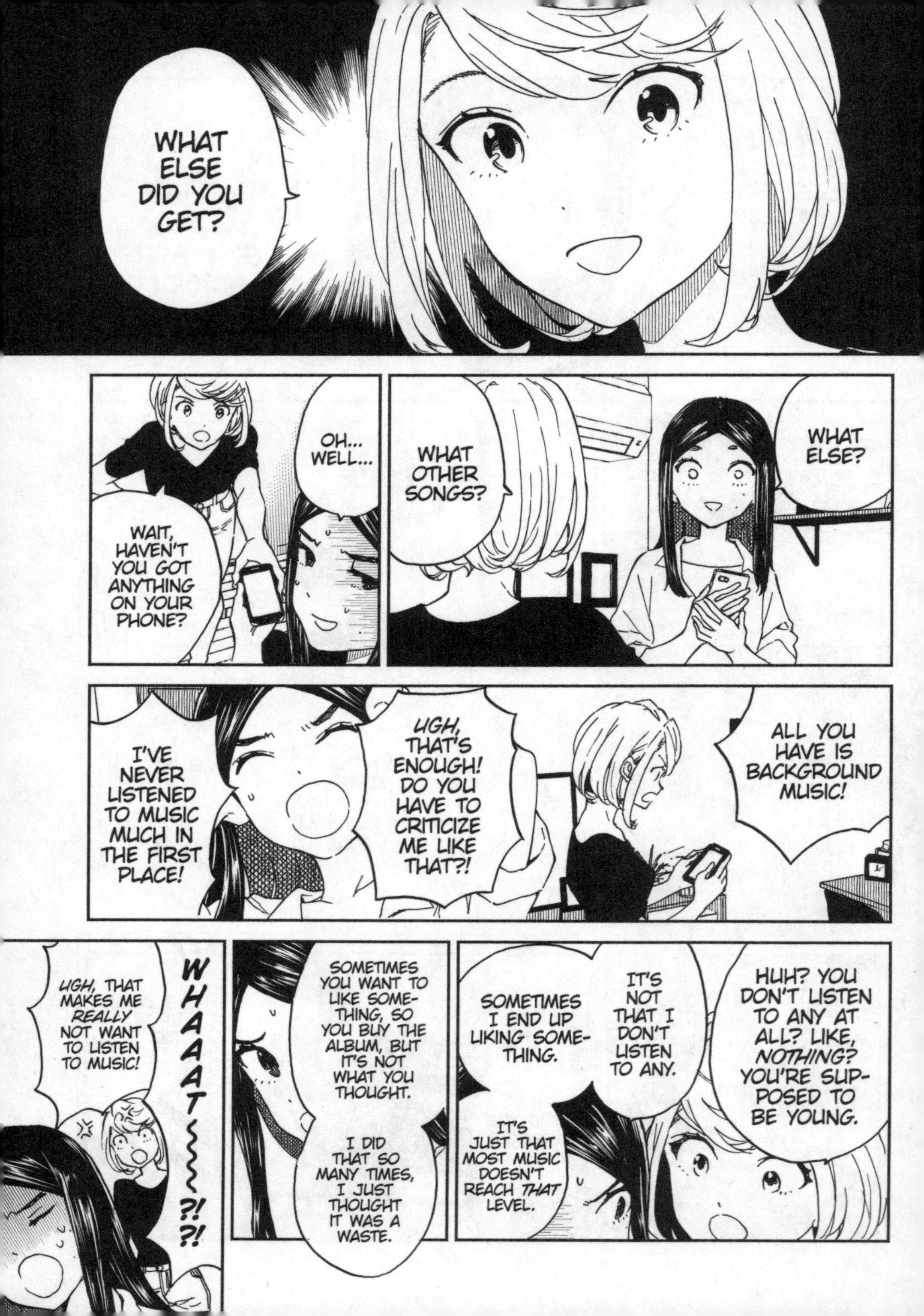
WHAT ELSE DID YOU GET?
WHAT ELSE?
WHAT OTHER SONGS?
OH... WELL...
WAIT, HAVEN'T YOU GOT ANYTHING ON YOUR PHONE?
ALL YOU HAVE IS BACKGROUND MUSIC!
UGH, THAT'S ENOUGH! DO YOU HAVE TO CRITICIZE ME LIKE THAT?!
I'VE NEVER LISTENED TO MUSIC MUCH IN THE FIRST PLACE!
HUH? YOU DON'T LISTEN TO ANY AT ALL? LIKE, *NOTHING*? YOU'RE SUPPOSED TO BE YOUNG.
IT'S NOT THAT I DON'T LISTEN TO ANY.
SOMETIMES I END UP LIKING SOMETHING.
IT'S JUST THAT MOST MUSIC DOESN'T REACH *THAT* LEVEL.
SOMETIMES YOU WANT TO LIKE SOMETHING, SO YOU BUY THE ALBUM, BUT IT'S NOT WHAT YOU THOUGHT.
I DID THAT SO MANY TIMES, I JUST THOUGHT IT WAS A WASTE.
WHAAAAT~~~?!?!
UGH, THAT MAKES ME *REALLY* NOT WANT TO LISTEN TO MUSIC!

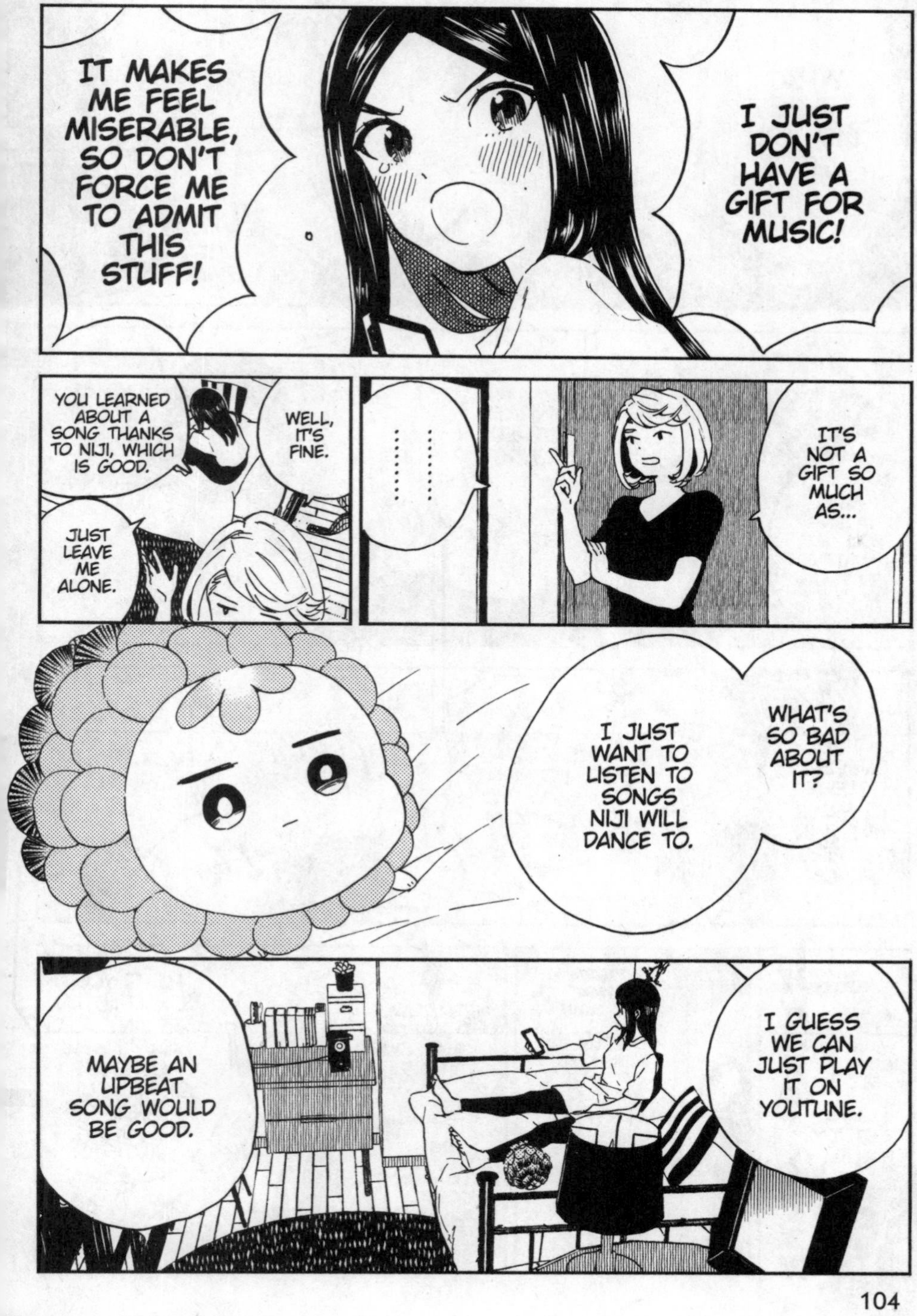
I JUST DON'T HAVE A GIFT FOR MUSIC!
IT MAKES ME FEEL MISERABLE, SO DON'T FORCE ME TO ADMIT THIS STUFF!
IT'S NOT A GIFT SO MUCH AS...
......
WELL, IT'S FINE.
YOU LEARNED ABOUT A SONG THANKS TO NIJI, WHICH IS GOOD.
JUST LEAVE ME ALONE.
WHAT'S SO BAD ABOUT IT?
I JUST WANT TO LISTEN TO SONGS NIJI WILL DANCE TO.
I GUESS WE CAN JUST PLAY IT ON YOUTUNE.
MAYBE AN UPBEAT SONG WOULD BE GOOD.

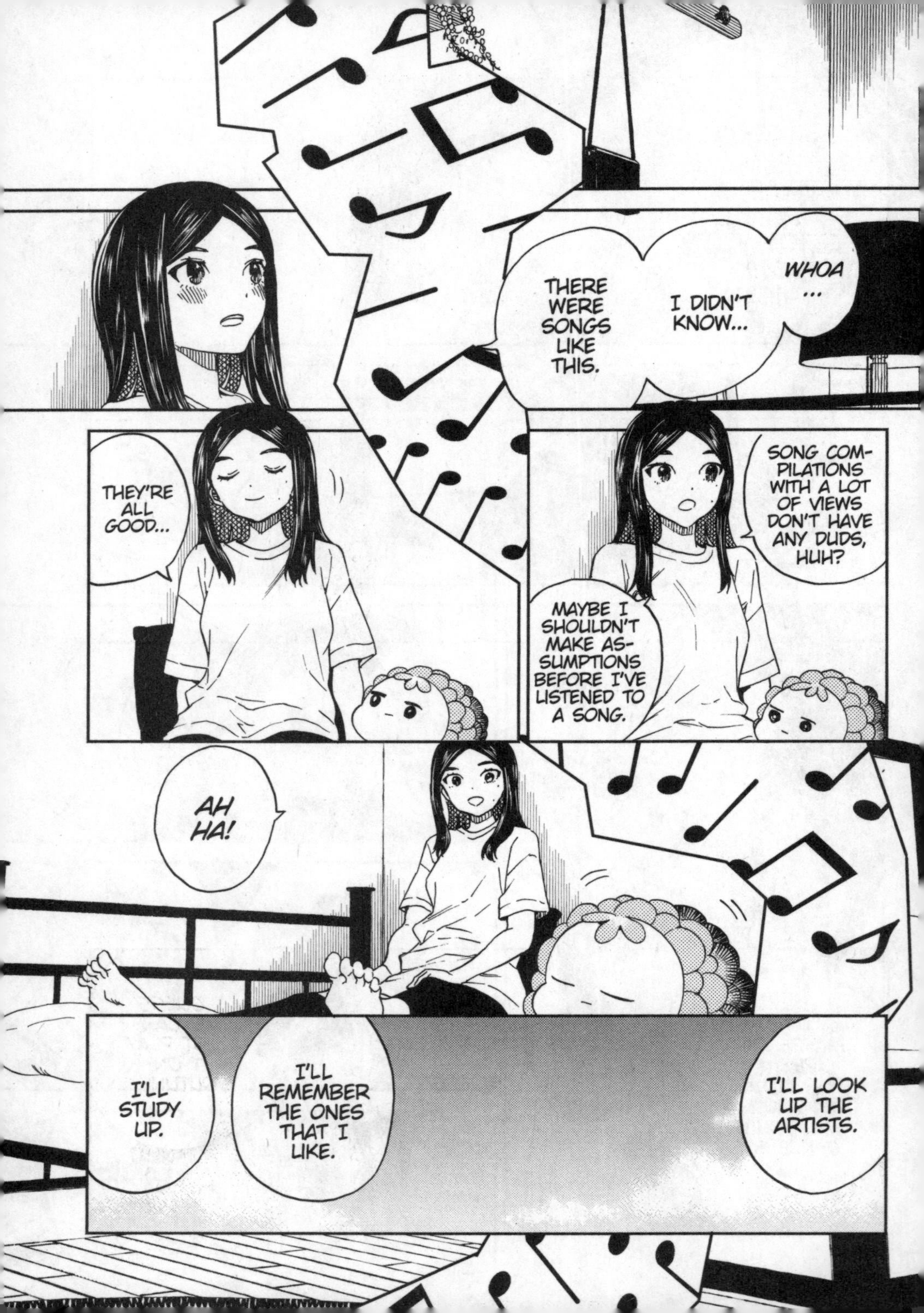
WHOA...
I DIDN'T KNOW...
THERE WERE SONGS LIKE THIS.
SONG COMPILATIONS WITH A LOT OF VIEWS DON'T HAVE ANY DUDS, HUH?
MAYBE I SHOULDN'T MAKE ASSUMPTIONS BEFORE I'VE LISTENED TO A SONG.
THEY'RE ALL GOOD...
AH HA!
I'LL LOOK UP THE ARTISTS.
I'LL REMEMBER THE ONES THAT I LIKE.
I'LL STUDY UP.

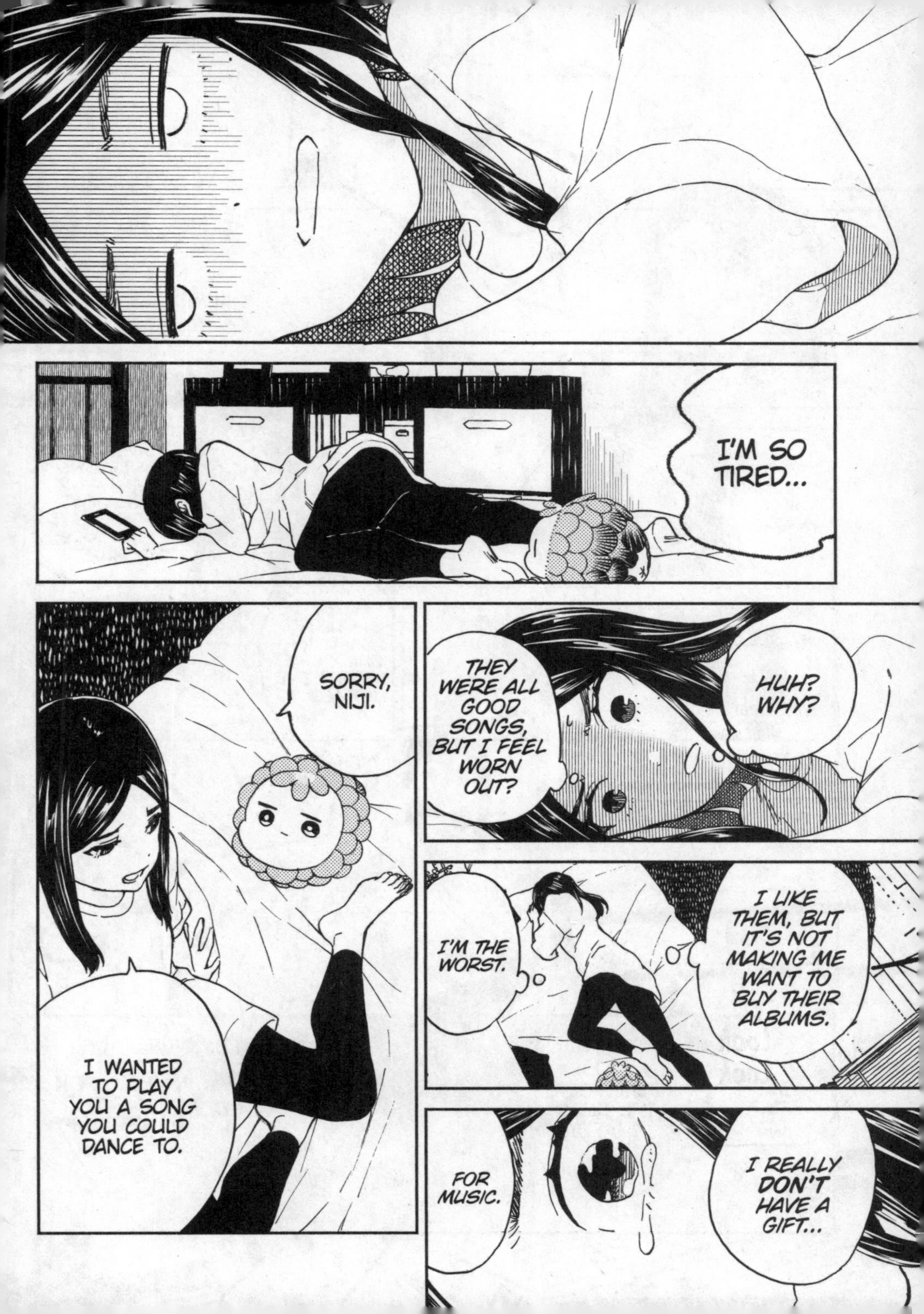
I'M SO TIRED...
HUH? WHY?
THEY WERE ALL GOOD SONGS, BUT I FEEL WORN OUT?
I LIKE THEM, BUT IT'S NOT MAKING ME WANT TO BUY THEIR ALBUMS.
I'M THE WORST.
I REALLY DON'T HAVE A GIFT...
FOR MUSIC.
SORRY, NIJI.
I WANTED TO PLAY YOU A SONG YOU COULD DANCE TO.

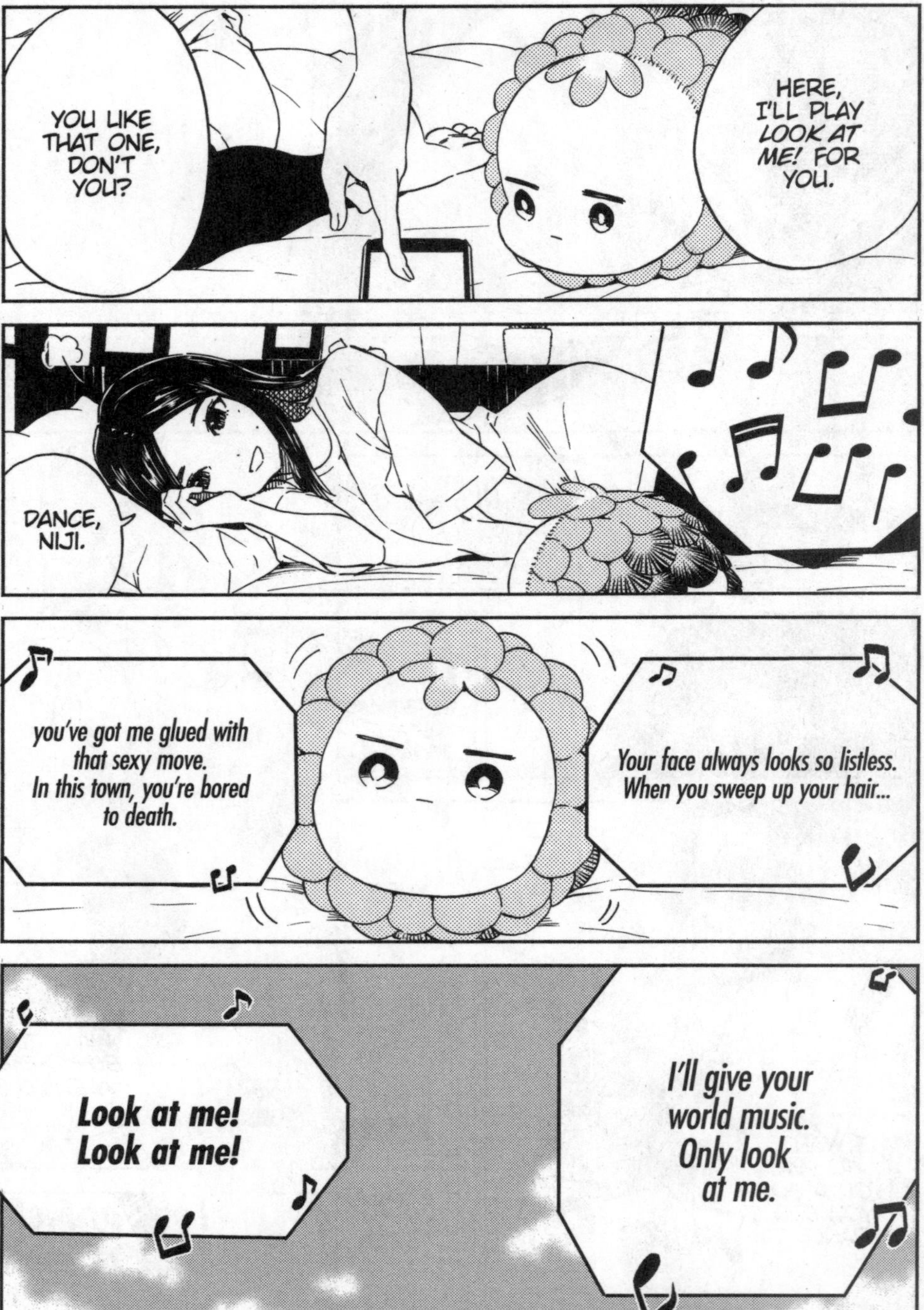
HERE, I'LL PLAY LOOK AT ME! FOR YOU.
YOU LIKE THAT ONE, DON'T YOU?
DANCE, NIJI.
Your face always looks so listless. When you sweep up your hair...
you've got me glued with that sexy move. In this town, you're bored to death.
I'll give your world music. Only look at me.
Look at me! Look at me!

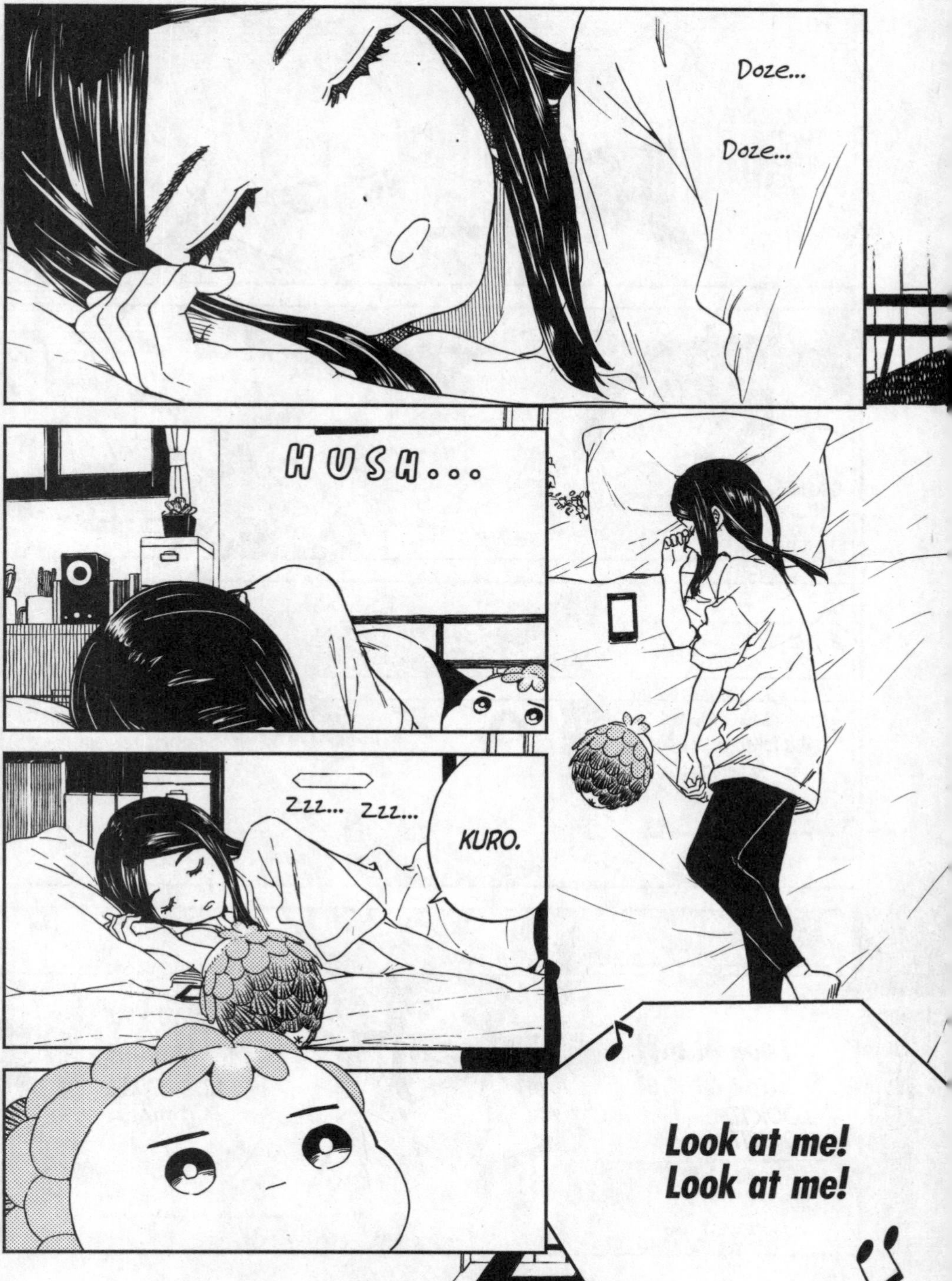
Doze...
Doze...
Look at me! Look at me!
HUSH...
KURO.
Zzz... Zzz...

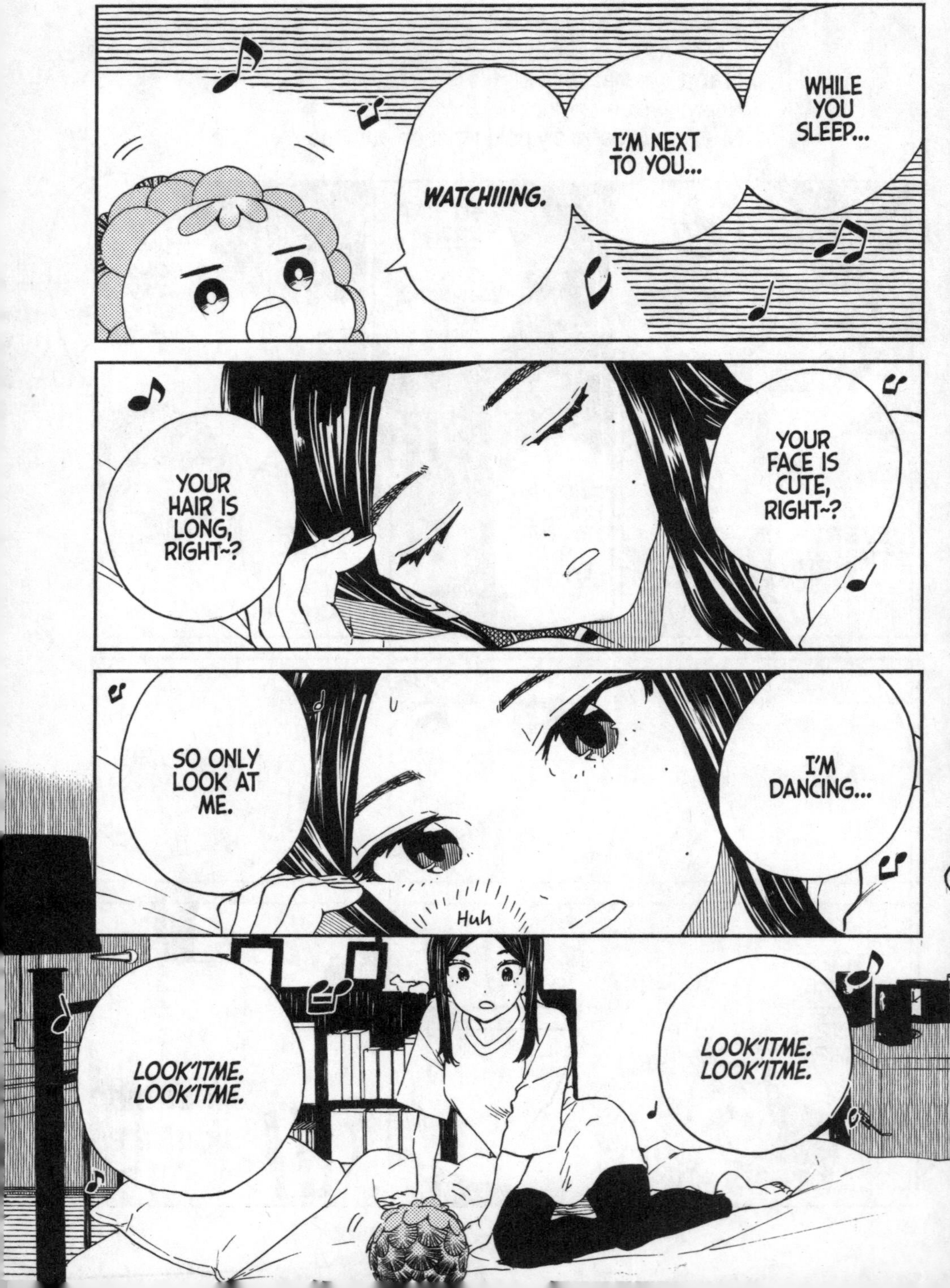
WHILE YOU SLEEP...
I'M NEXT TO YOU...
WATCHIIING.
YOUR FACE IS CUTE, RIGHT~?
YOUR HAIR IS LONG, RIGHT~?
I'M DANCING...
SO ONLY LOOK AT ME.
Huh
LOOK'ITME. LOOK'ITME.
LOOK'ITME. LOOK'ITME.

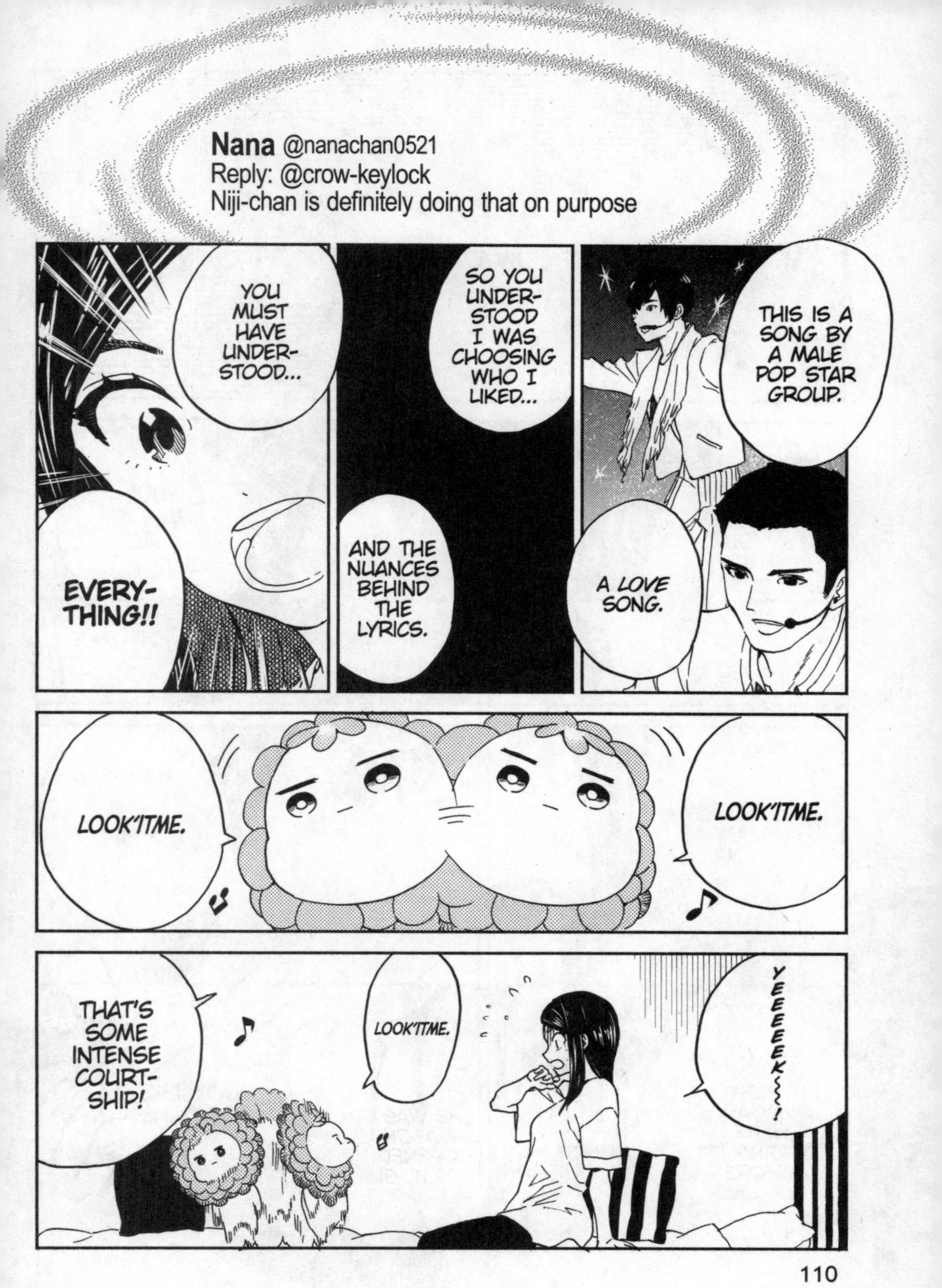
Nana @nanachan0521
Reply: @crow-keylock
Niji-chan is definitely doing that on purpose
THIS IS A SONG BY A MALE POP STAR GROUP.
A LOVE SONG.
SO YOU UNDERSTOOD I WAS CHOOSING WHO I LIKED...
AND THE NUANCES BEHIND THE LYRICS.
YOU MUST HAVE UNDERSTOOD...
EVERYTHING!!
LOOK'ITME.
LOOK'ITME.
YEEEEEK~~!
LOOK'ITME.
THAT'S SOME INTENSE COURTSHIP!

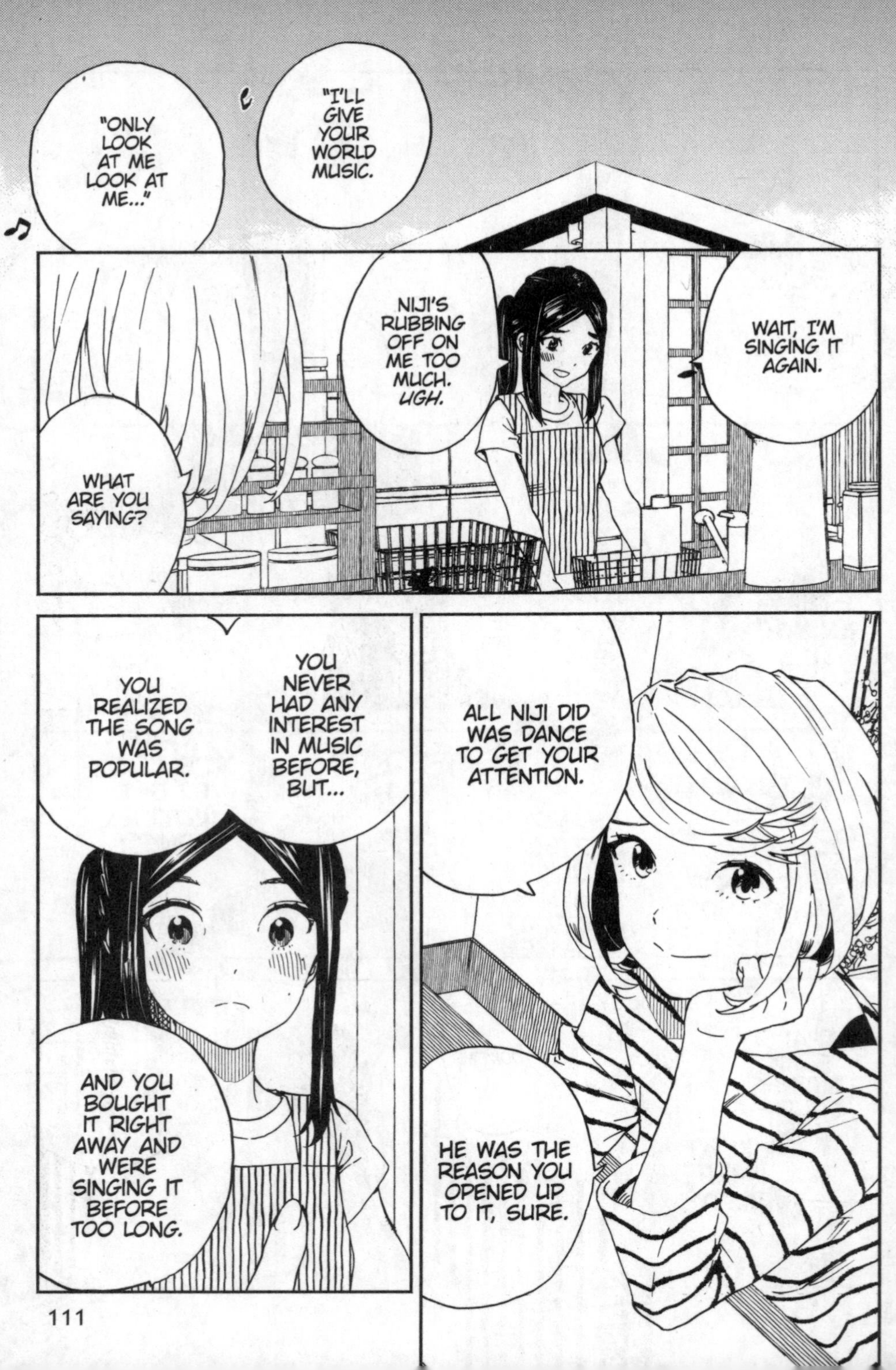
"I'LL GIVE YOUR WORLD MUSIC.
"ONLY LOOK AT ME LOOK AT ME..."
WAIT, I'M SINGING IT AGAIN.
NIJI'S RUBBING OFF ON ME TOO MUCH. UGH.
WHAT ARE YOU SAYING?
ALL NIJI DID WAS DANCE TO GET YOUR ATTENTION.
HE WAS THE REASON YOU OPENED UP TO IT, SURE.
YOU NEVER HAD ANY INTEREST IN MUSIC BEFORE, BUT...
YOU REALIZED THE SONG WAS POPULAR.
AND YOU BOUGHT IT RIGHT AWAY AND WERE SINGING IT BEFORE TOO LONG.

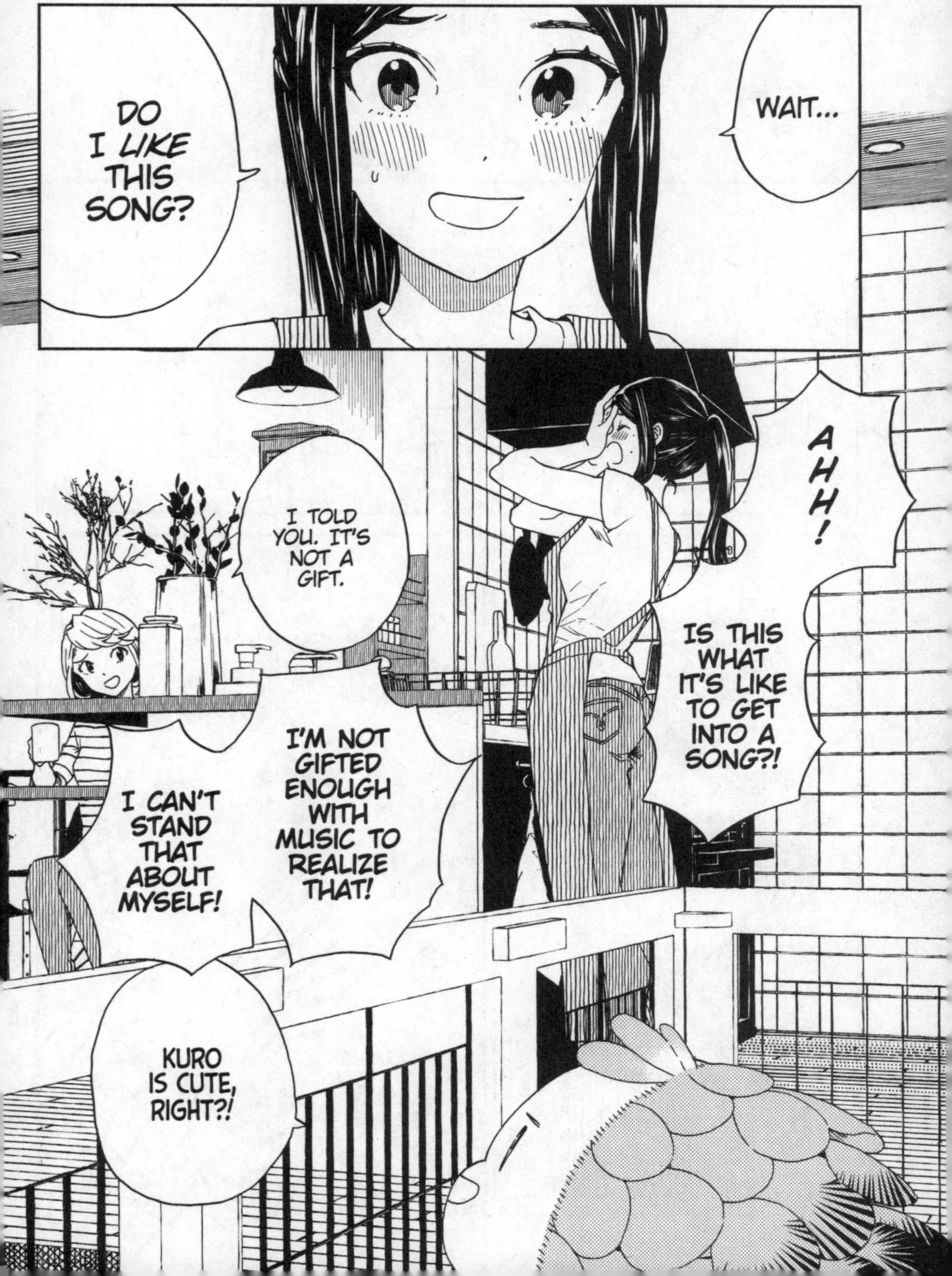
WAIT...
DO I *LIKE* THIS SONG?
AHH!
IS THIS WHAT IT'S LIKE TO GET INTO A SONG?!
I TOLD YOU. IT'S NOT A GIFT.
I'M NOT GIFTED ENOUGH WITH MUSIC TO REALIZE THAT!
I CAN'T STAND THAT ABOUT MYSELF!
KURO IS CUTE, RIGHT?!

Rainbow and Black

Story & Art by **Eri Takenashi**

NOW LOADING...

#25 Plucking

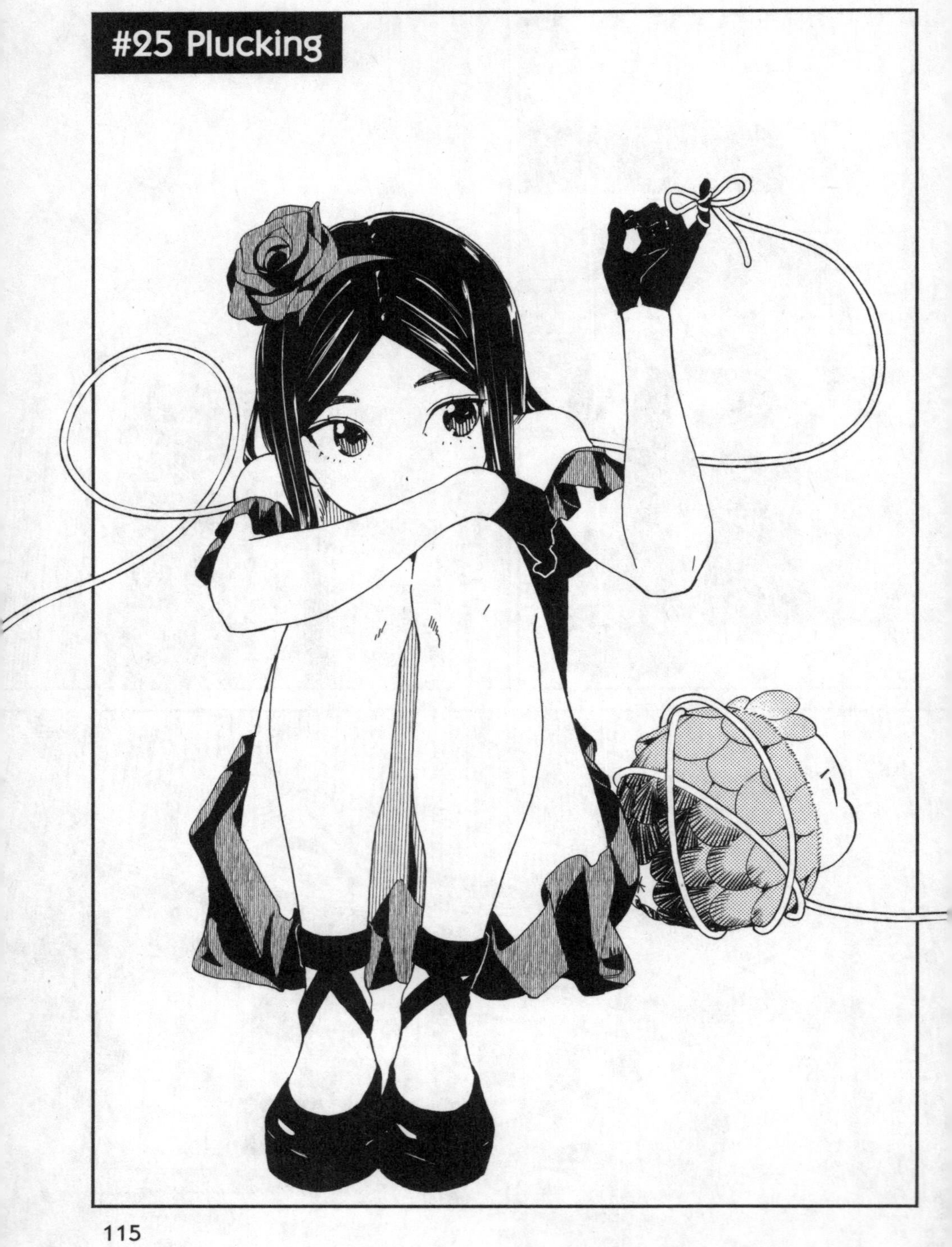

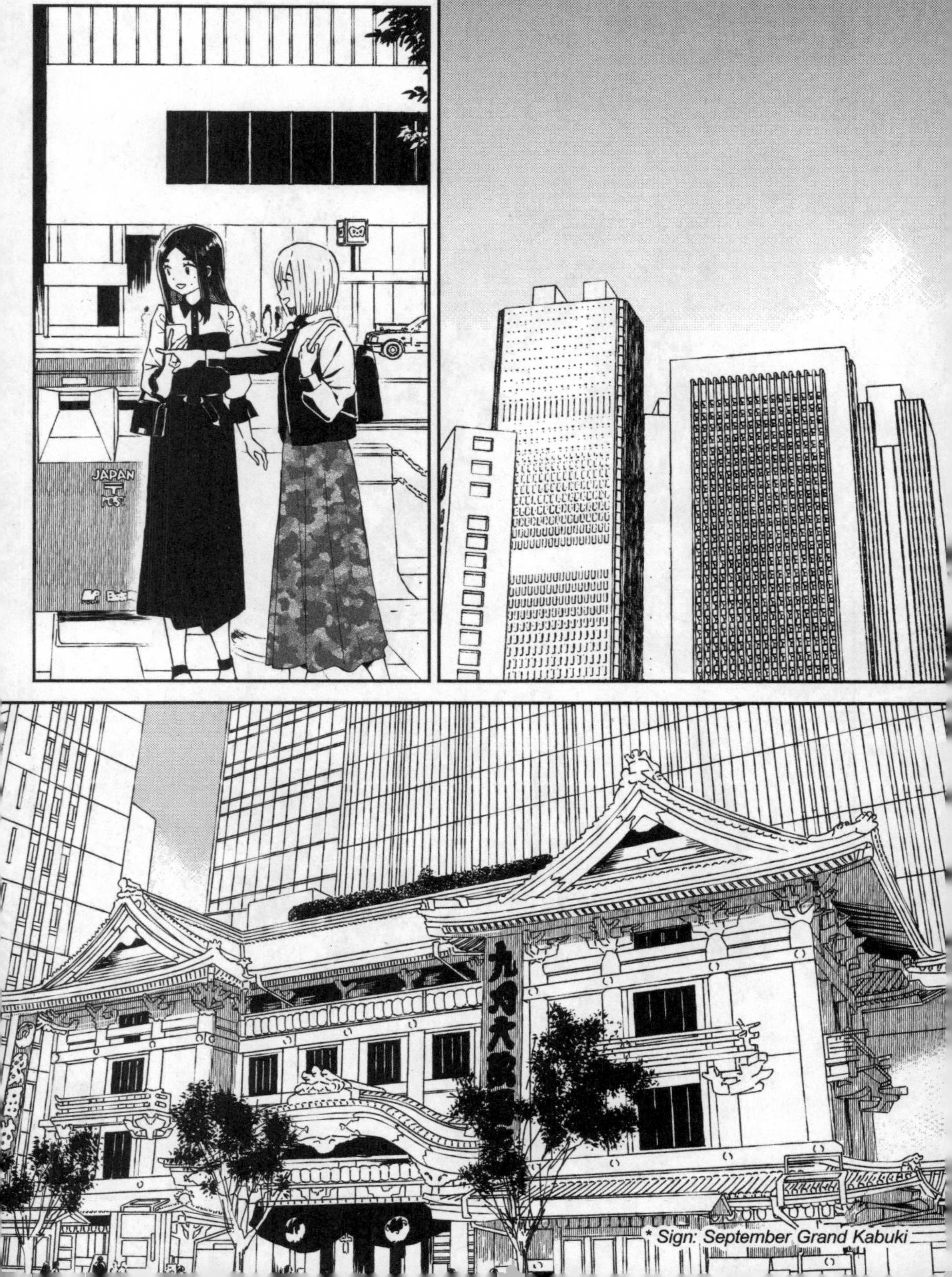
JAPAN
〒
POST
* Sign: September Grand Kabuki

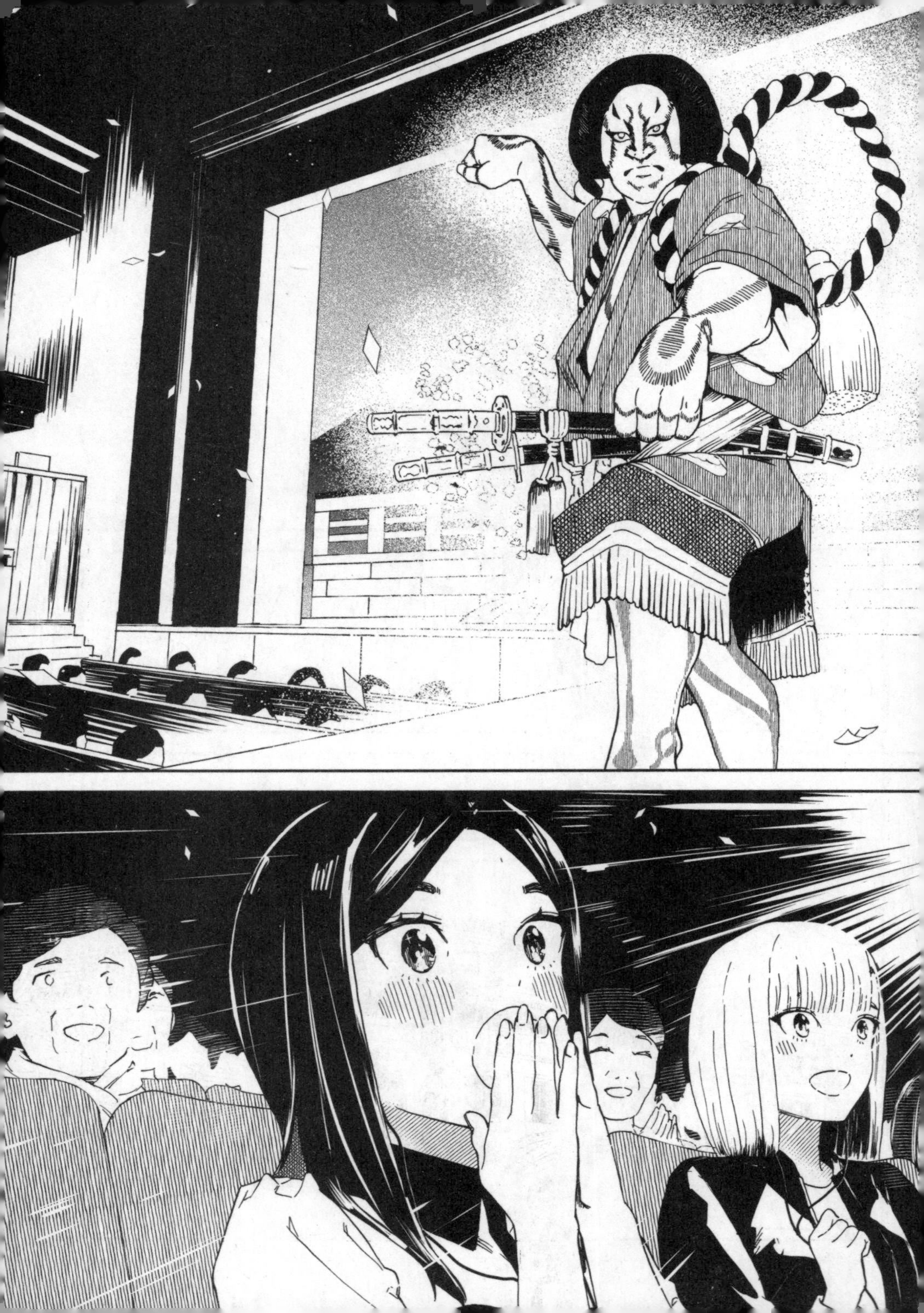

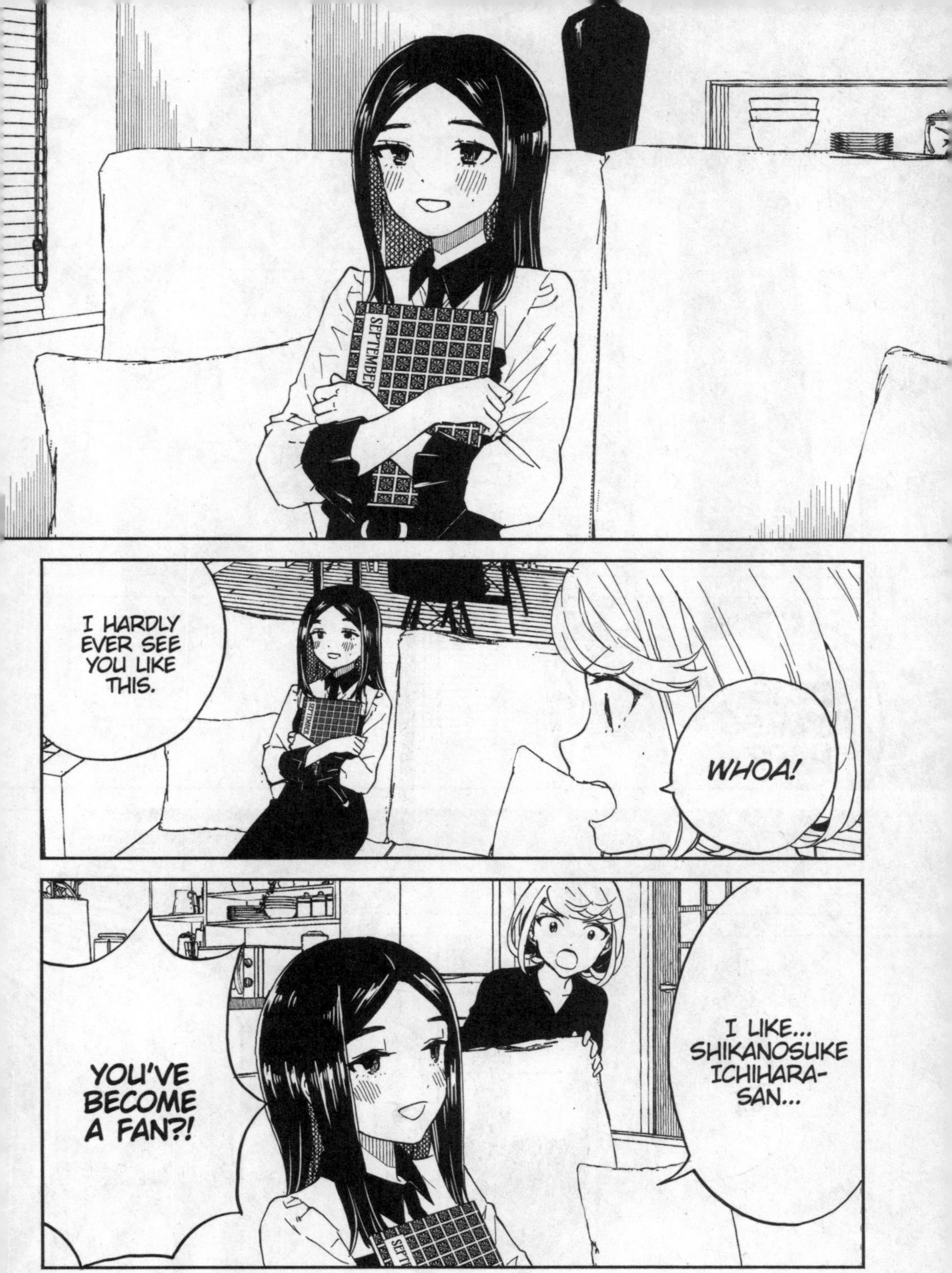
SEPTEMBER
WHOA!
I HARDLY EVER SEE YOU LIKE THIS.
I LIKE... SHIKANOSUKE ICHIHARA-SAN...
YOU'VE BECOME A FAN?!

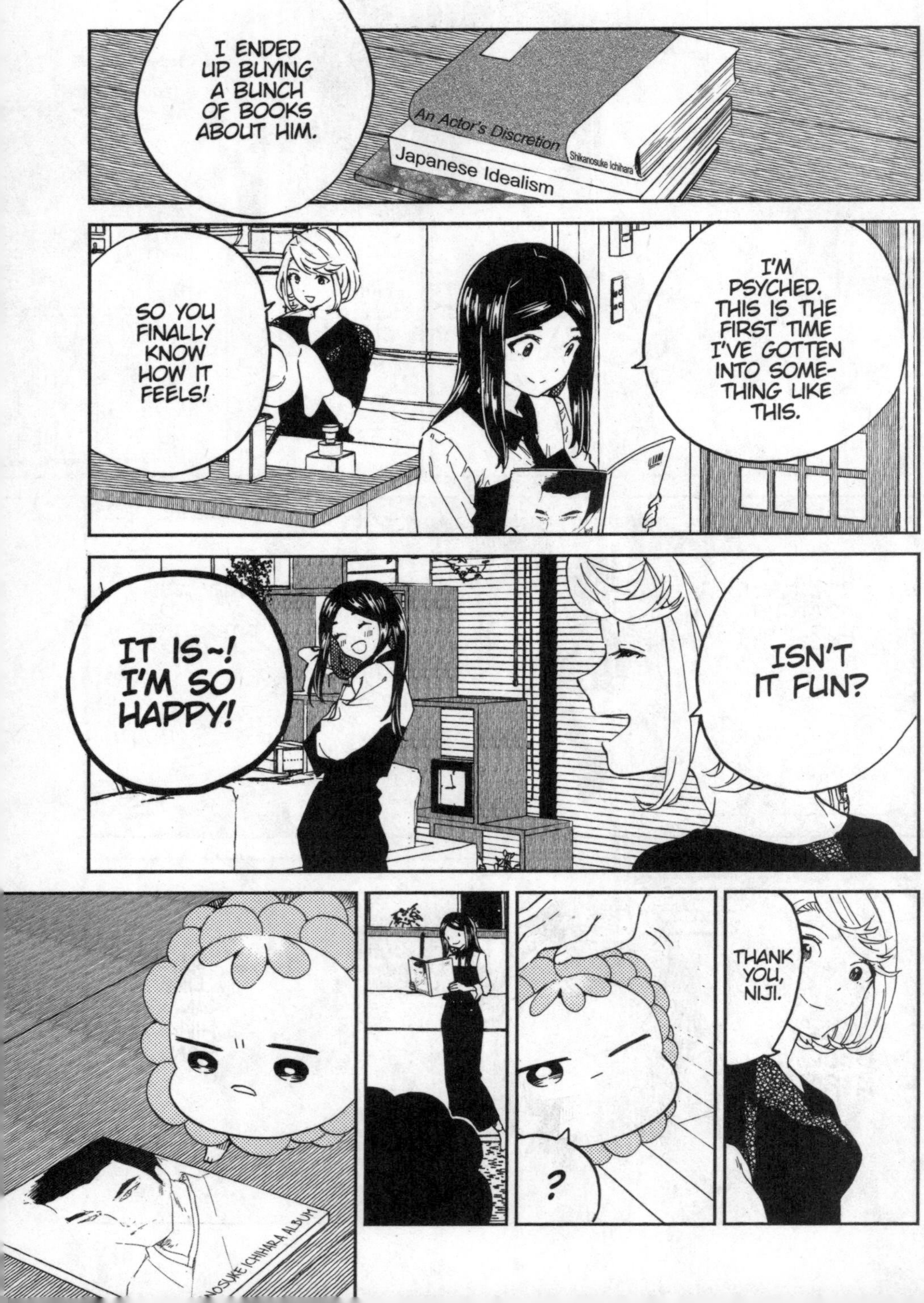
I ENDED UP BUYING A BUNCH OF BOOKS ABOUT HIM.
An Actor's Discretion
Shikanosuke Ichihara
Japanese Idealism
I'M PSYCHED. THIS IS THE FIRST TIME I'VE GOTTEN INTO SOME-THING LIKE THIS.
SO YOU FINALLY KNOW HOW IT FEELS!
ISN'T IT FUN?
IT IS~! I'M SO HAPPY!
THANK YOU, NIJI.
?
NOSUKE ICHIHARA ALBUM

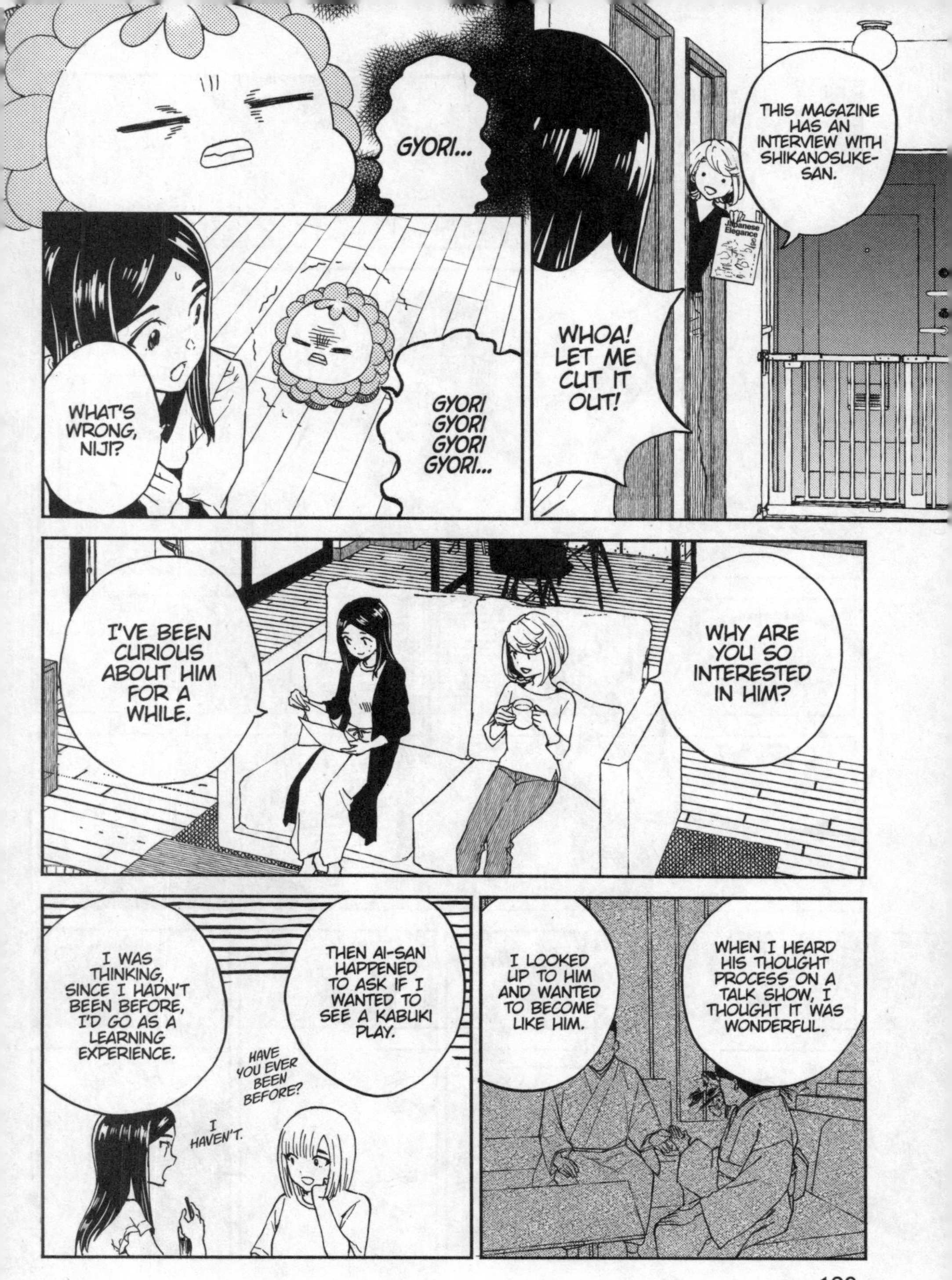
THIS MAGAZINE HAS AN INTERVIEW WITH SHIKANOSUKE-SAN.
Japanese Elegance
WHOA! LET ME CUT IT OUT!
GYORI...
GYORI GYORI GYORI GYORI...
WHAT'S WRONG, NIJI?
WHY ARE YOU SO INTERESTED IN HIM?
I'VE BEEN CURIOUS ABOUT HIM FOR A WHILE.
WHEN I HEARD HIS THOUGHT PROCESS ON A TALK SHOW, I THOUGHT IT WAS WONDERFUL.
I LOOKED UP TO HIM AND WANTED TO BECOME LIKE HIM.
THEN AI-SAN HAPPENED TO ASK IF I WANTED TO SEE A KABUKI PLAY.
HAVE YOU EVER BEEN BEFORE?
I HAVEN'T.
I WAS THINKING, SINCE I HADN'T BEEN BEFORE, I'D GO AS A LEARNING EXPERIENCE.

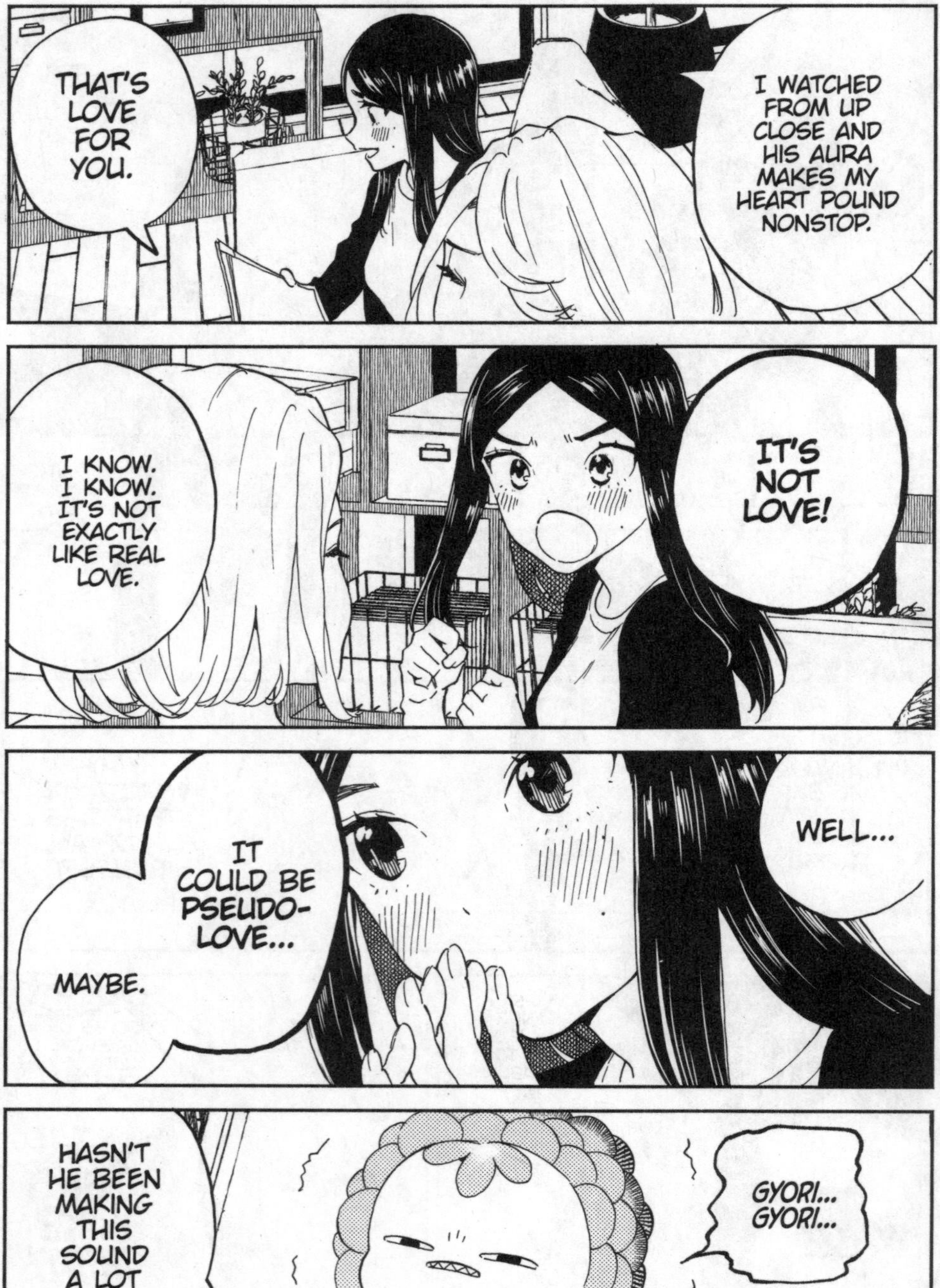
I WATCHED FROM UP CLOSE AND HIS AURA MAKES MY HEART POUND NONSTOP.
THAT'S LOVE FOR YOU.
IT'S NOT LOVE!
I KNOW. I KNOW. IT'S NOT EXACTLY LIKE REAL LOVE.
WELL...
IT COULD BE PSEUDO-LOVE...
MAYBE.
GYORI... GYORI...
HASN'T HE BEEN MAKING THIS SOUND A LOT LATELY?

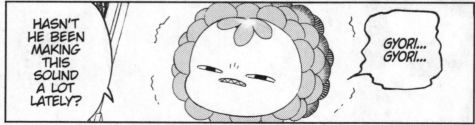

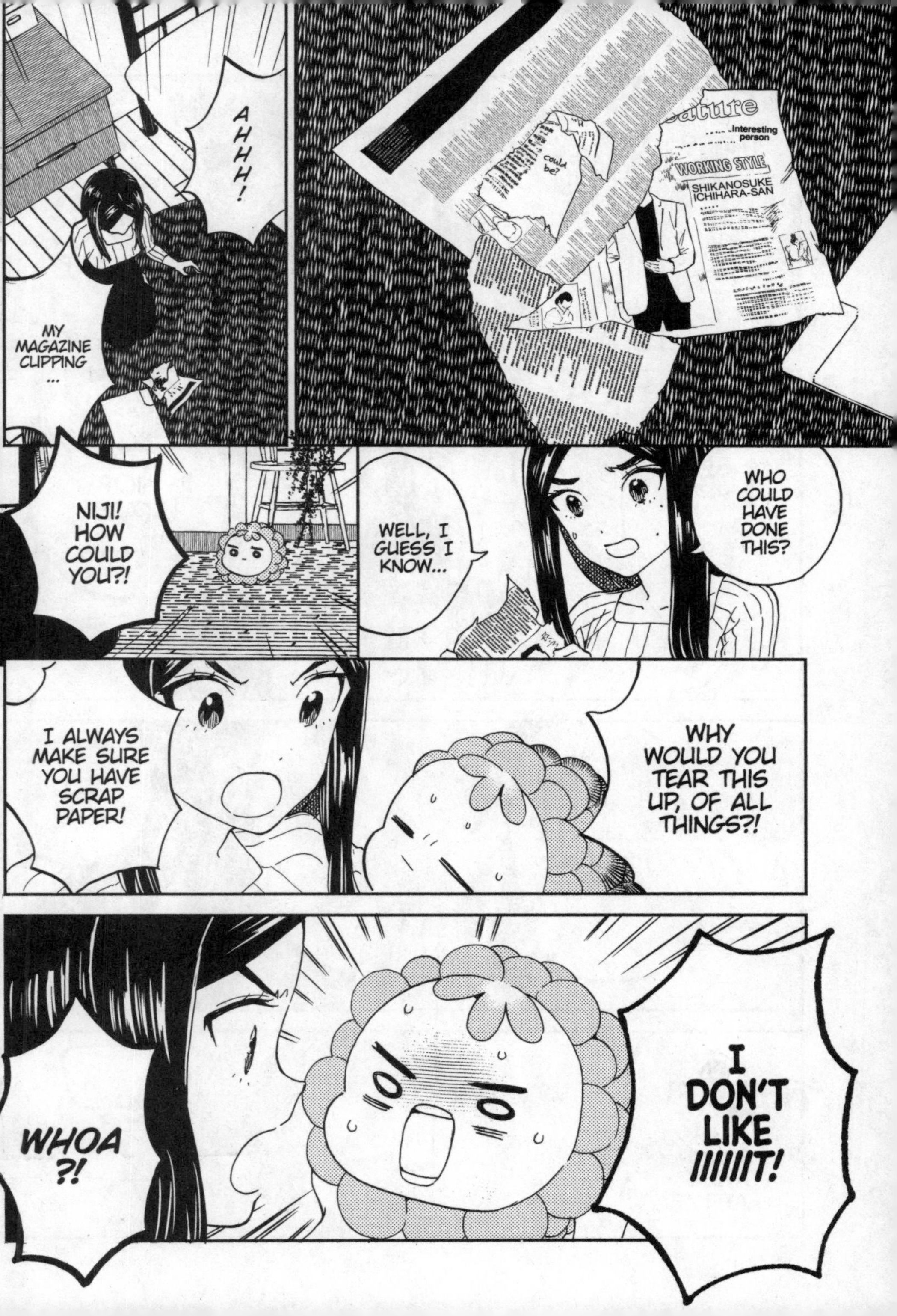

Interesting person
WORKING STYLE
SHIKANOSUKE ICHIHARA-SAN
could be?
AHHH!
MY MAGAZINE CLIPPING ...
WHO COULD HAVE DONE THIS?
WELL, I GUESS I KNOW...
NIJI! HOW COULD YOU?!
WHY WOULD YOU TEAR THIS UP, OF ALL THINGS?!
I ALWAYS MAKE SURE YOU HAVE SCRAP PAPER!
I DON'T LIKE IIIIIIIT!
WHOA?!

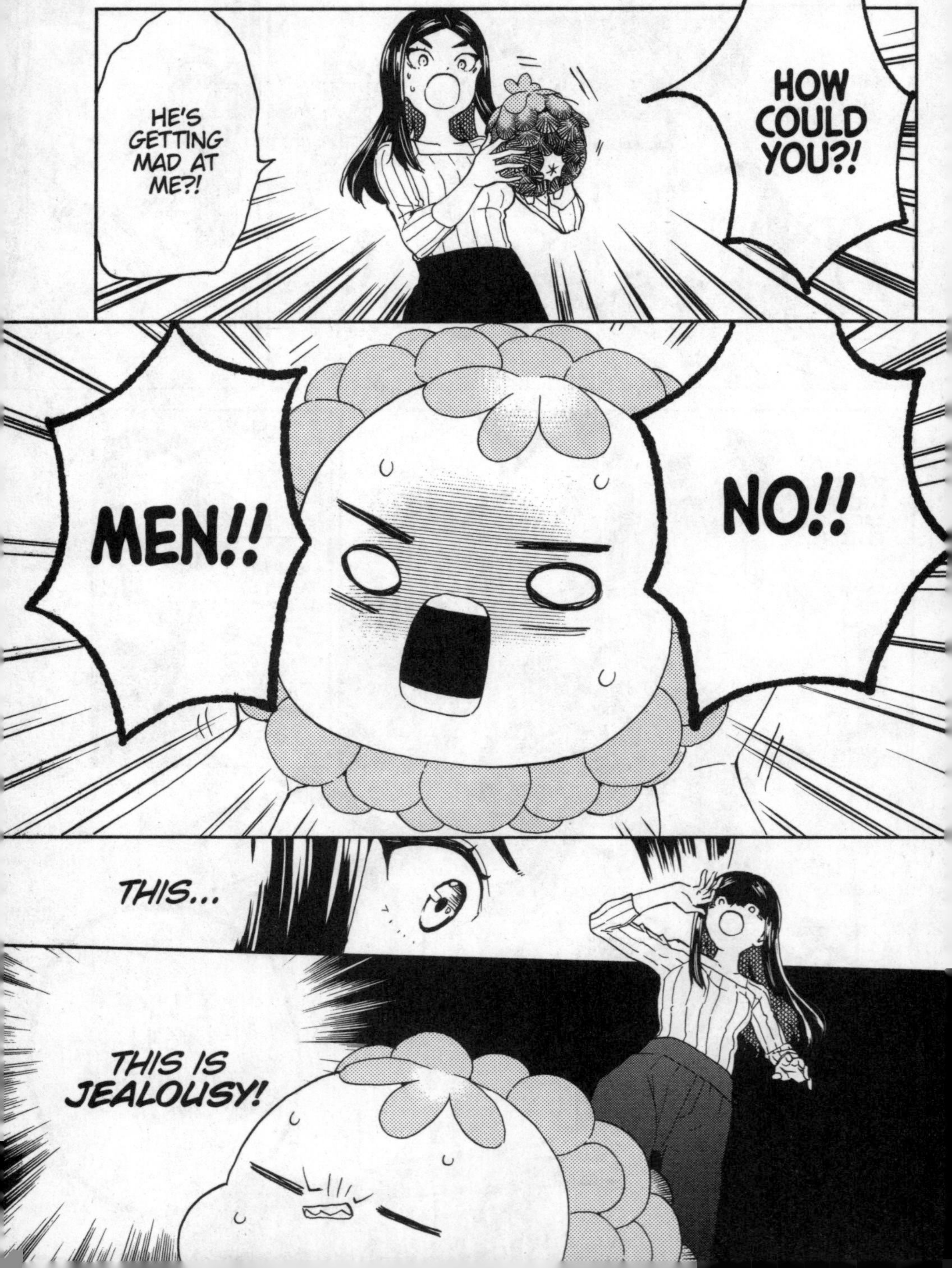
HOW COULD YOU?!
HE'S GETTING MAD AT ME?!
NO!!
MEN!!
THIS...
THIS IS JEALOUSY!

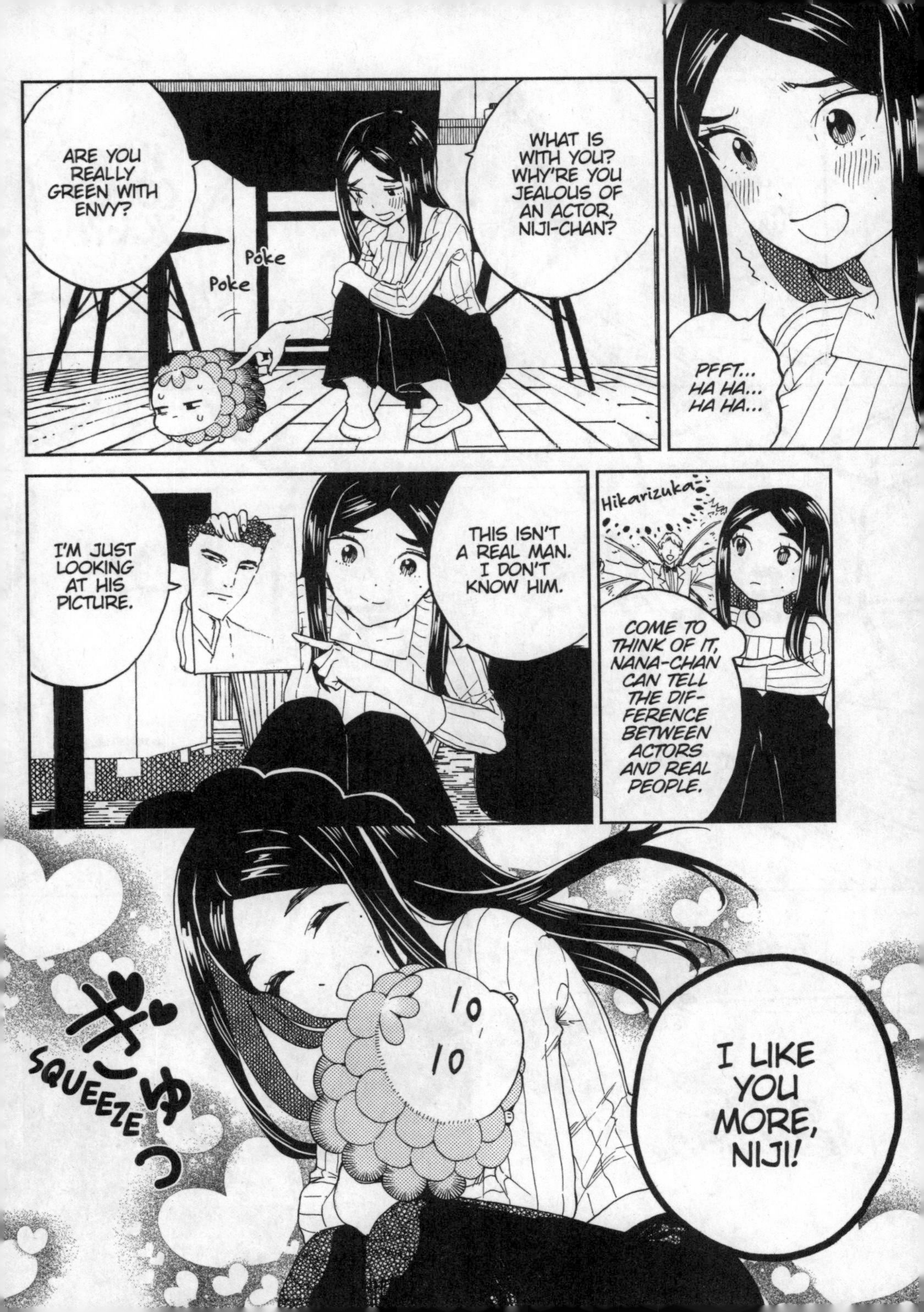
PFFT... HA HA... HA HA...
WHAT IS WITH YOU? WHY'RE YOU JEALOUS OF AN ACTOR, NIJI-CHAN?
ARE YOU REALLY GREEN WITH ENVY?
Poke
Poke
Hikarizuka
COME TO THINK OF IT, NANA-CHAN CAN TELL THE DIF-FERENCE BETWEEN ACTORS AND REAL PEOPLE.
THIS ISN'T A REAL MAN. I DON'T KNOW HIM.
I'M JUST LOOKING AT HIS PICTURE.
I LIKE YOU MORE, NIJI!
ぎゅっ
SQUEEZE

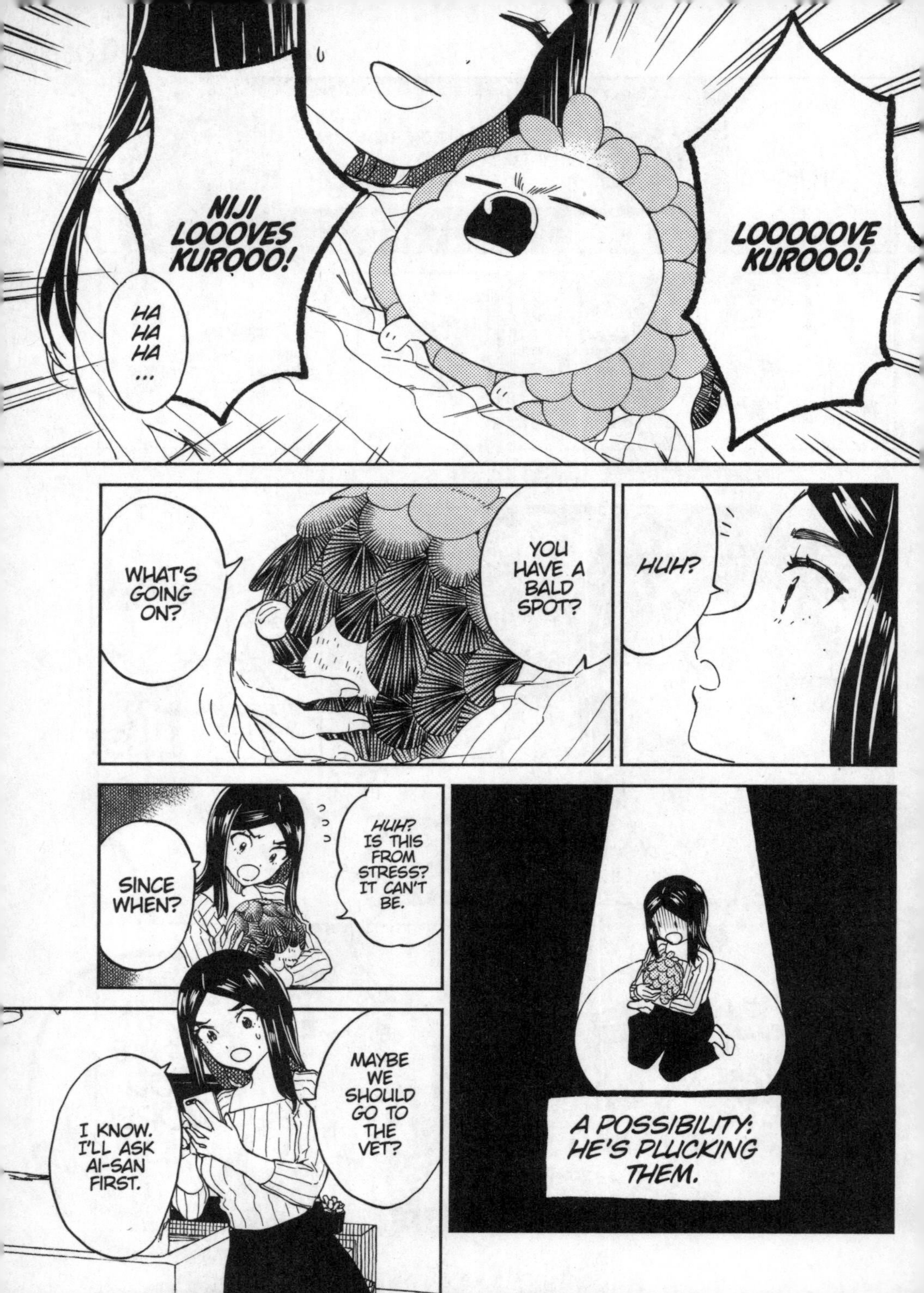
LOOOOOVE KUROOO!
NIJI LOOOVES KUROOO!
HA HA HA ...
HUH?
YOU HAVE A BALD SPOT?
WHAT'S GOING ON?
A POSSIBILITY: HE'S PLUCKING THEM.
HUH? IS THIS FROM STRESS? IT CAN'T BE.
SINCE WHEN?
MAYBE WE SHOULD GO TO THE VET?
I KNOW. I'LL ASK AI-SAN FIRST.

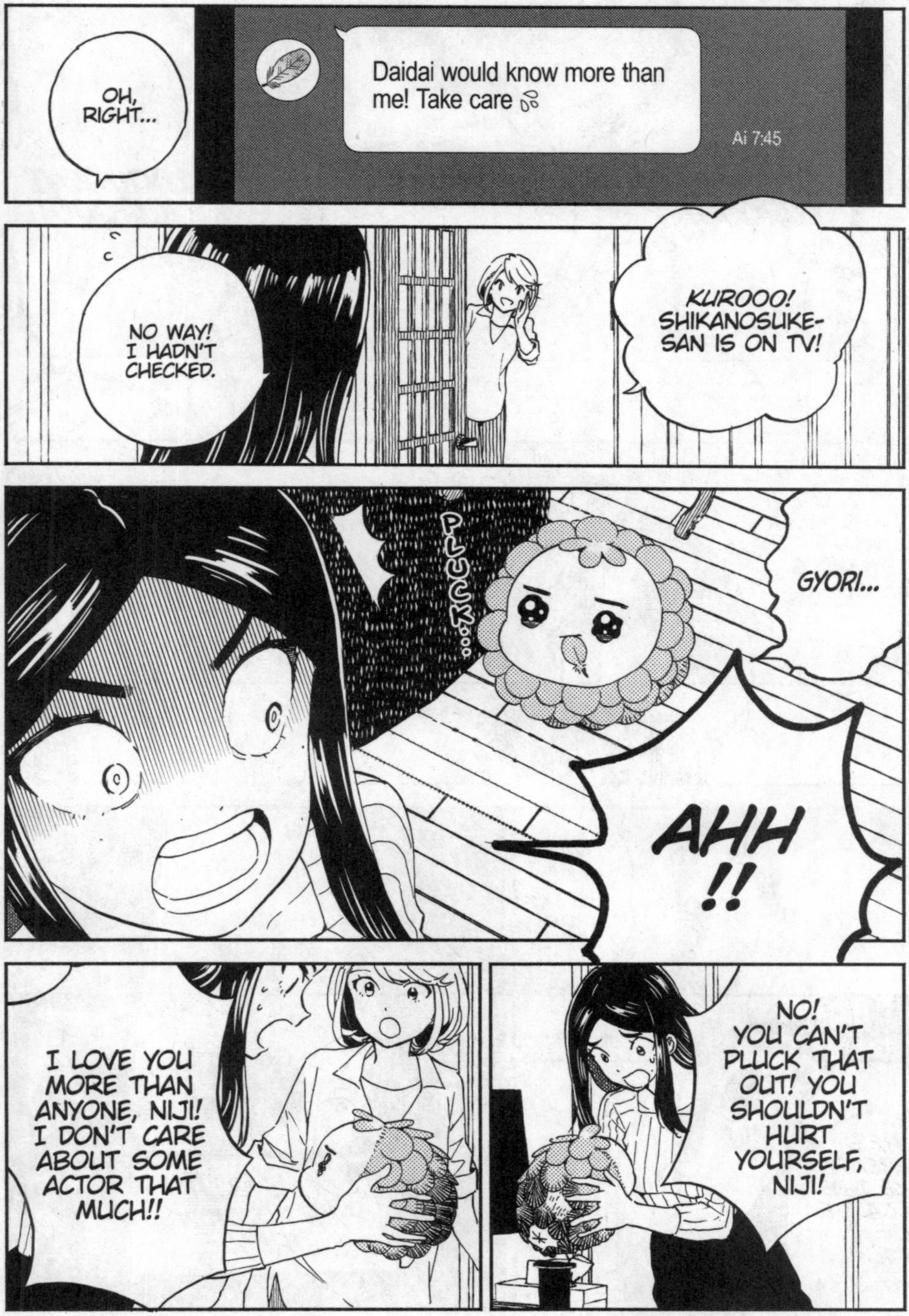
Daidai would know more than me! Take care
Ai 7:45
OH, RIGHT...
KUROOO! SHIKANOSUKE-SAN IS ON TV!
NO WAY! I HADN'T CHECKED.
GYORI...
PLUCK...
AHH!!
NO! YOU CAN'T PLUCK THAT OUT! YOU SHOULDN'T HURT YOURSELF, NIJI!
I LOVE YOU MORE THAN ANYONE, NIJI! I DON'T CARE ABOUT SOME ACTOR THAT MUCH!!

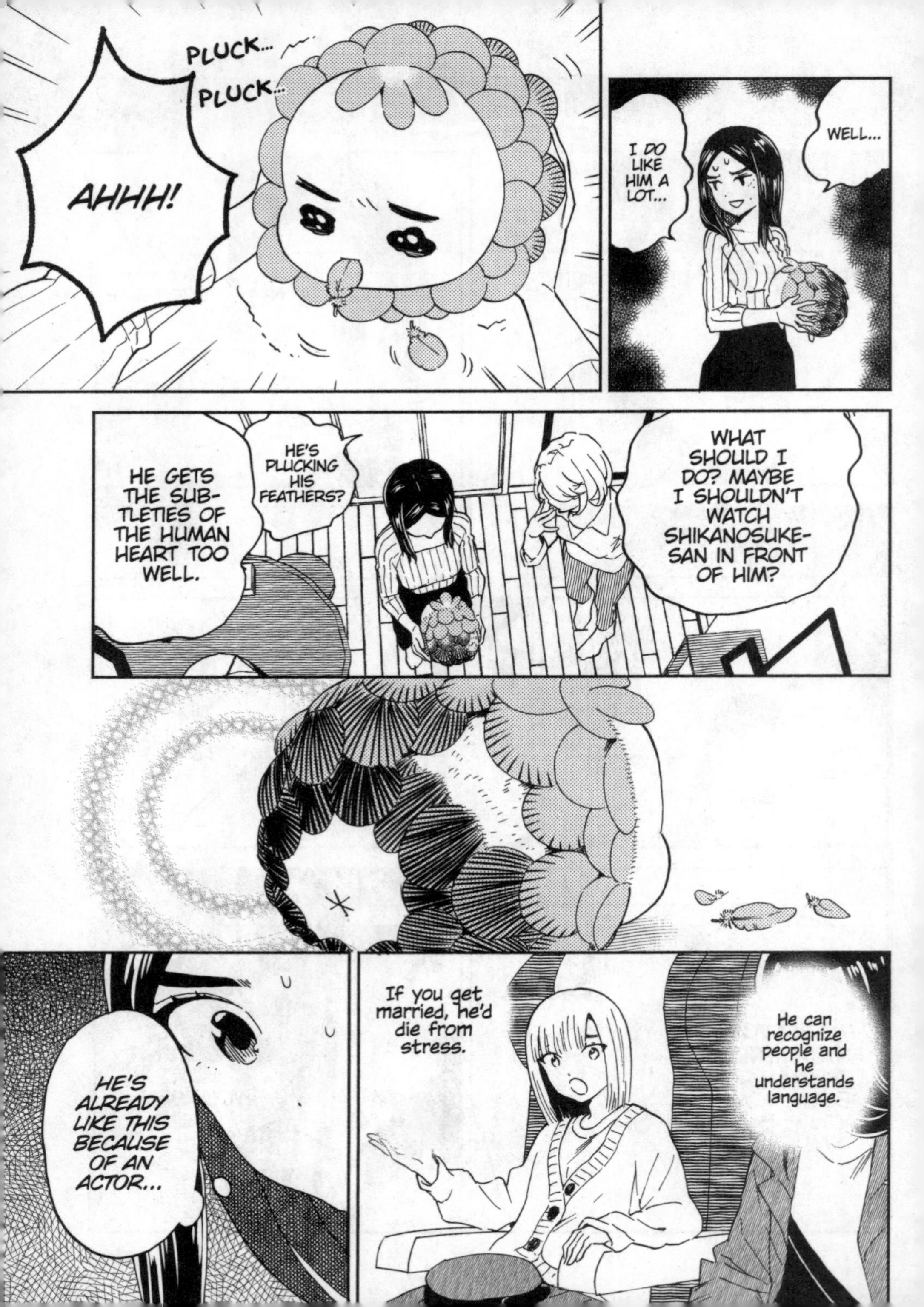
WELL...
I DO LIKE HIM A LOT...
PLUCK...
PLUCK...
AHHH!
WHAT SHOULD I DO? MAYBE I SHOULDN'T WATCH SHIKANOSUKE-SAN IN FRONT OF HIM?
HE'S PLUCKING HIS FEATHERS?
HE GETS THE SUBTLETIES OF THE HUMAN HEART TOO WELL.
He can recognize people and he understands language.
If you get married, he'd die from stress.
HE'S ALREADY LIKE THIS BECAUSE OF AN ACTOR...

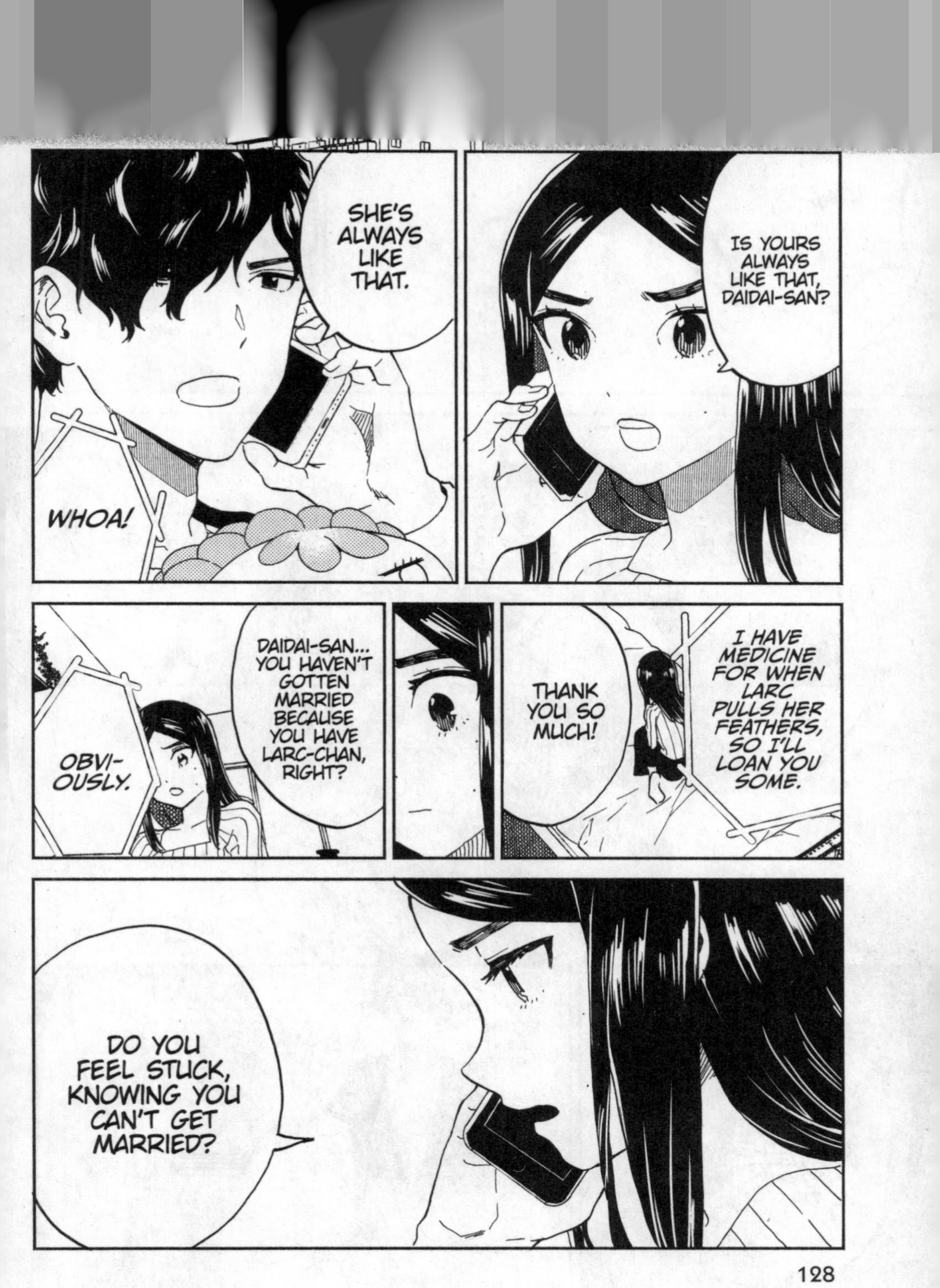
IS YOURS ALWAYS LIKE THAT, DAIDAI-SAN?
SHE'S ALWAYS LIKE THAT.
WHOA!
I HAVE MEDICINE FOR WHEN LARC PULLS HER FEATHERS, SO I'LL LOAN YOU SOME.
THANK YOU SO MUCH!
DAIDAI-SAN... YOU HAVEN'T GOTTEN MARRIED BECAUSE YOU HAVE LARC-CHAN, RIGHT?
OBVI-OUSLY.
DO YOU FEEL STUCK, KNOWING YOU CAN'T GET MARRIED?

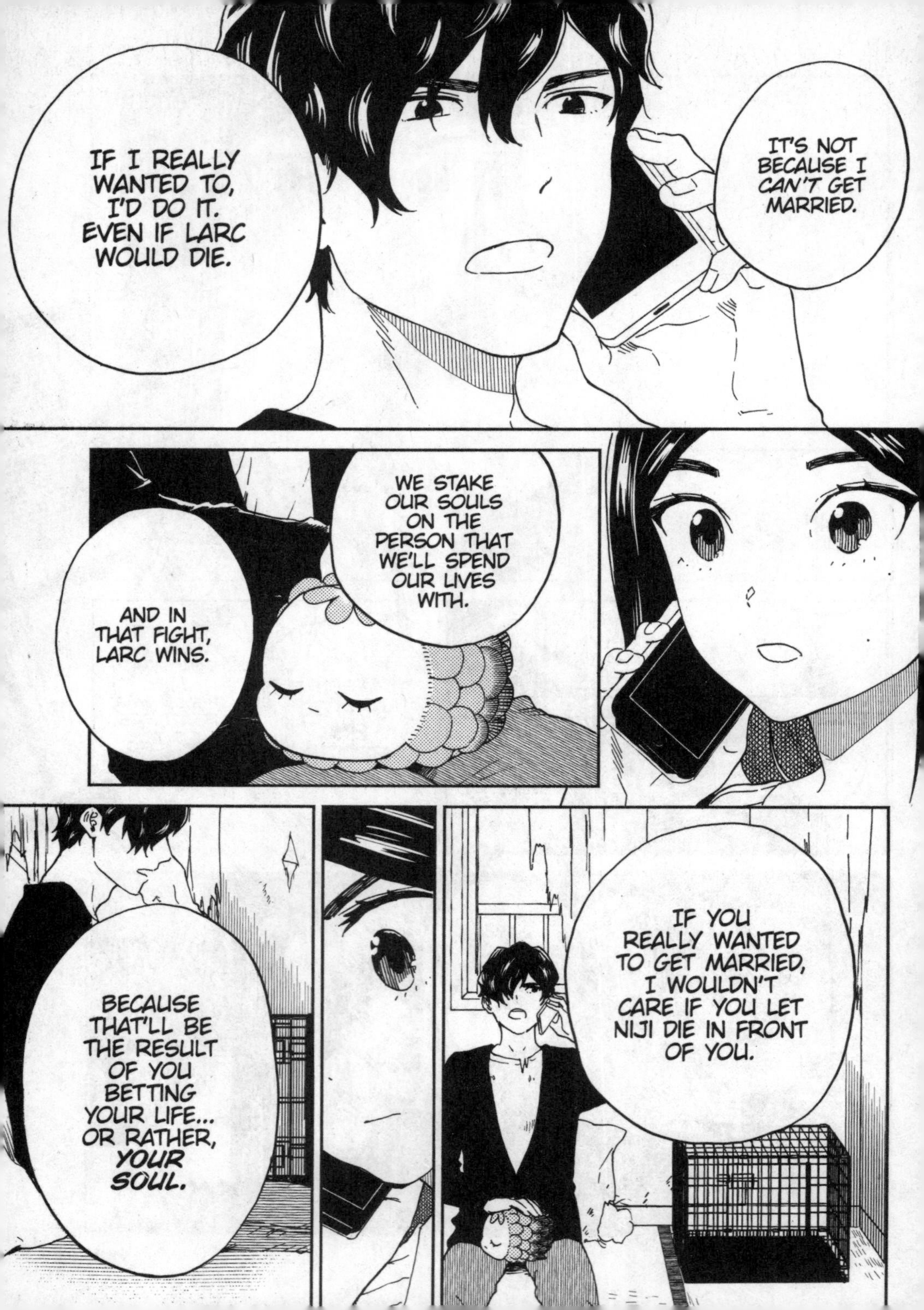
IT'S NOT BECAUSE I CAN'T GET MARRIED.
IF I REALLY WANTED TO, I'D DO IT. EVEN IF LARC WOULD DIE.
WE STAKE OUR SOULS ON THE PERSON THAT WE'LL SPEND OUR LIVES WITH.
AND IN THAT FIGHT, LARC WINS.
IF YOU REALLY WANTED TO GET MARRIED, I WOULDN'T CARE IF YOU LET NIJI DIE IN FRONT OF YOU.
BECAUSE THAT'LL BE THE RESULT OF YOU BETTING YOUR LIFE... OR RATHER, *YOUR SOUL*.

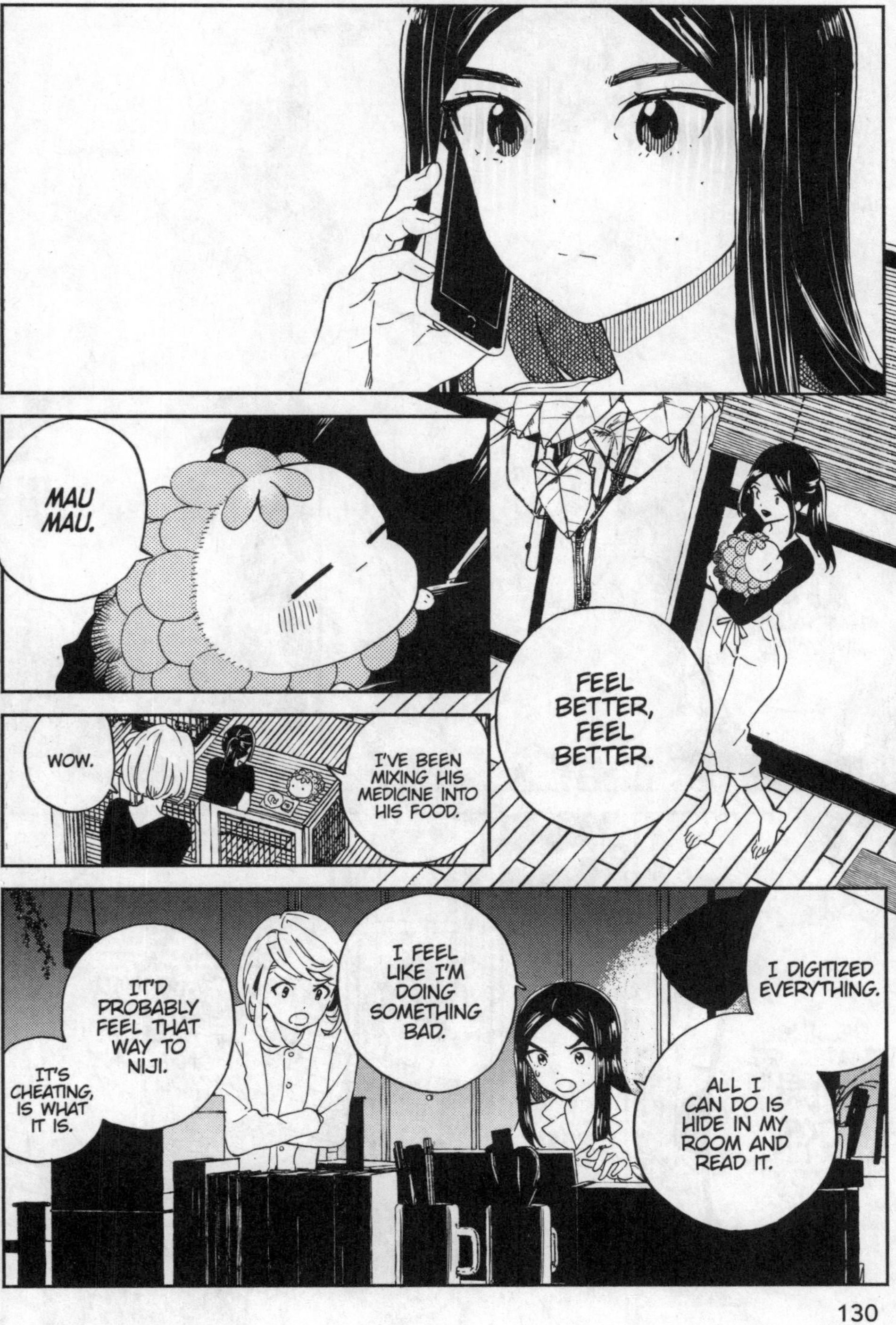
FEEL BETTER, FEEL BETTER.
MAU MAU.
I'VE BEEN MIXING HIS MEDICINE INTO HIS FOOD.
WOW.
I DIGITIZED EVERYTHING.
ALL I CAN DO IS HIDE IN MY ROOM AND READ IT.
I FEEL LIKE I'M DOING SOMETHING BAD.
IT'D PROBABLY FEEL THAT WAY TO NIJI.
IT'S CHEATING, IS WHAT IT IS.

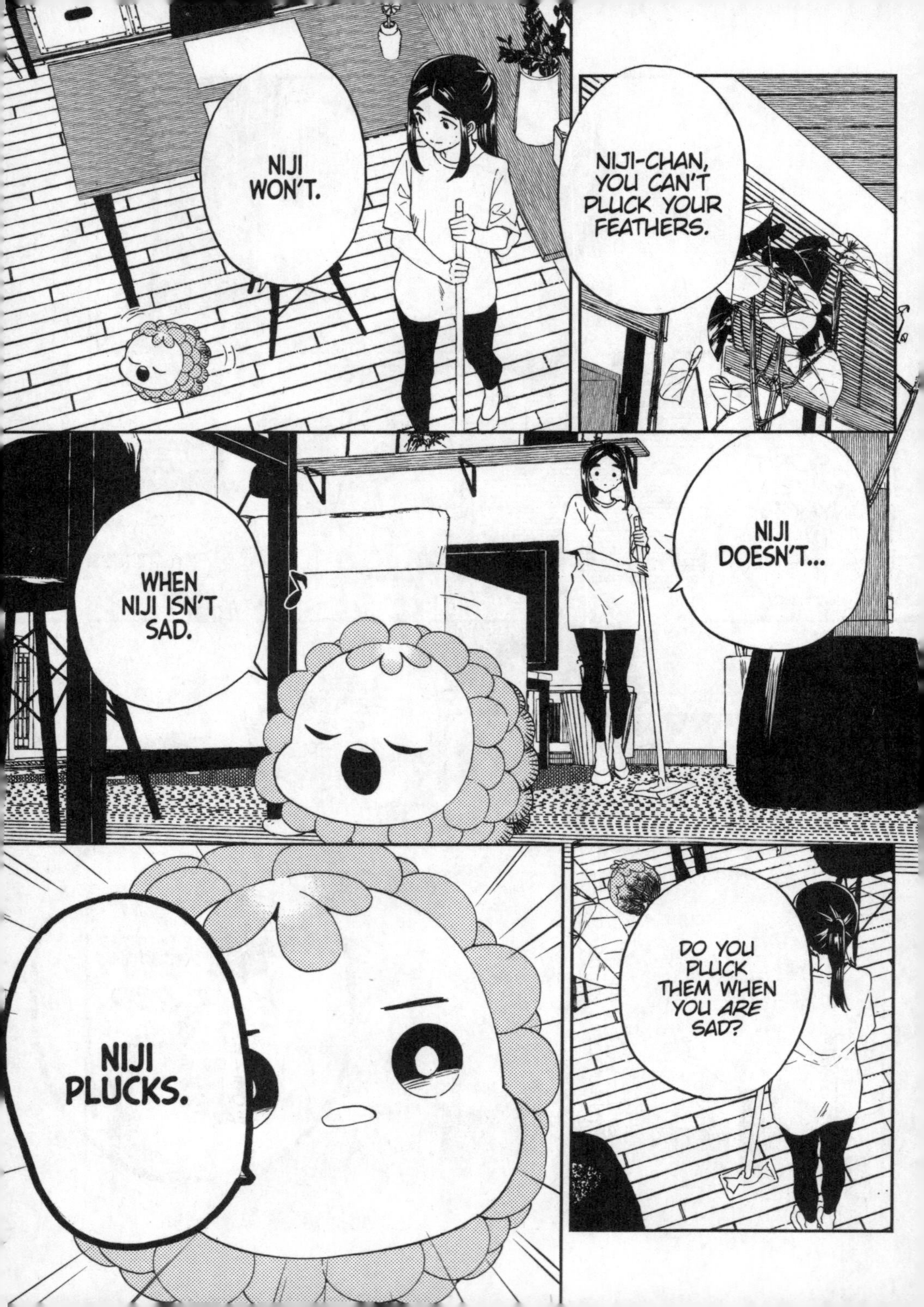
NIJI-CHAN, YOU CAN'T PLUCK YOUR FEATHERS.
NIJI WON'T.
NIJI DOESN'T...
WHEN NIJI ISN'T SAD.
DO YOU PLUCK THEM WHEN YOU *ARE* SAD?
NIJI PLUCKS.

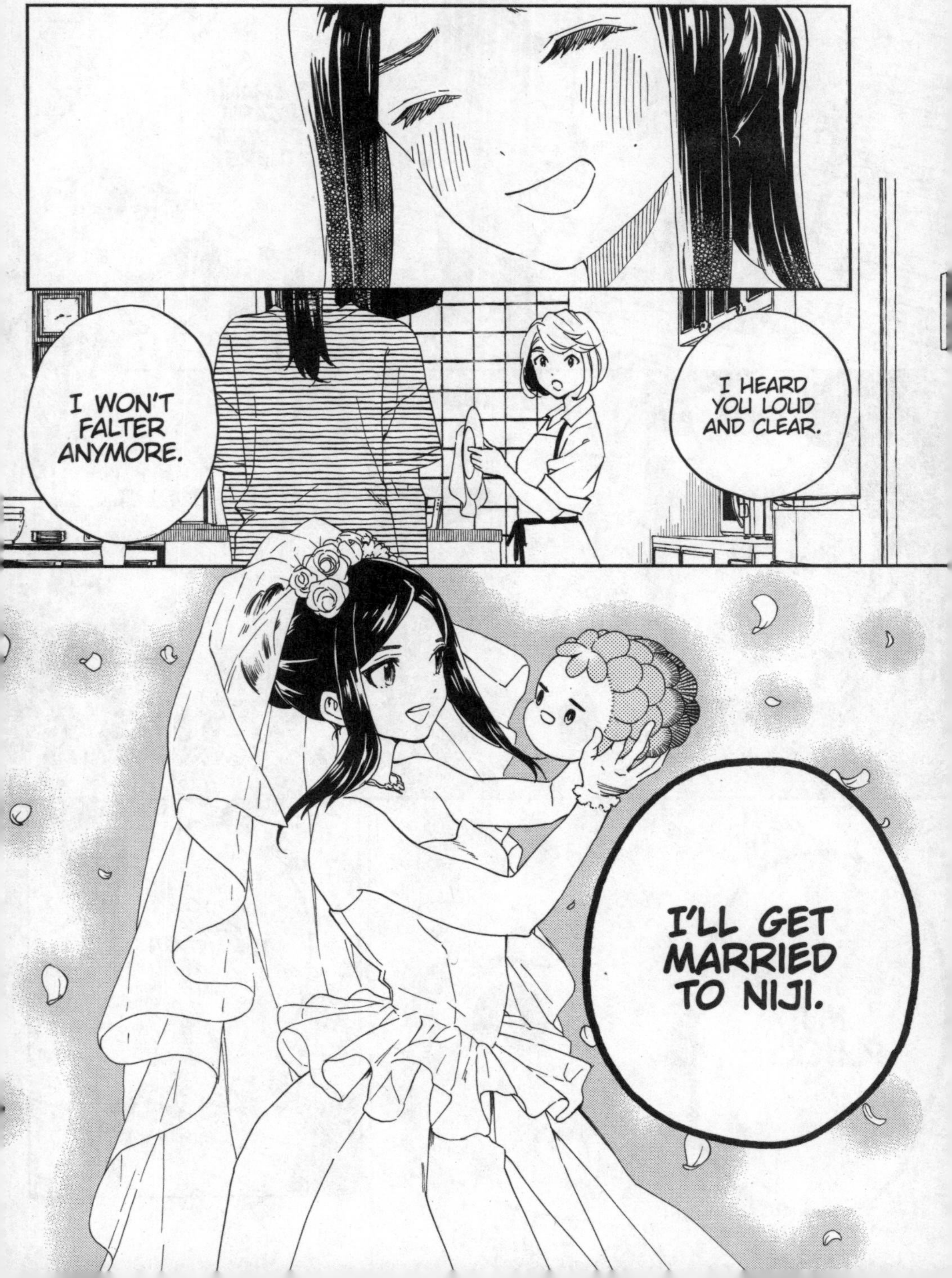
I HEARD YOU LOUD AND CLEAR.
I WON'T FALTER ANYMORE.
I'LL GET MARRIED TO NIJI.

Rainbow and Black

Story & Art by **Eri Takenashi**

NOW LOADING...

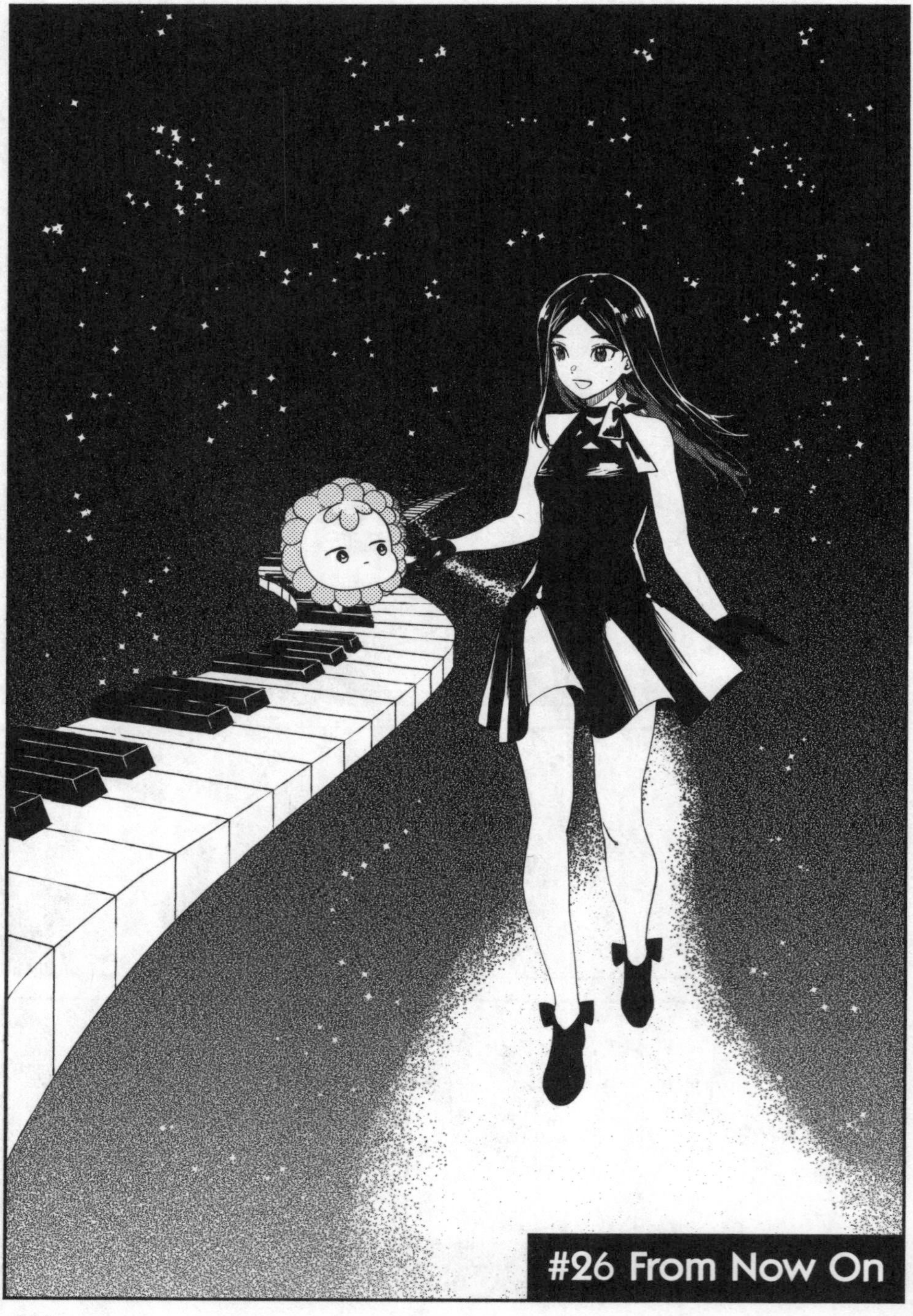
#26 From Now On

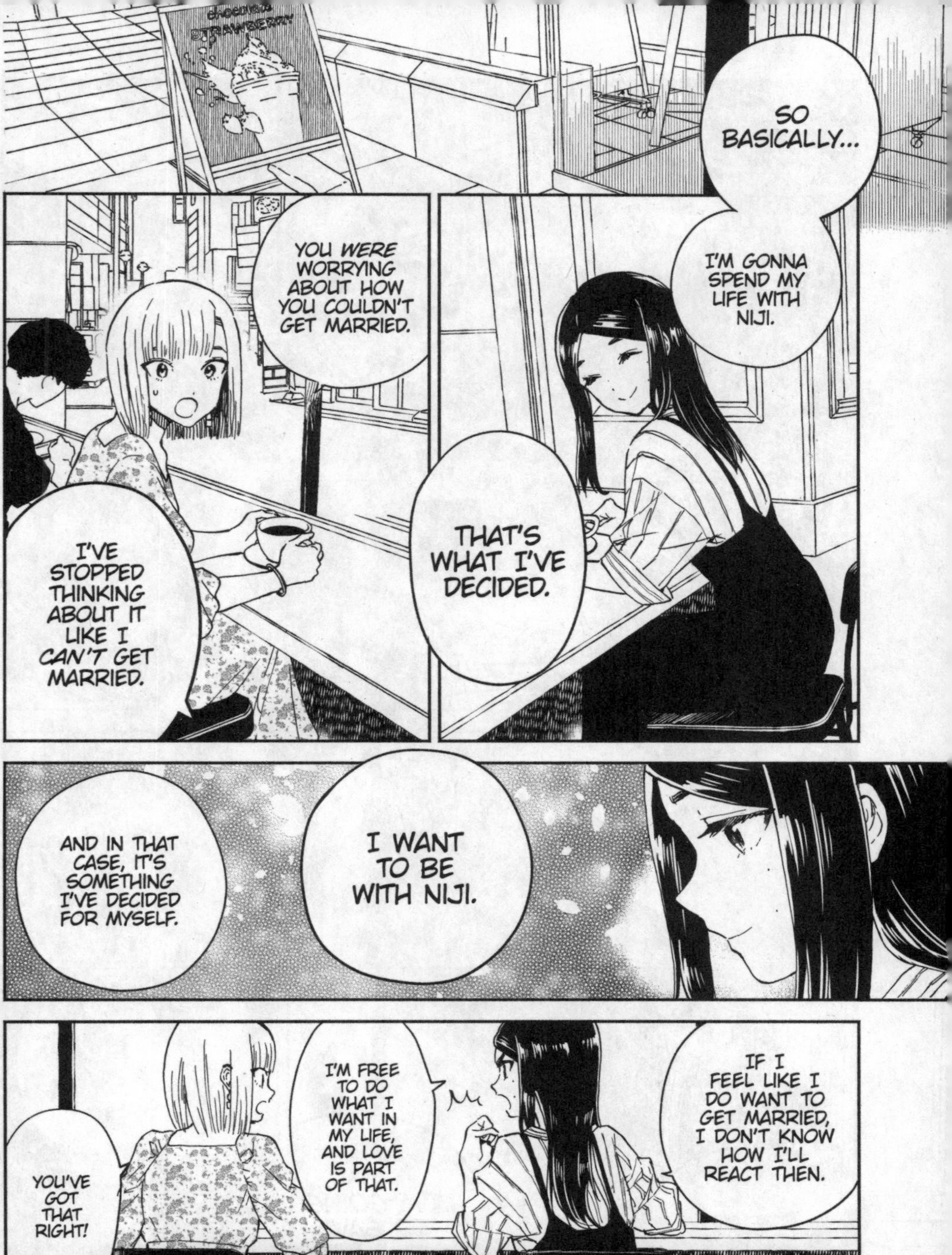
STRAWBERRY
SO BASICALLY...
I'M GONNA SPEND MY LIFE WITH NIJI.
THAT'S WHAT I'VE DECIDED.
YOU *WERE* WORRYING ABOUT HOW YOU COULDN'T GET MARRIED.
I'VE STOPPED THINKING ABOUT IT LIKE I *CAN'T* GET MARRIED.
I WANT TO BE WITH NIJI.
AND IN THAT CASE, IT'S SOMETHING I'VE DECIDED FOR MYSELF.
IF I FEEL LIKE I DO WANT TO GET MARRIED, I DON'T KNOW HOW I'LL REACT THEN.
I'M FREE TO DO WHAT I WANT IN MY LIFE, AND LOVE IS PART OF THAT.
YOU'VE GOT THAT RIGHT!

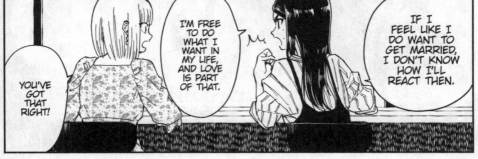

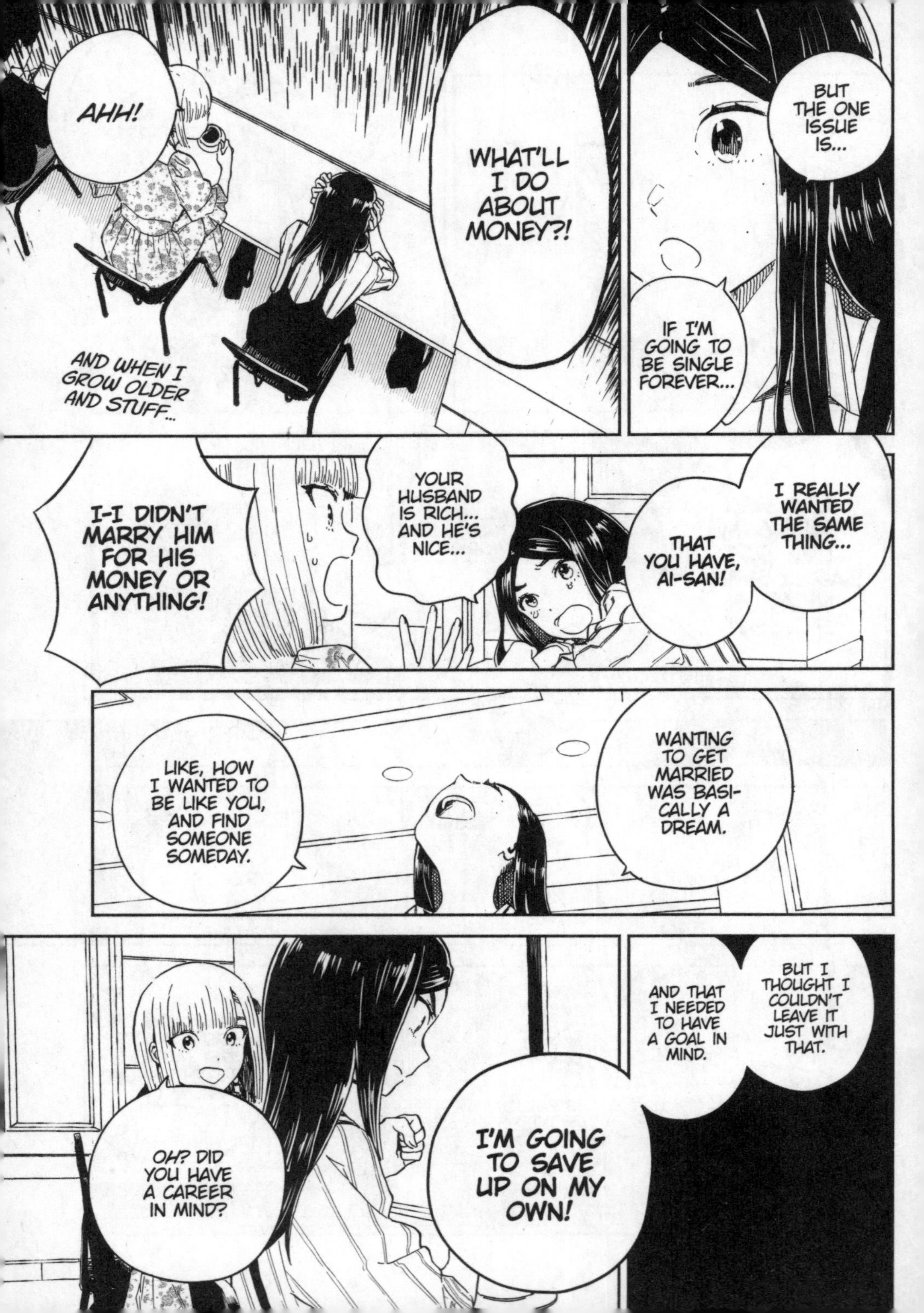
BUT THE ONE ISSUE IS...
IF I'M GOING TO BE SINGLE FOREVER...
WHAT'LL I DO ABOUT MONEY?!
AHH!
AND WHEN I GROW OLDER AND STUFF...
I REALLY WANTED THE SAME THING...
THAT YOU HAVE, AI-SAN!
YOUR HUSBAND IS RICH... AND HE'S NICE...
I-I DIDN'T MARRY HIM FOR HIS MONEY OR ANYTHING!
WANTING TO GET MARRIED WAS BASI-CALLY A DREAM.
LIKE, HOW I WANTED TO BE LIKE YOU, AND FIND SOMEONE SOMEDAY.
BUT I THOUGHT I COULDN'T LEAVE IT JUST WITH THAT.
AND THAT I NEEDED TO HAVE A GOAL IN MIND.
I'M GOING TO SAVE UP ON MY OWN!
OH? DID YOU HAVE A CAREER IN MIND?

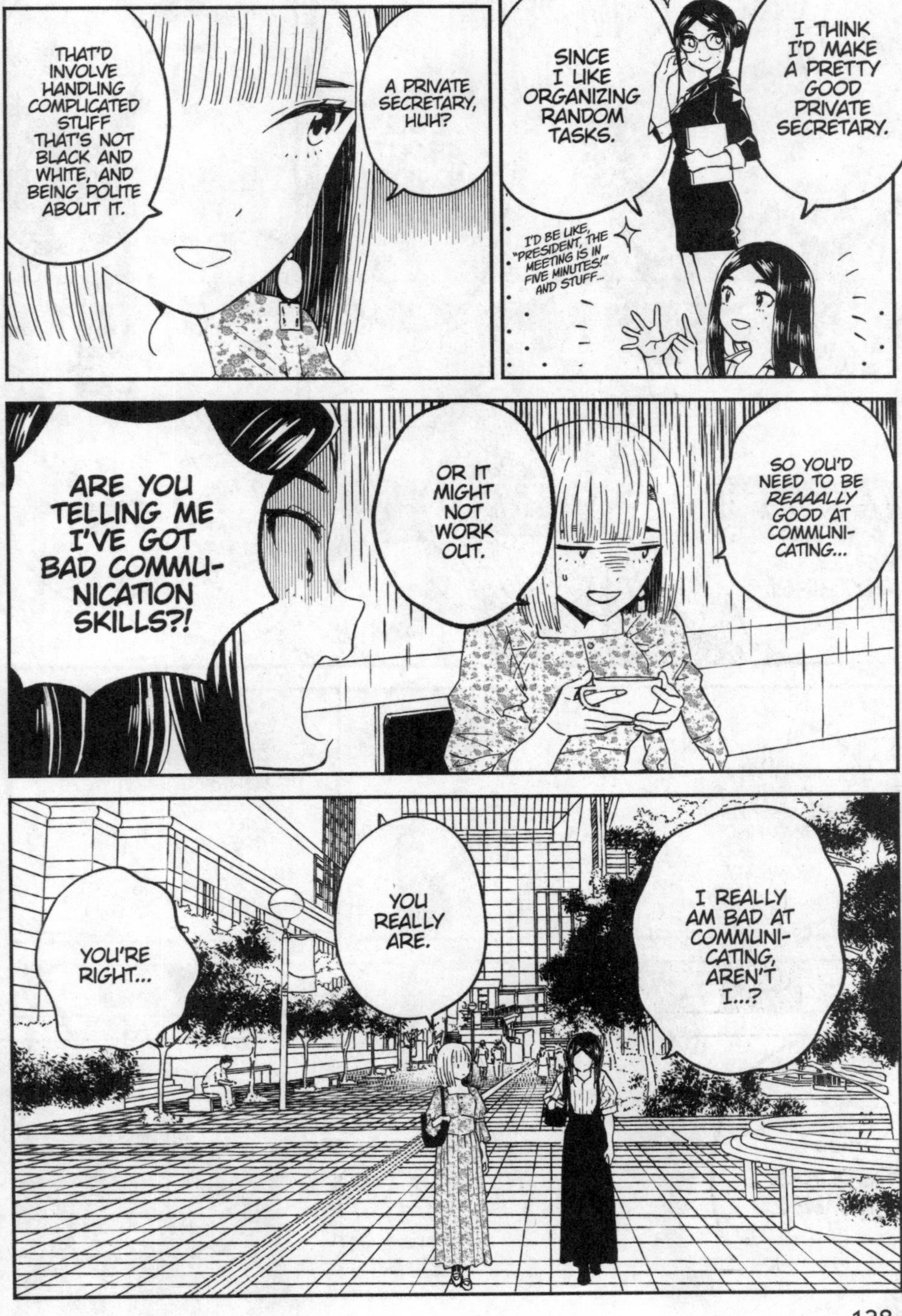
I THINK I'D MAKE A PRETTY GOOD PRIVATE SECRETARY.
SINCE I LIKE ORGANIZING RANDOM TASKS.
I'D BE LIKE, "PRESIDENT, THE MEETING IS IN FIVE MINUTES!" AND STUFF...
A PRIVATE SECRETARY, HUH?
THAT'D INVOLVE HANDLING COMPLICATED STUFF THAT'S NOT BLACK AND WHITE, AND BEING POLITE ABOUT IT.
SO YOU'D NEED TO BE *REAAALLY* GOOD AT COMMUNI-CATING...
OR IT MIGHT NOT WORK OUT.
ARE YOU TELLING ME I'VE GOT BAD COMMU-NICATION SKILLS?!
I REALLY AM BAD AT COMMUNI-CATING, AREN'T I...?
YOU REALLY ARE.
YOU'RE RIGHT...

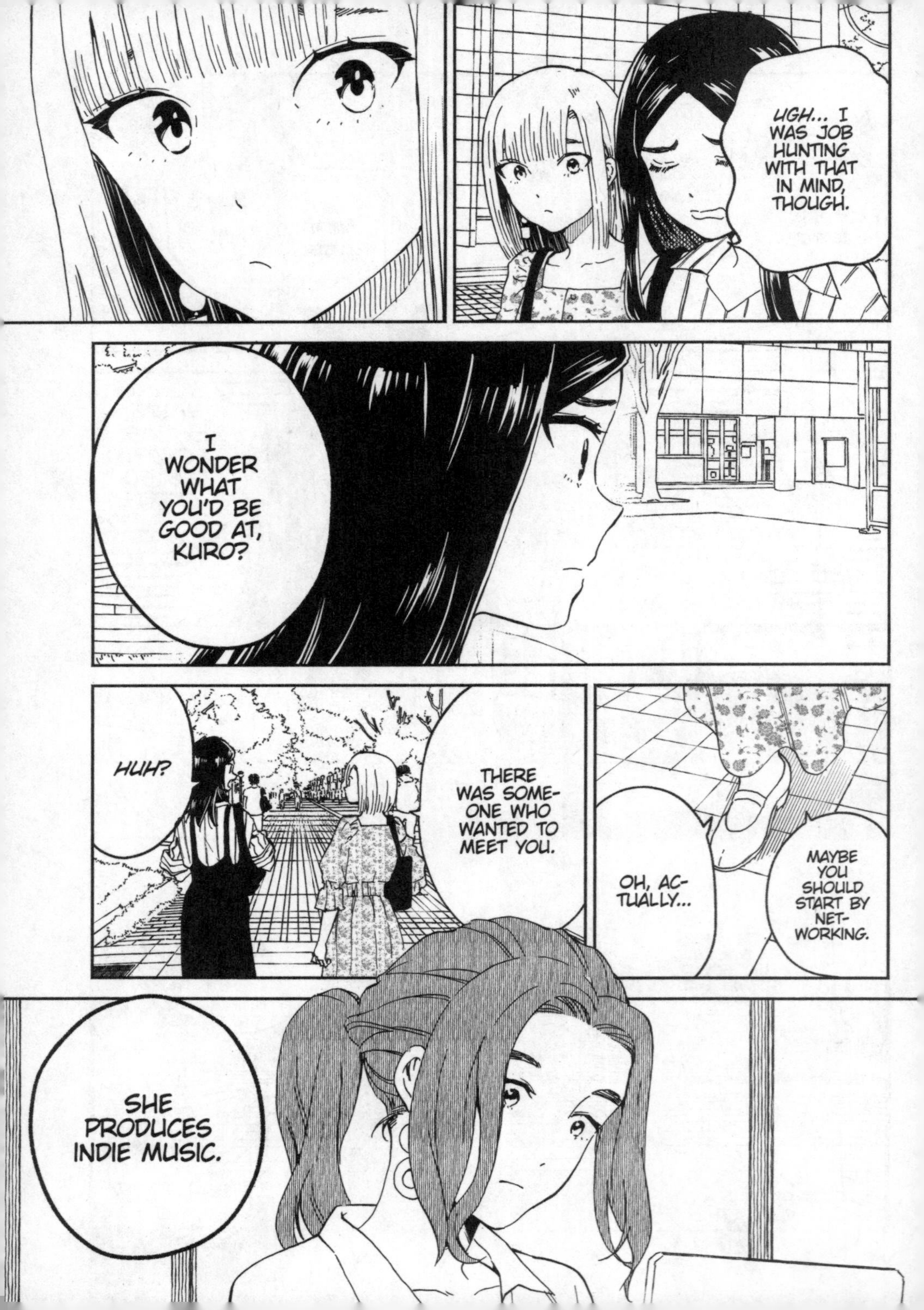
UGH... I WAS JOB HUNTING WITH THAT IN MIND, THOUGH.
I WONDER WHAT YOU'D BE GOOD AT, KURO?
MAYBE YOU SHOULD START BY NET-WORKING.
OH, AC-TUALLY...
THERE WAS SOME-ONE WHO WANTED TO MEET YOU.
HUH?
SHE PRODUCES INDIE MUSIC.

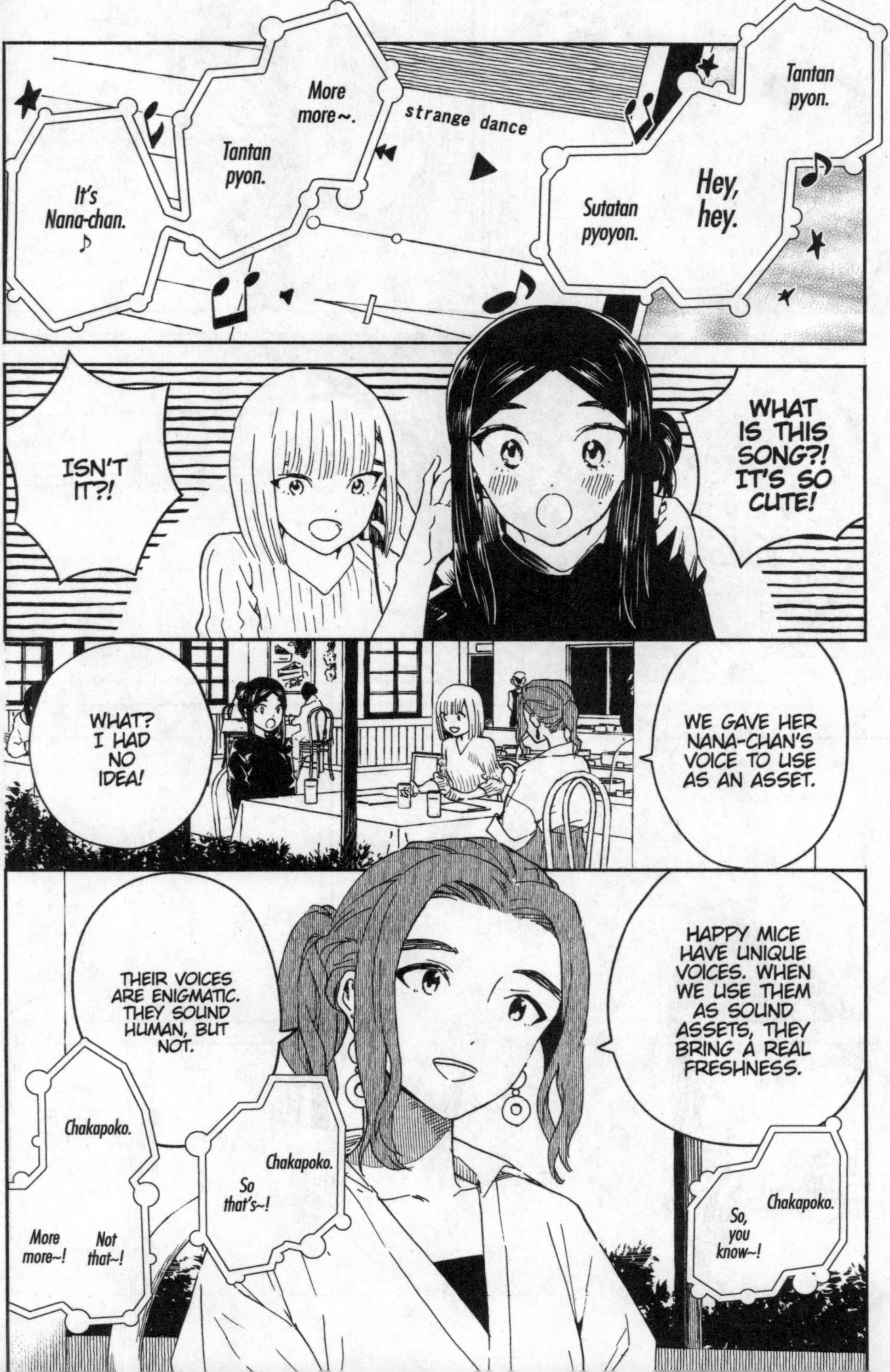
Tantan pyon.
Hey, hey.
Sutatan pyoyon.
strange dance
More more~.
Tantan pyon.
It's Nana-chan. ♪
WHAT IS THIS SONG?! IT'S SO CUTE!
ISN'T IT?!
WE GAVE HER NANA-CHAN'S VOICE TO USE AS AN ASSET.
WHAT? I HAD NO IDEA!
HAPPY MICE HAVE UNIQUE VOICES. WHEN WE USE THEM AS SOUND ASSETS, THEY BRING A REAL FRESHNESS.
THEIR VOICES ARE ENIGMATIC. THEY SOUND HUMAN, BUT NOT.
Chakapoko.
So, you know~!
Chakapoko.
So that's~!
Chakapoko.
Not that~!
More more~!

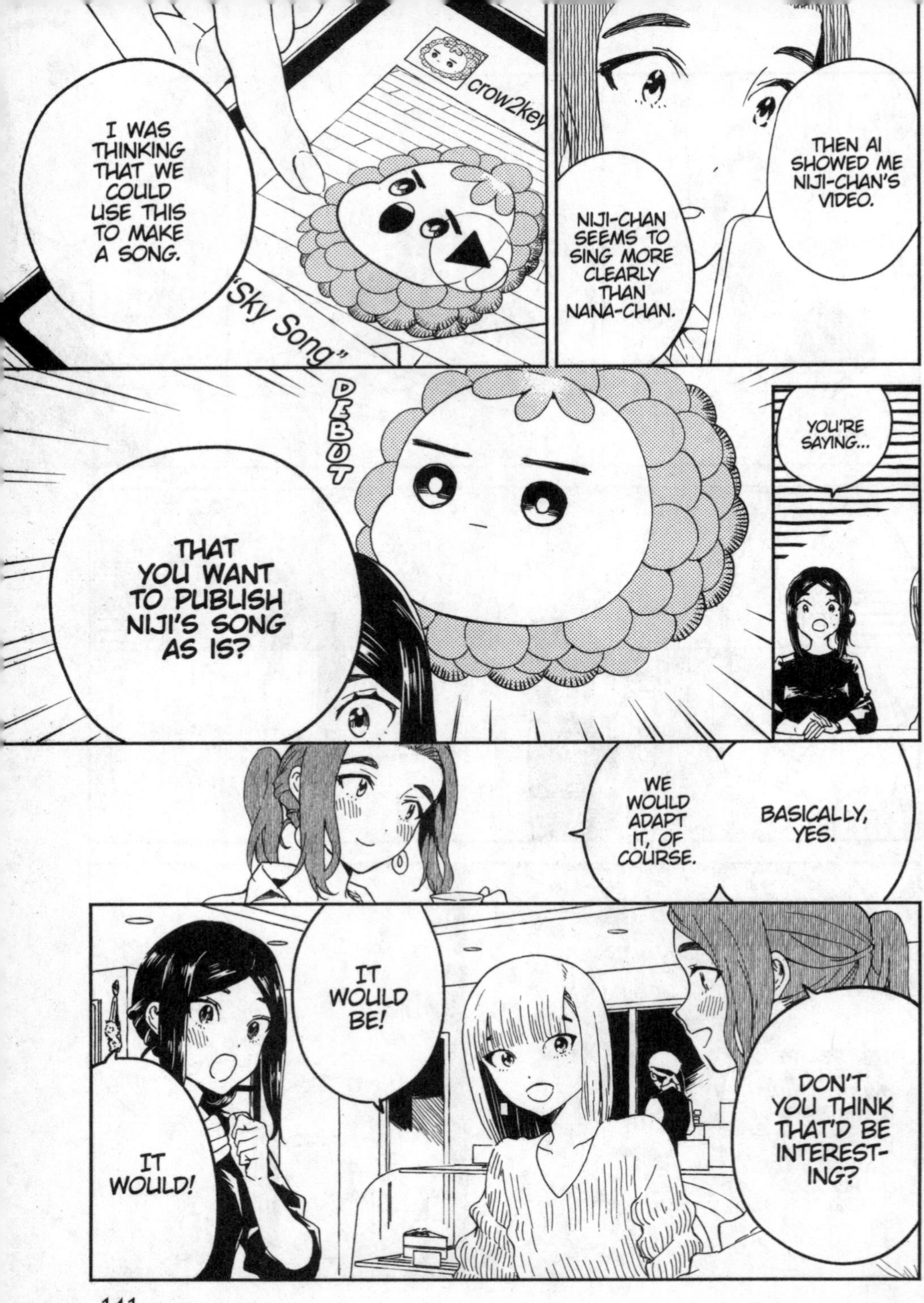
THEN AI SHOWED ME NIJI-CHAN'S VIDEO.
NIJI-CHAN SEEMS TO SING MORE CLEARLY THAN NANA-CHAN.
crow2key
I WAS THINKING THAT WE COULD USE THIS TO MAKE A SONG.
"Sky Song"
YOU'RE SAYING...
DEBUT
THAT YOU WANT TO PUBLISH NIJI'S SONG AS IS?
BASICALLY, YES.
WE WOULD ADAPT IT, OF COURSE.
DON'T YOU THINK THAT'D BE INTERESTING?
IT WOULD BE!
IT WOULD!

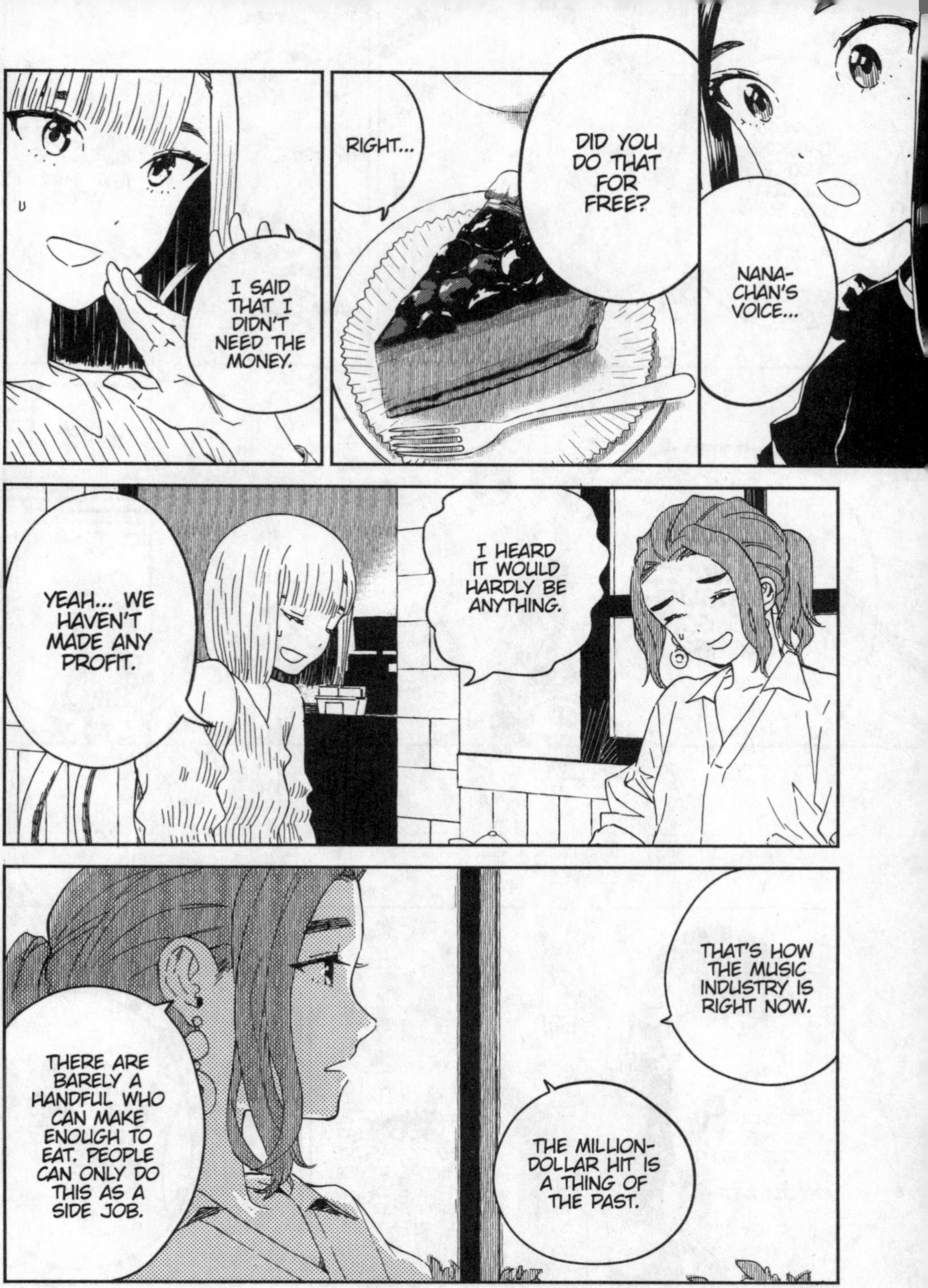
NANA-CHAN'S VOICE...
DID YOU DO THAT FOR FREE?
RIGHT...
I SAID THAT I DIDN'T NEED THE MONEY.
I HEARD IT WOULD HARDLY BE ANYTHING.
YEAH... WE HAVEN'T MADE ANY PROFIT.
THAT'S HOW THE MUSIC INDUSTRY IS RIGHT NOW.
THE MILLION-DOLLAR HIT IS A THING OF THE PAST.
THERE ARE BARELY A HANDFUL WHO CAN MAKE ENOUGH TO EAT. PEOPLE CAN ONLY DO THIS AS A SIDE JOB.

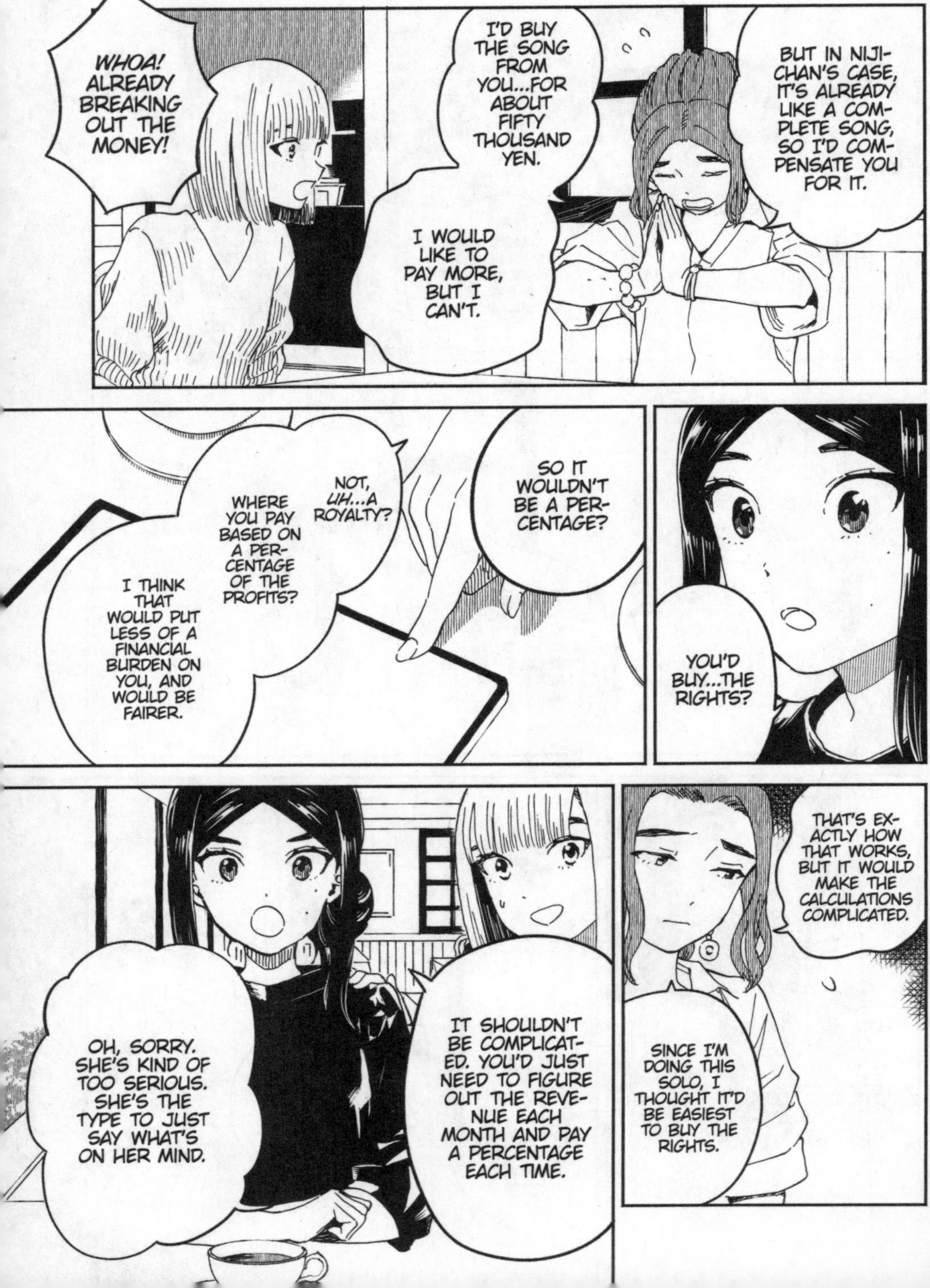
BUT IN NIJI-CHAN'S CASE, IT'S ALREADY LIKE A COMPLETE SONG, SO I'D COMPENSATE YOU FOR IT.
I'D BUY THE SONG FROM YOU...FOR ABOUT FIFTY THOUSAND YEN.
I WOULD LIKE TO PAY MORE, BUT I CAN'T.
WHOA! ALREADY BREAKING OUT THE MONEY!
YOU'D BUY...THE RIGHTS?
SO IT WOULDN'T BE A PERCENTAGE?
NOT, *UH*...A ROYALTY?
WHERE YOU PAY BASED ON A PERCENTAGE OF THE PROFITS?
I THINK THAT WOULD PUT LESS OF A FINANCIAL BURDEN ON YOU, AND WOULD BE FAIRER.
THAT'S EXACTLY HOW THAT WORKS, BUT IT WOULD MAKE THE CALCULATIONS COMPLICATED.
SINCE I'M DOING THIS SOLO, I THOUGHT IT'D BE EASIEST TO BUY THE RIGHTS.
IT SHOULDN'T BE COMPLICATED. YOU'D JUST NEED TO FIGURE OUT THE REVENUE EACH MONTH AND PAY A PERCENTAGE EACH TIME.
OH, SORRY. SHE'S KIND OF TOO SERIOUS. SHE'S THE TYPE TO JUST SAY WHAT'S ON HER MIND.

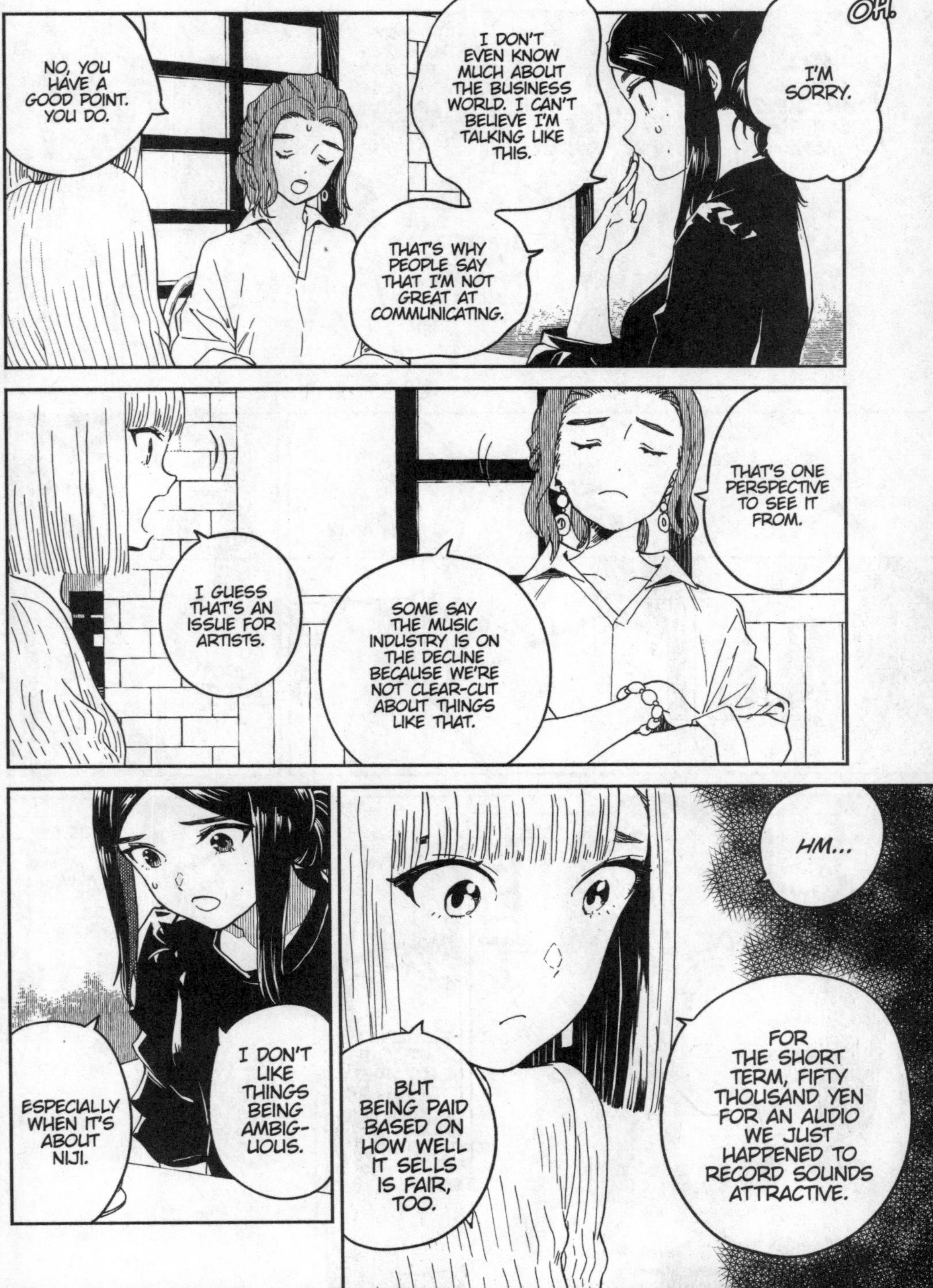
OH.
I'M SORRY.
I DON'T EVEN KNOW MUCH ABOUT THE BUSINESS WORLD. I CAN'T BELIEVE I'M TALKING LIKE THIS.
THAT'S WHY PEOPLE SAY THAT I'M NOT GREAT AT COMMUNICATING.
NO, YOU HAVE A GOOD POINT. YOU DO.
THAT'S ONE PERSPECTIVE TO SEE IT FROM.
SOME SAY THE MUSIC INDUSTRY IS ON THE DECLINE BECAUSE WE'RE NOT CLEAR-CUT ABOUT THINGS LIKE THAT.
I GUESS THAT'S AN ISSUE FOR ARTISTS.
HM...
FOR THE SHORT TERM, FIFTY THOUSAND YEN FOR AN AUDIO WE JUST HAPPENED TO RECORD SOUNDS ATTRACTIVE.
BUT BEING PAID BASED ON HOW WELL IT SELLS IS FAIR, TOO.
I DON'T LIKE THINGS BEING AMBIG-UOUS.
ESPECIALLY WHEN IT'S ABOUT NIJI.

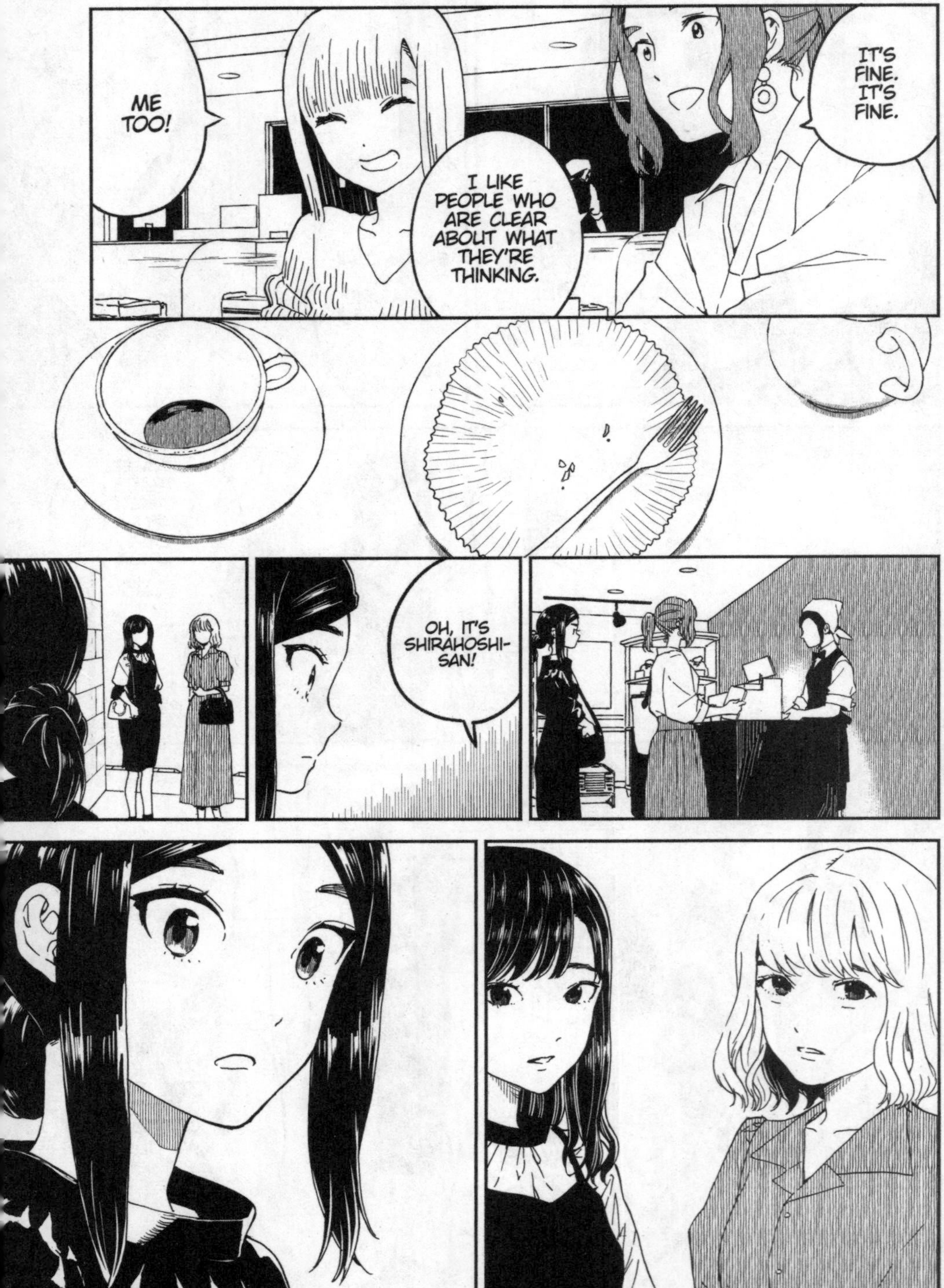
IT'S FINE. IT'S FINE.
I LIKE PEOPLE WHO ARE CLEAR ABOUT WHAT THEY'RE THINKING.
ME TOO!
OH, IT'S SHIRAHOSHI-SAN!

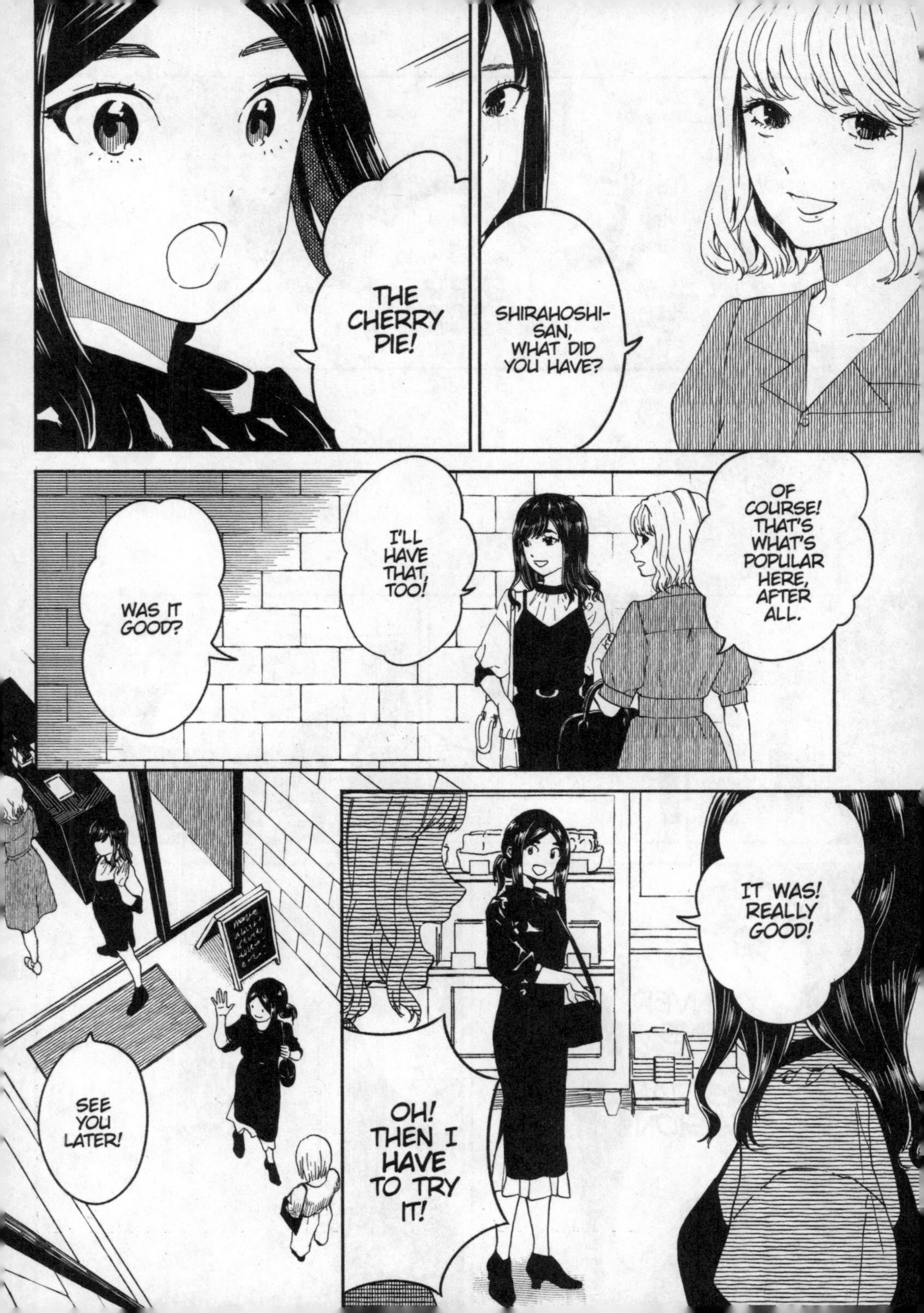
SHIRAHOSHI-SAN, WHAT DID YOU HAVE?
THE CHERRY PIE!
OF COURSE! THAT'S WHAT'S POPULAR HERE, AFTER ALL.
I'LL HAVE THAT, TOO!
WAS IT GOOD?
IT WAS! REALLY GOOD!
OH! THEN I HAVE TO TRY IT!
SEE YOU LATER!

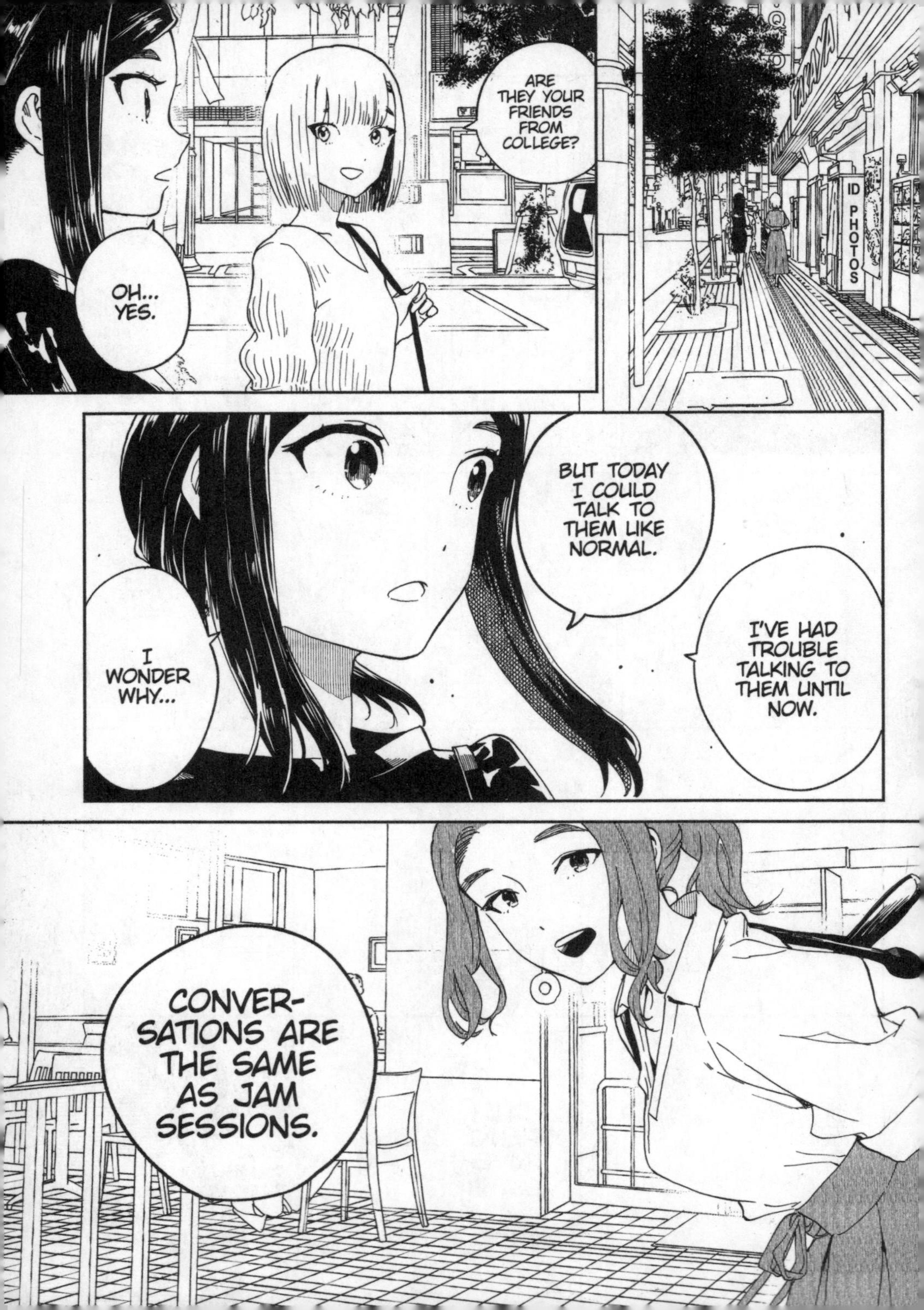
ARE THEY YOUR FRIENDS FROM COLLEGE?
OH... YES.
I'VE HAD TROUBLE TALKING TO THEM UNTIL NOW.
BUT TODAY I COULD TALK TO THEM LIKE NORMAL.
I WONDER WHY...
CONVER-SATIONS ARE THE SAME AS JAM SESSIONS.

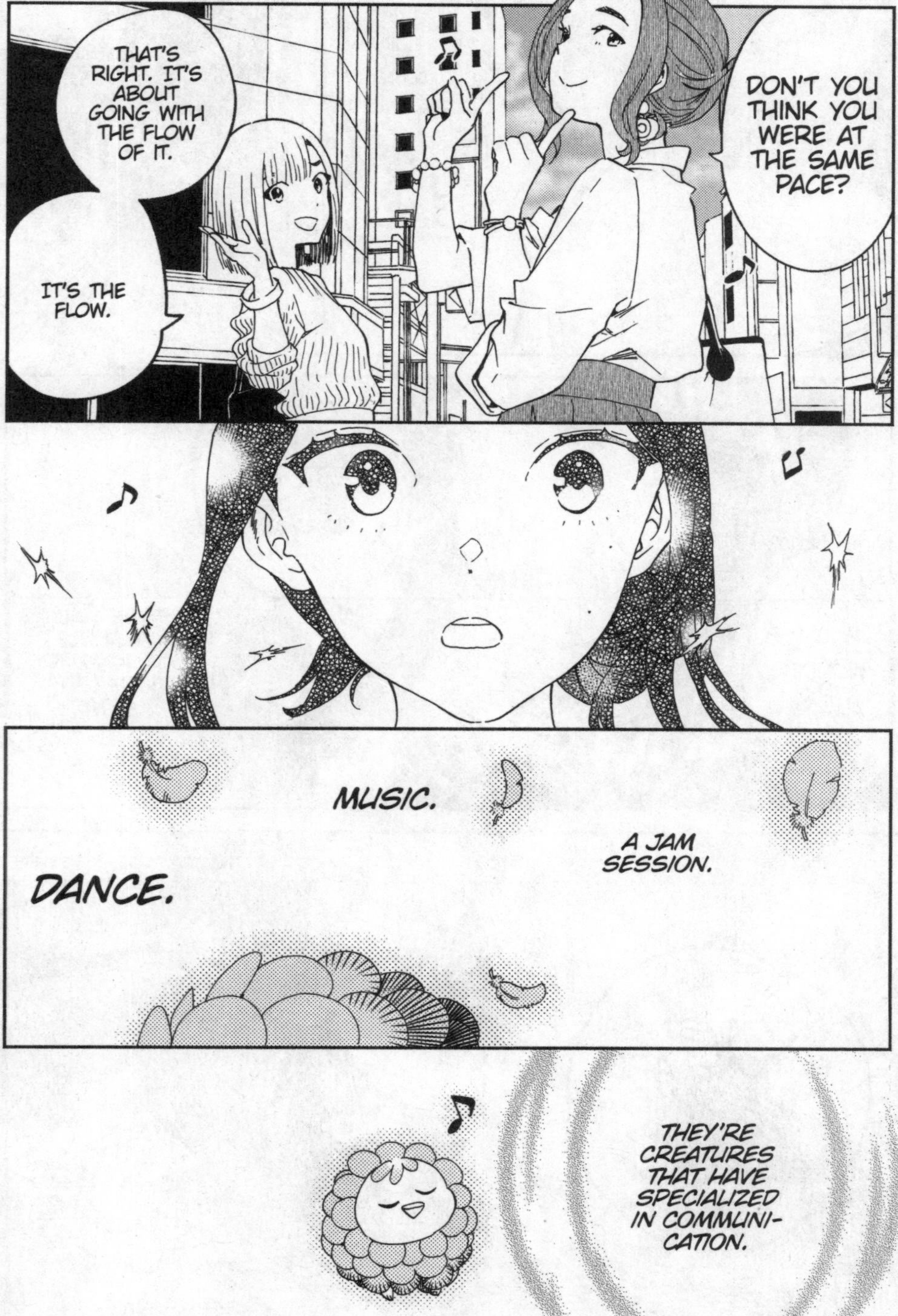
DON'T YOU THINK YOU WERE AT THE SAME PACE?
THAT'S RIGHT. IT'S ABOUT GOING WITH THE FLOW OF IT.
IT'S THE FLOW.
MUSIC.
A JAM SESSION.
DANCE.
THEY'RE CREATURES THAT HAVE SPECIALIZED IN COMMUNI-CATION.

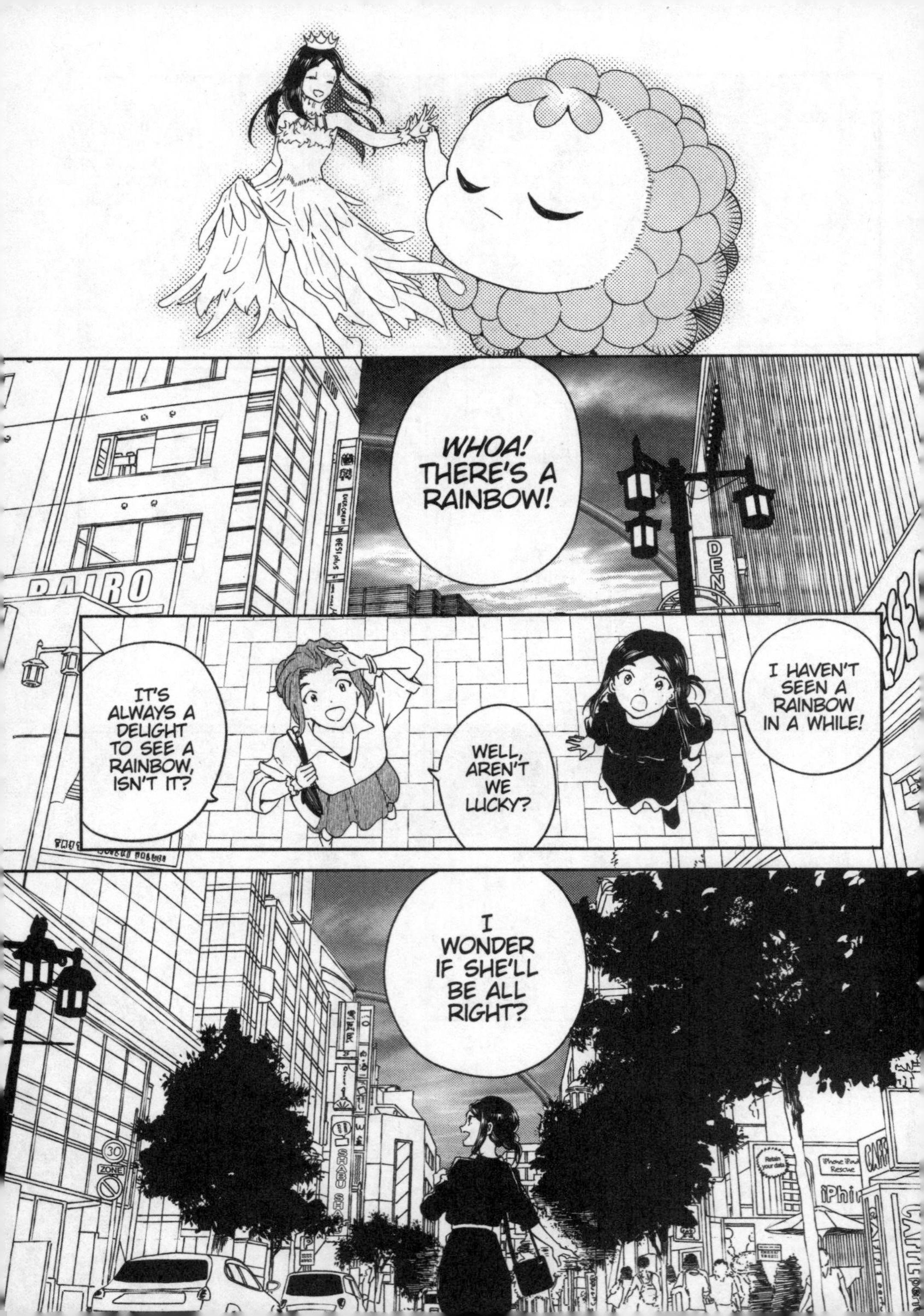
WHOA! THERE'S A RAINBOW!
I HAVEN'T SEEN A RAINBOW IN A WHILE!
WELL, AREN'T WE LUCKY?
IT'S ALWAYS A DELIGHT TO SEE A RAINBOW, ISN'T IT?
I WONDER IF SHE'LL BE ALL RIGHT?

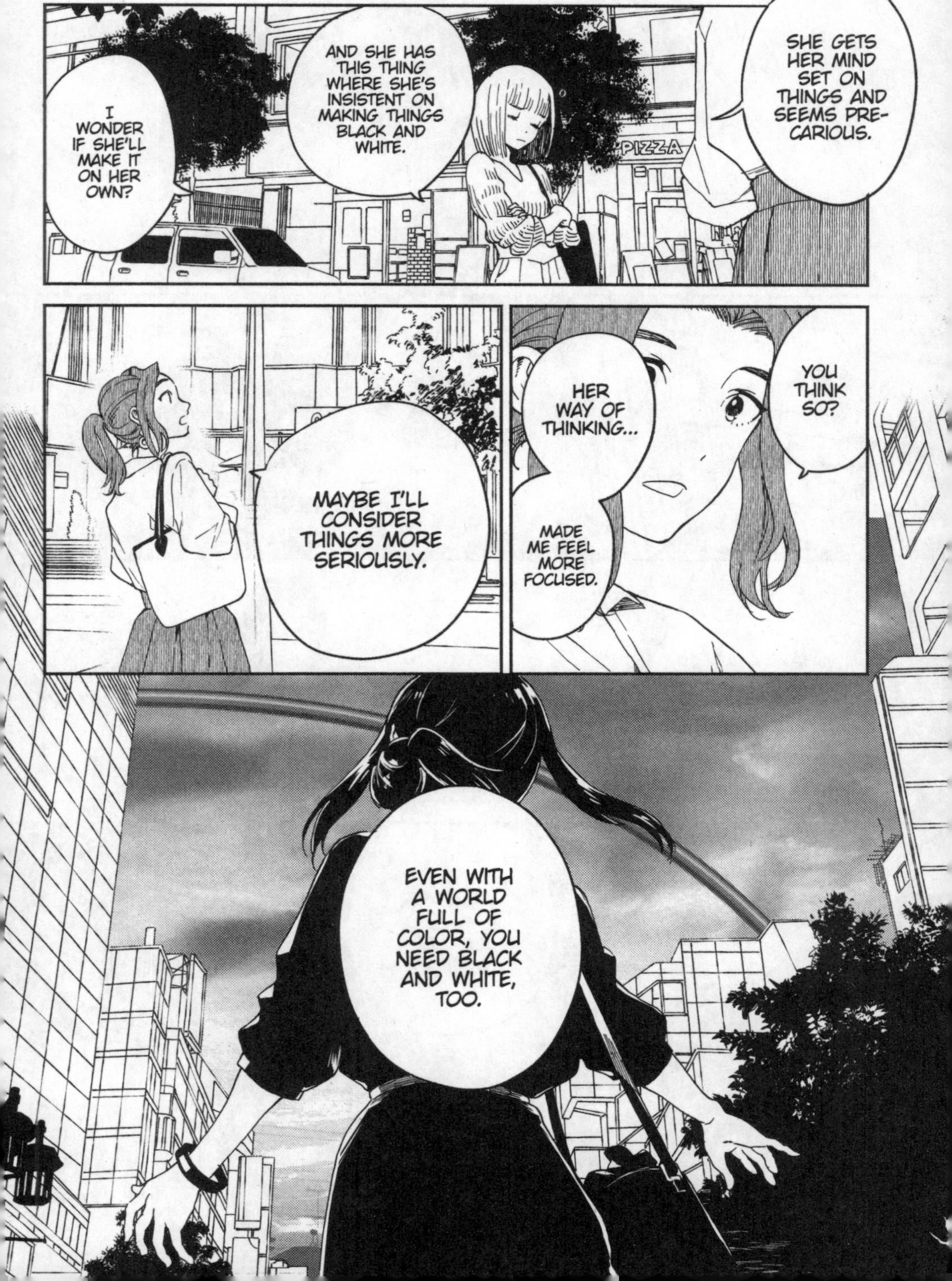
SHE GETS HER MIND SET ON THINGS AND SEEMS PRE-CARIOUS.
AND SHE HAS THIS THING WHERE SHE'S INSISTENT ON MAKING THINGS BLACK AND WHITE.
I WONDER IF SHE'LL MAKE IT ON HER OWN?
PIZZA
YOU THINK SO?
HER WAY OF THINKING...
MADE ME FEEL MORE FOCUSED.
MAYBE I'LL CONSIDER THINGS MORE SERIOUSLY.
EVEN WITH A WORLD FULL OF COLOR, YOU NEED BLACK AND WHITE, TOO.

Rainbow and Black

Story & Art by Eri Takenashi

NOW LOADING...

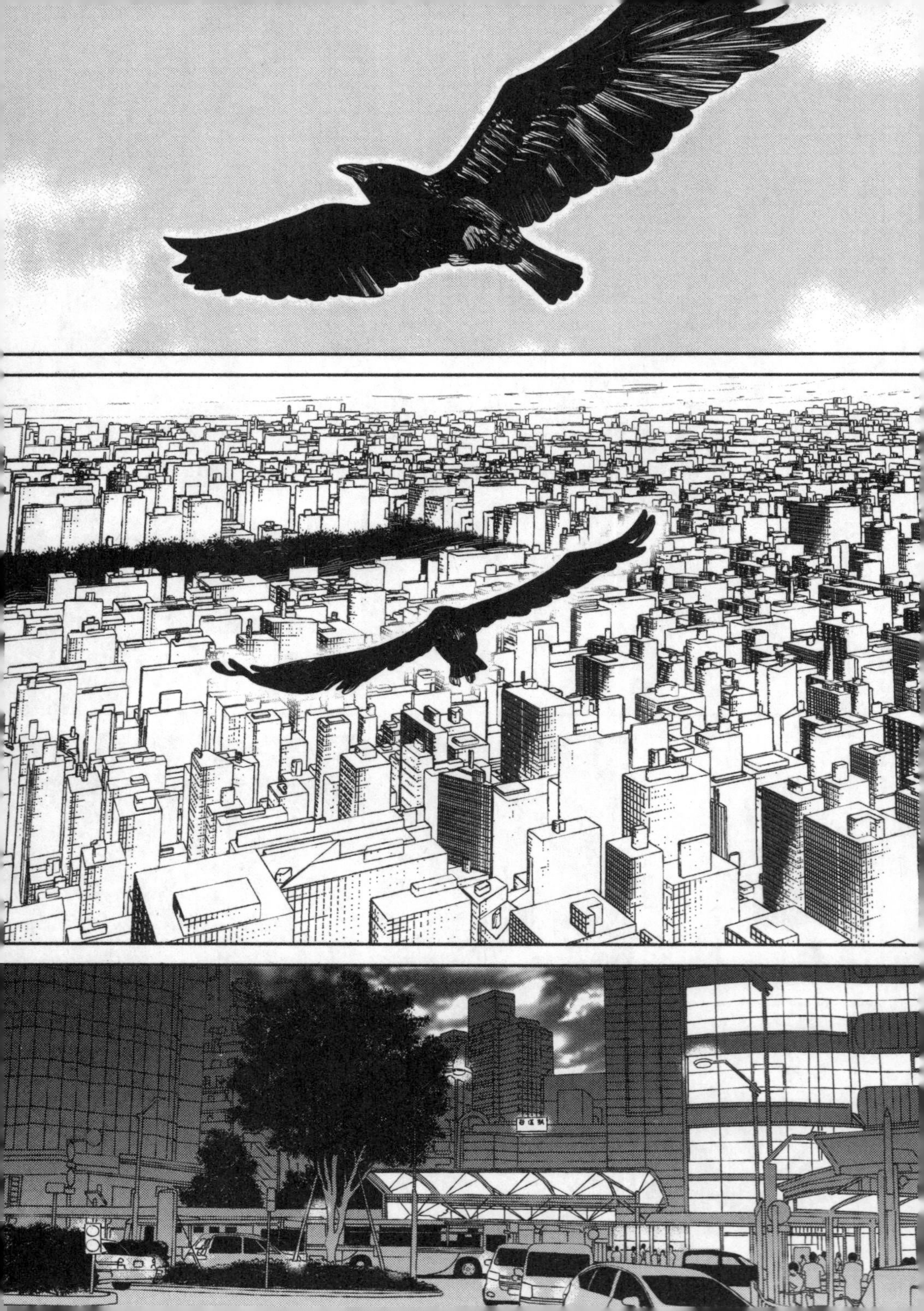

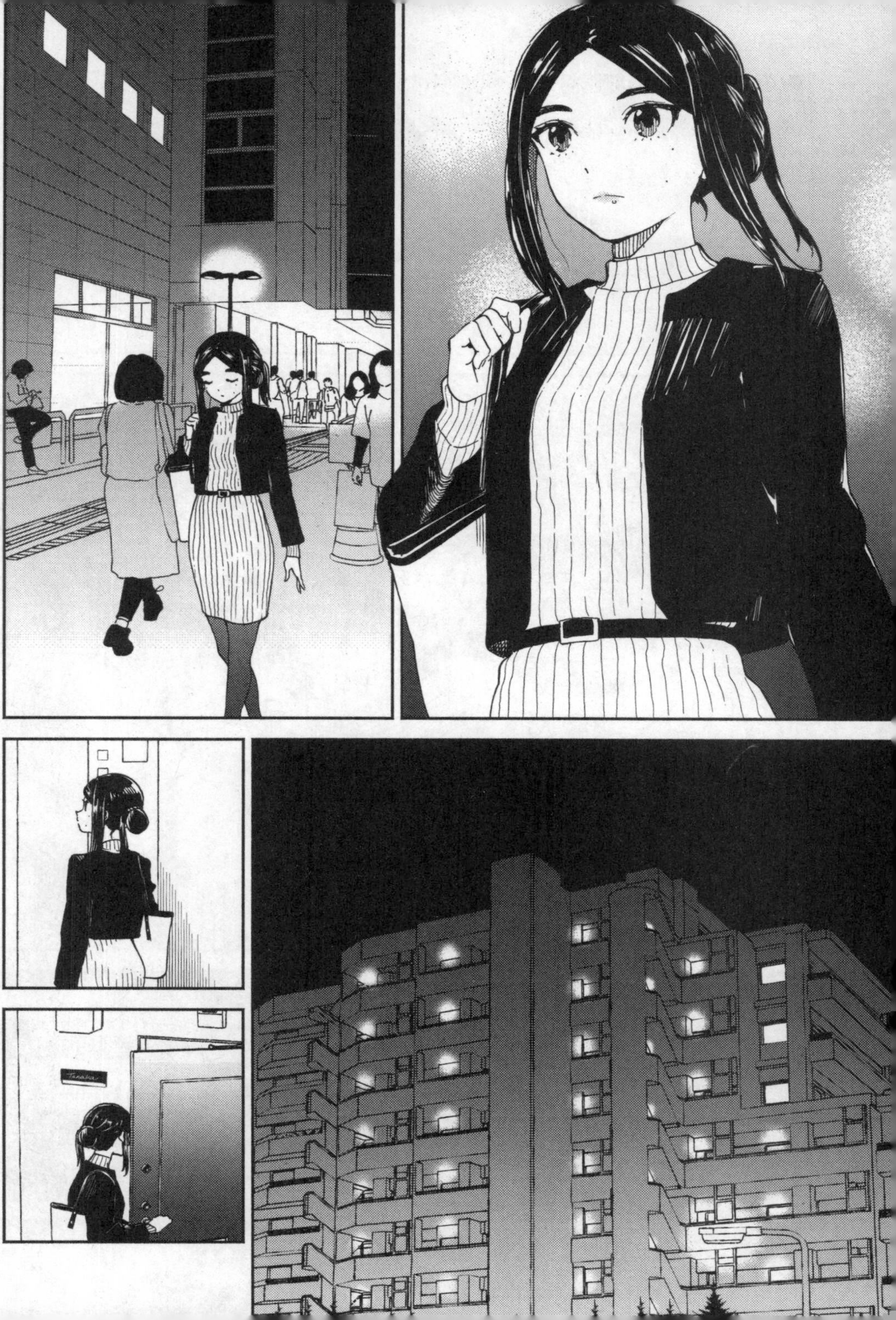
Tanaka

#27 Rainbow and Black

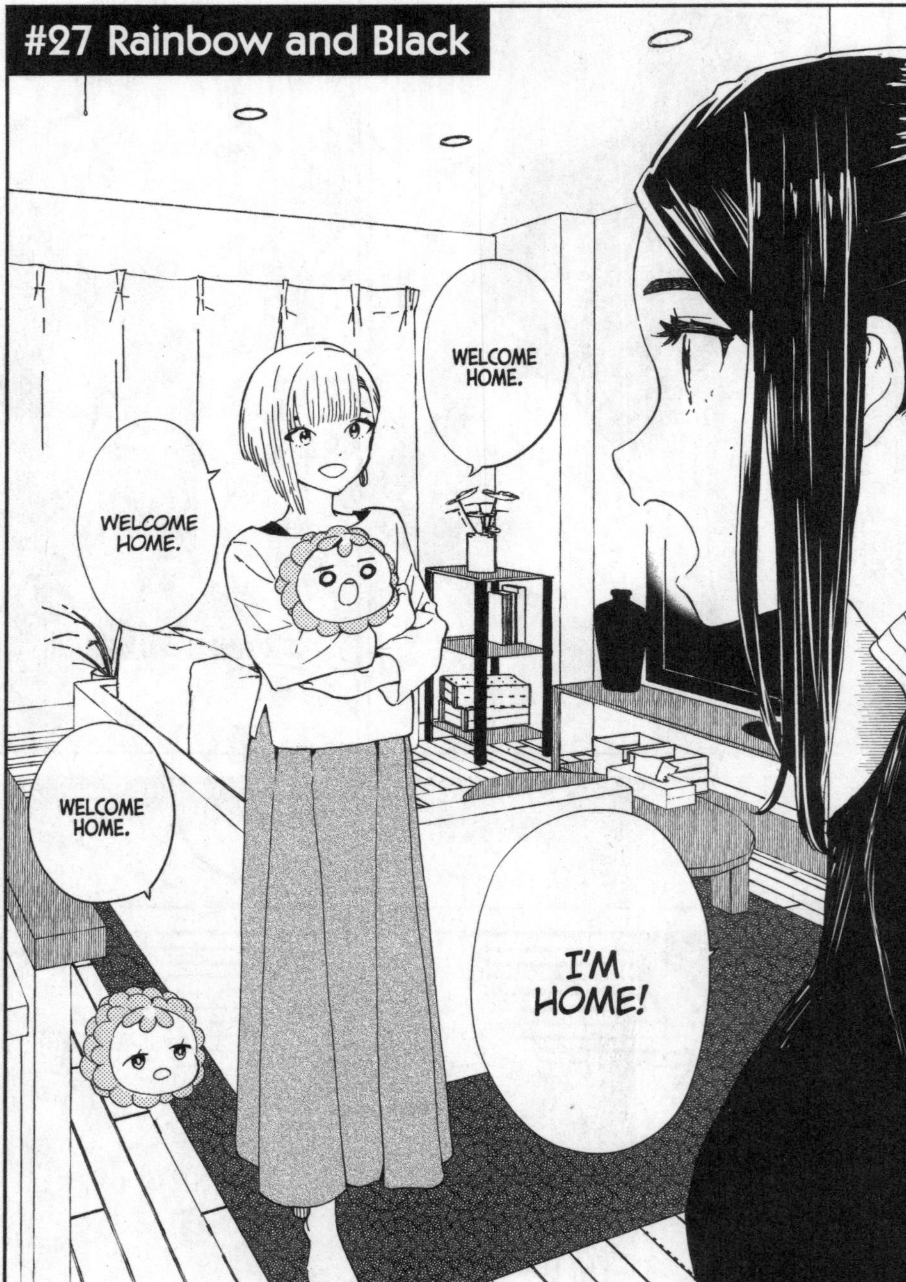
WELCOME HOME.
WELCOME HOME.
WELCOME HOME.
I'M HOME!

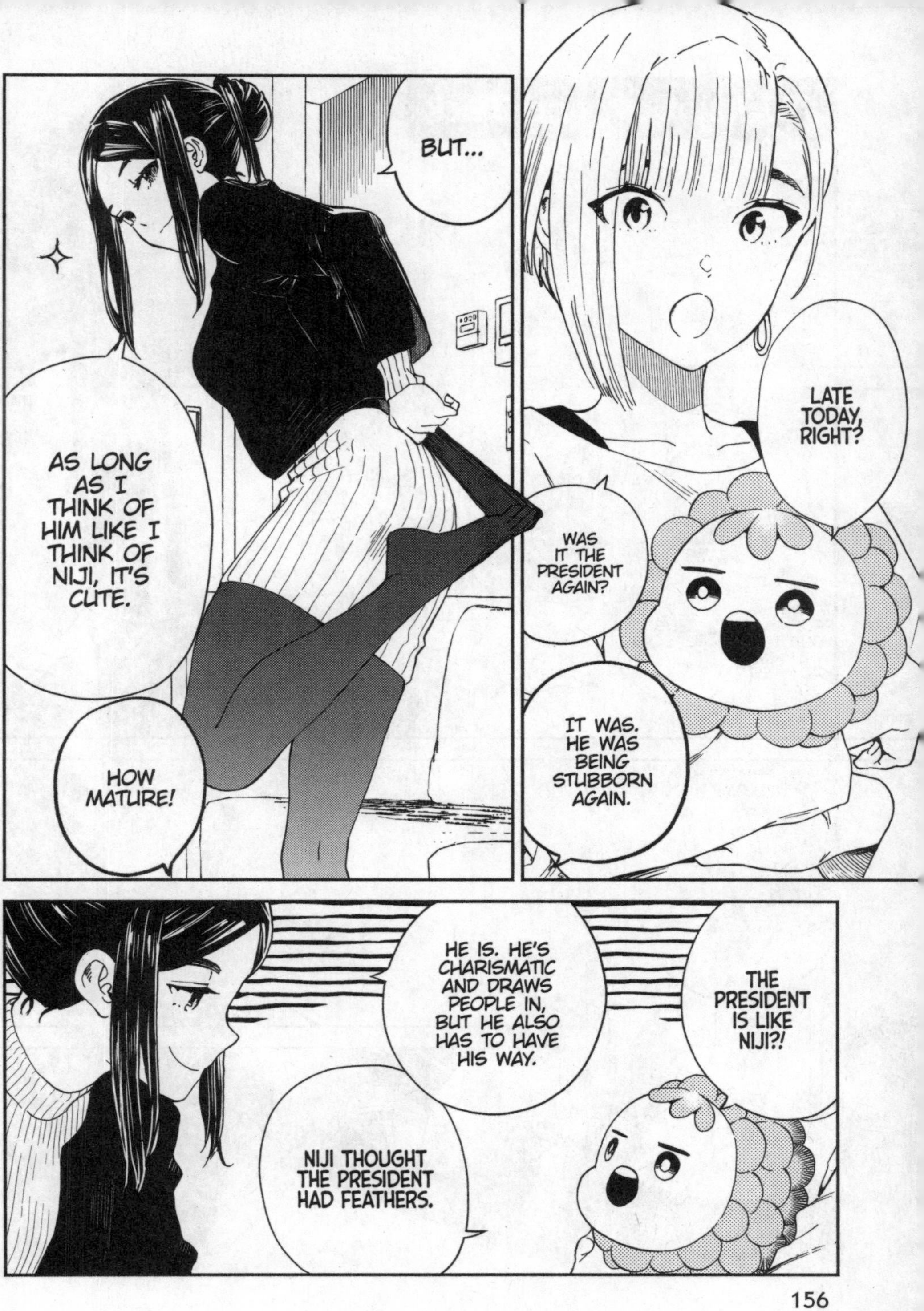
LATE TODAY, RIGHT?
WAS IT THE PRESIDENT AGAIN?
IT WAS. HE WAS BEING STUBBORN AGAIN.
BUT...
AS LONG AS I THINK OF HIM LIKE I THINK OF NIJI, IT'S CUTE.
HOW MATURE!
THE PRESIDENT IS LIKE NIJI?!
HE IS. HE'S CHARISMATIC AND DRAWS PEOPLE IN, BUT HE ALSO HAS TO HAVE HIS WAY.
NIJI THOUGHT THE PRESIDENT HAD FEATHERS.

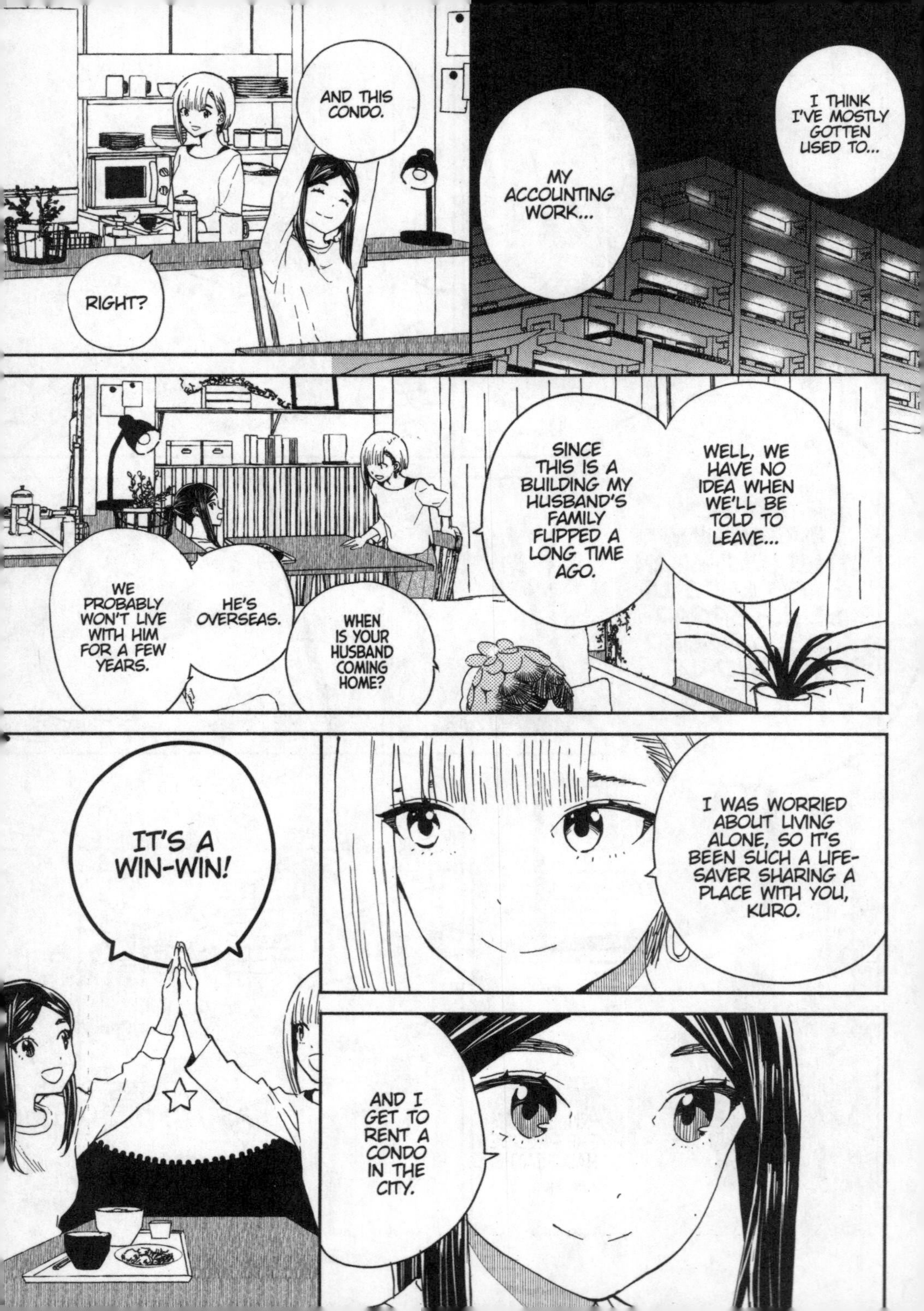
I THINK I'VE MOSTLY GOTTEN USED TO...
MY ACCOUNTING WORK...
AND THIS CONDO.
RIGHT?
WELL, WE HAVE NO IDEA WHEN WE'LL BE TOLD TO LEAVE...
SINCE THIS IS A BUILDING MY HUSBAND'S FAMILY FLIPPED A LONG TIME AGO.
WHEN IS YOUR HUSBAND COMING HOME?
HE'S OVERSEAS.
WE PROBABLY WON'T LIVE WITH HIM FOR A FEW YEARS.
I WAS WORRIED ABOUT LIVING ALONE, SO IT'S BEEN SUCH A LIFE-SAVER SHARING A PLACE WITH YOU, KURO.
AND I GET TO RENT A CONDO IN THE CITY.
IT'S A WIN-WIN!

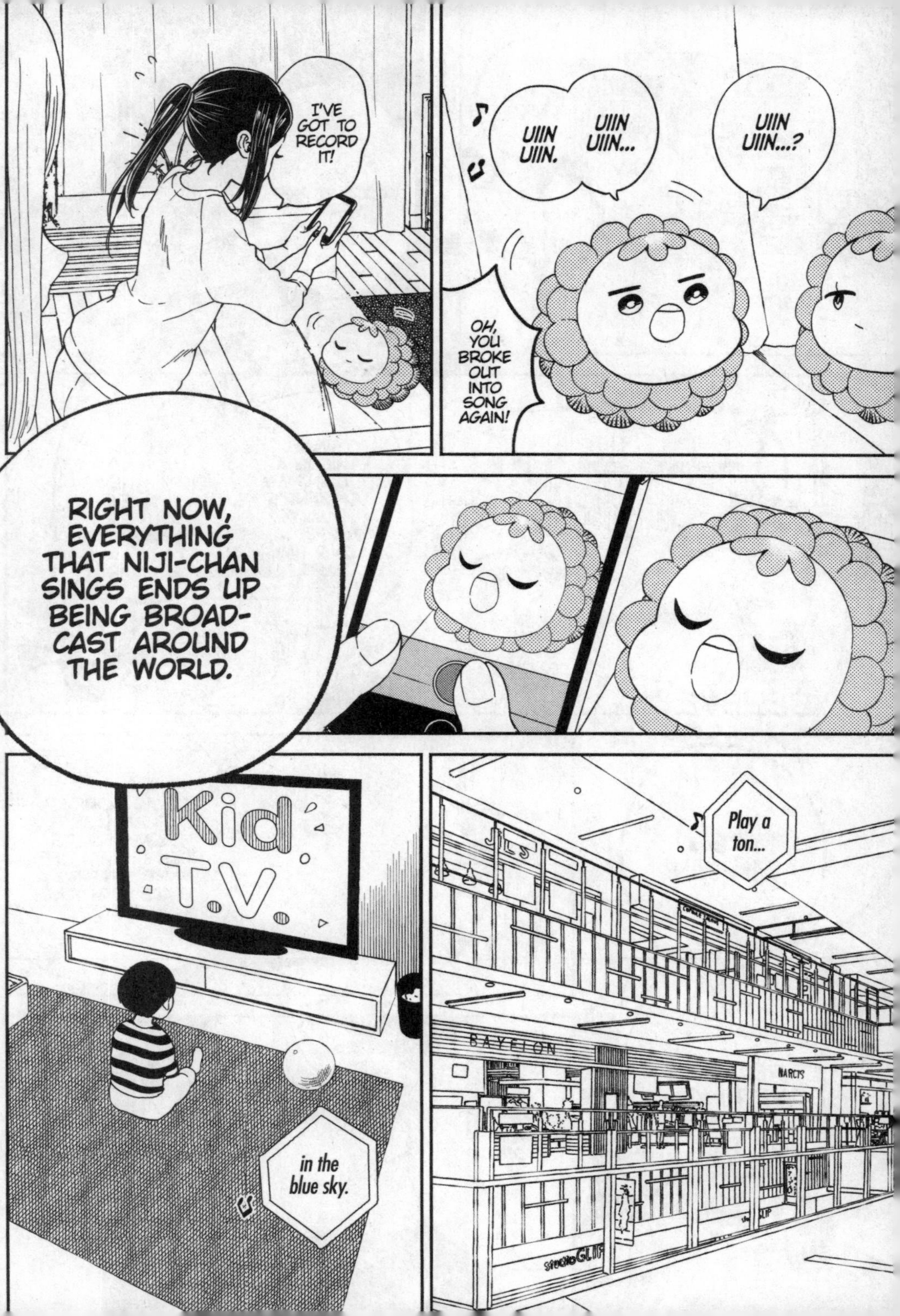
UIIN UIIN...?
UIIN UIIN...
UIIN UIIN.
OH, YOU BROKE OUT INTO SONG AGAIN!
I'VE GOT TO RECORD IT!
RIGHT NOW, EVERYTHING THAT NIJI-CHAN SINGS ENDS UP BEING BROAD-CAST AROUND THE WORLD.
Play a ton...
BAYELON
studio GLIP
Kid T.V.
in the blue sky.

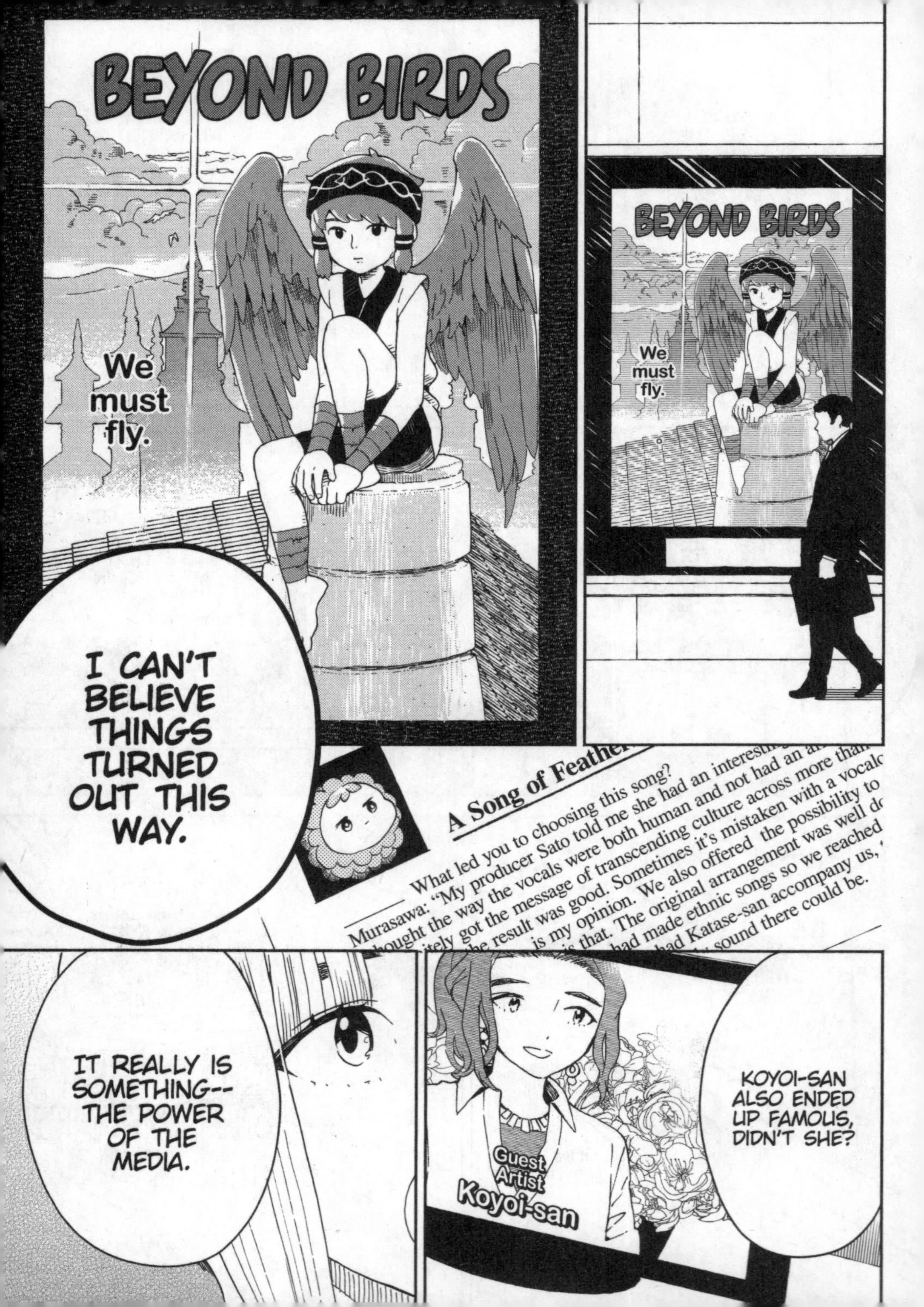
BEYOND BIRDS
We must fly.
BEYOND BIRDS
We must fly.
I CAN'T BELIEVE THINGS TURNED OUT THIS WAY.
A Song of Feathe
What led you to choosing this song?
Murasawa: "My producer Sato told me she had an interesti
thought the way the vocals were both human and not had an
itely got the message of transcending culture across more than
the result was good. Sometimes it's mistaken with a vocalo
is my opinion. We also offered the possibility to
is that. The original arrangement was well d
had made ethnic songs so we reached
had Katase-san accompany us,
sound there could be.
KOYOI-SAN ALSO ENDED UP FAMOUS, DIDN'T SHE?
Guest Artist
Koyoi-san
IT REALLY IS SOMETHING-- THE POWER OF THE MEDIA.

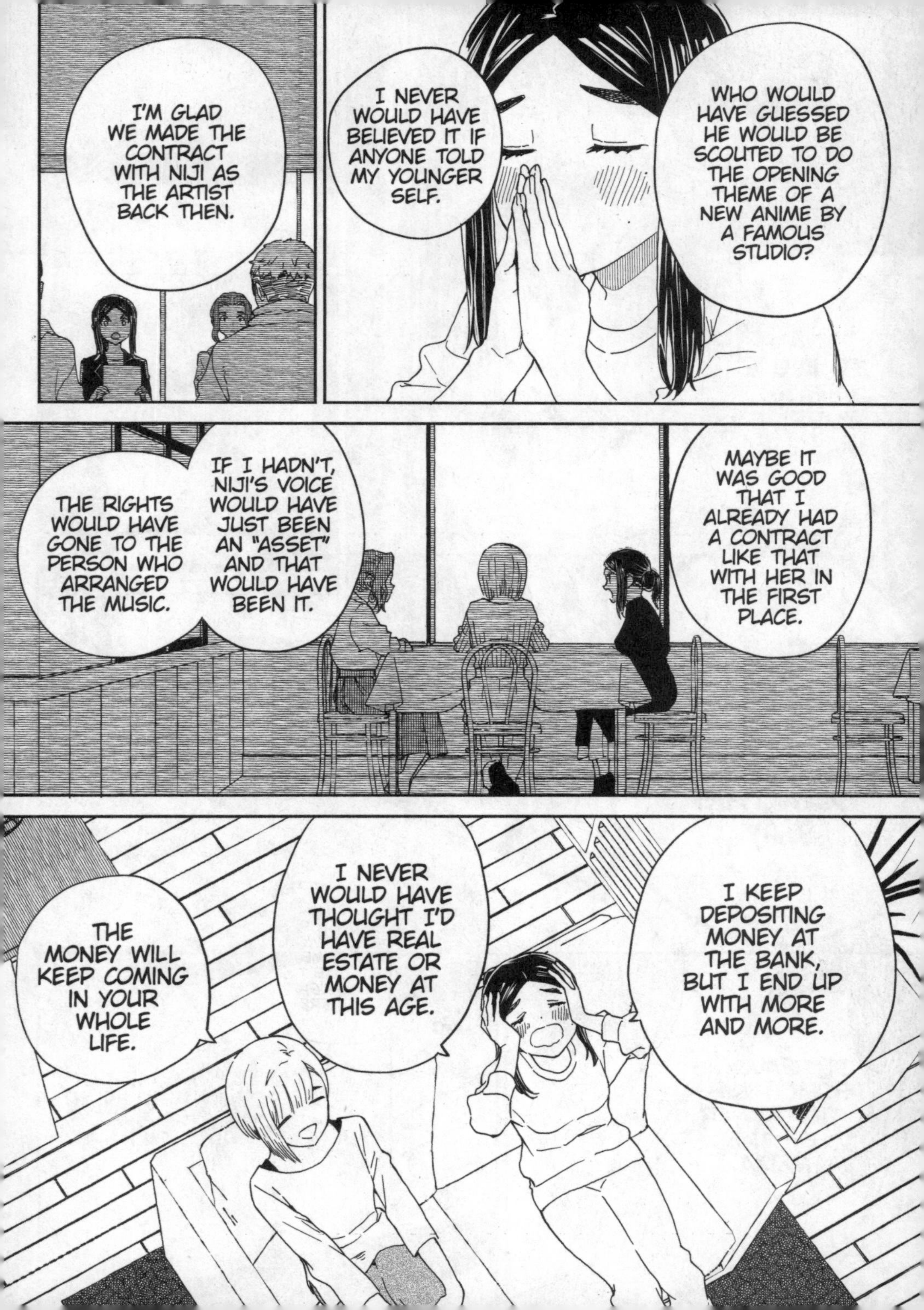
WHO WOULD HAVE GUESSED HE WOULD BE SCOUTED TO DO THE OPENING THEME OF A NEW ANIME BY A FAMOUS STUDIO?
I NEVER WOULD HAVE BELIEVED IT IF ANYONE TOLD MY YOUNGER SELF.
I'M GLAD WE MADE THE CONTRACT WITH NIJI AS THE ARTIST BACK THEN.
MAYBE IT WAS GOOD THAT I ALREADY HAD A CONTRACT LIKE THAT WITH HER IN THE FIRST PLACE.
IF I HADN'T, NIJI'S VOICE WOULD HAVE JUST BEEN AN "ASSET" AND THAT WOULD HAVE BEEN IT.
THE RIGHTS WOULD HAVE GONE TO THE PERSON WHO ARRANGED THE MUSIC.
I KEEP DEPOSITING MONEY AT THE BANK, BUT I END UP WITH MORE AND MORE.
I NEVER WOULD HAVE THOUGHT I'D HAVE REAL ESTATE OR MONEY AT THIS AGE.
THE MONEY WILL KEEP COMING IN YOUR WHOLE LIFE.

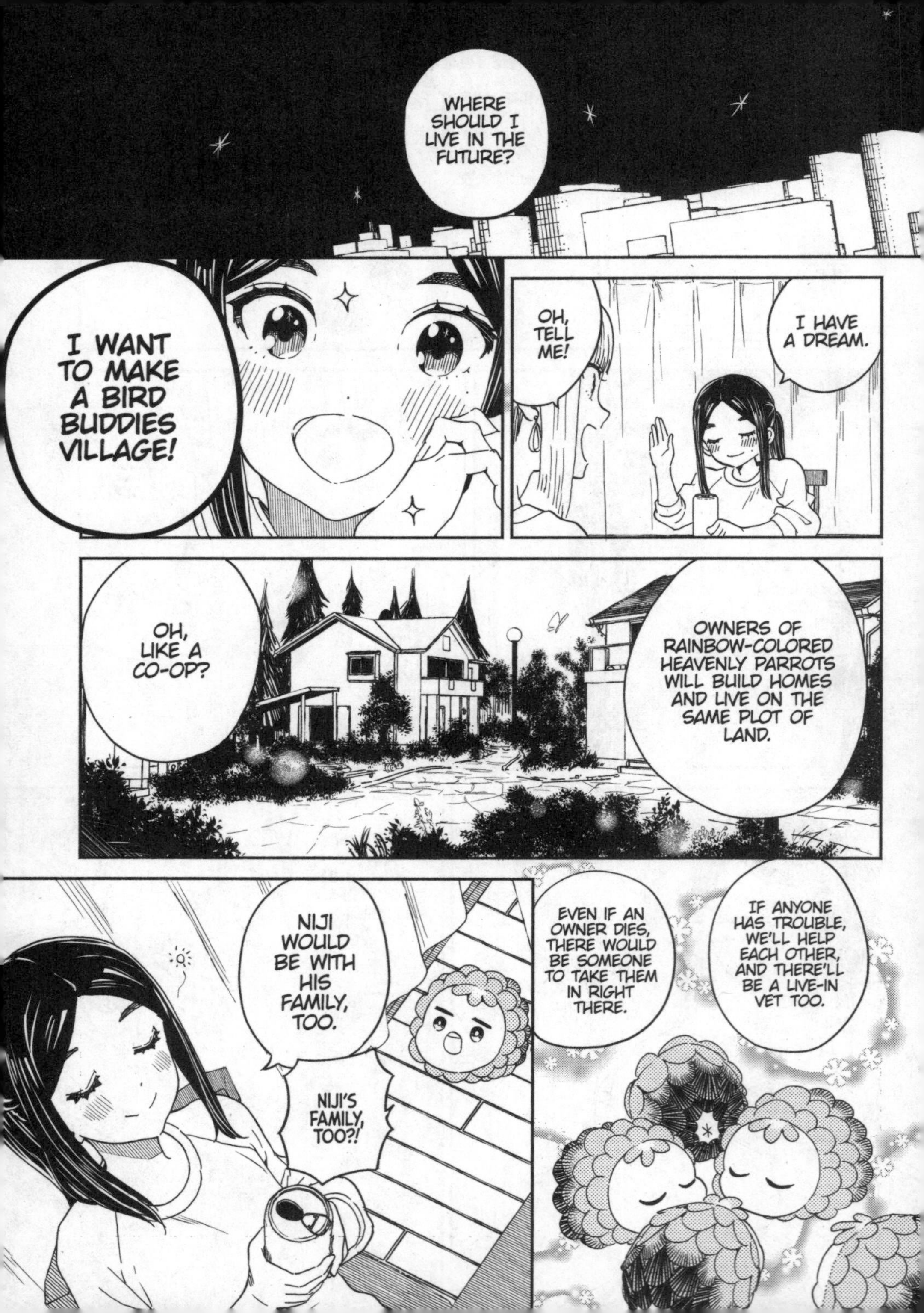
WHERE SHOULD I LIVE IN THE FUTURE?
I HAVE A DREAM.
OH, TELL ME!
I WANT TO MAKE A BIRD BUDDIES VILLAGE!
OWNERS OF RAINBOW-COLORED HEAVENLY PARROTS WILL BUILD HOMES AND LIVE ON THE SAME PLOT OF LAND.
OH, LIKE A CO-OP?
IF ANYONE HAS TROUBLE, WE'LL HELP EACH OTHER, AND THERE'LL BE A LIVE-IN VET TOO.
EVEN IF AN OWNER DIES, THERE WOULD BE SOMEONE TO TAKE THEM IN RIGHT THERE.
NIJI WOULD BE WITH HIS FAMILY, TOO.
NIJI'S FAMILY, TOO?!

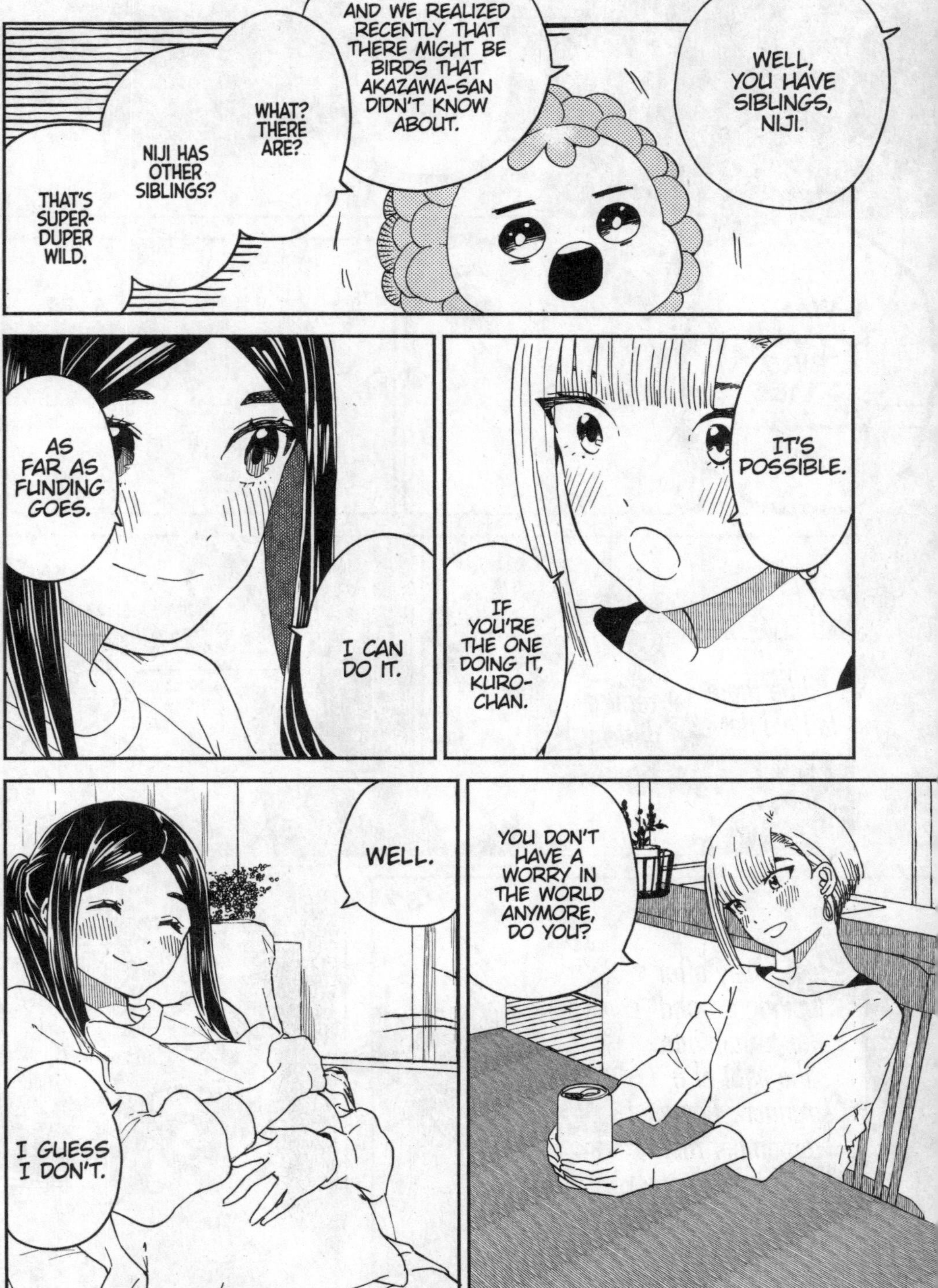
WELL, YOU HAVE SIBLINGS, NIJI.
AND WE REALIZED RECENTLY THAT THERE MIGHT BE BIRDS THAT AKAZAWA-SAN DIDN'T KNOW ABOUT.
WHAT? THERE ARE?
NIJI HAS OTHER SIBLINGS?
THAT'S SUPER-DUPER WILD.
IT'S POSSIBLE.
IF YOU'RE THE ONE DOING IT, KURO-CHAN.
I CAN DO IT.
AS FAR AS FUNDING GOES.
YOU DON'T HAVE A WORRY IN THE WORLD ANYMORE, DO YOU?
WELL.
I GUESS I DON'T.

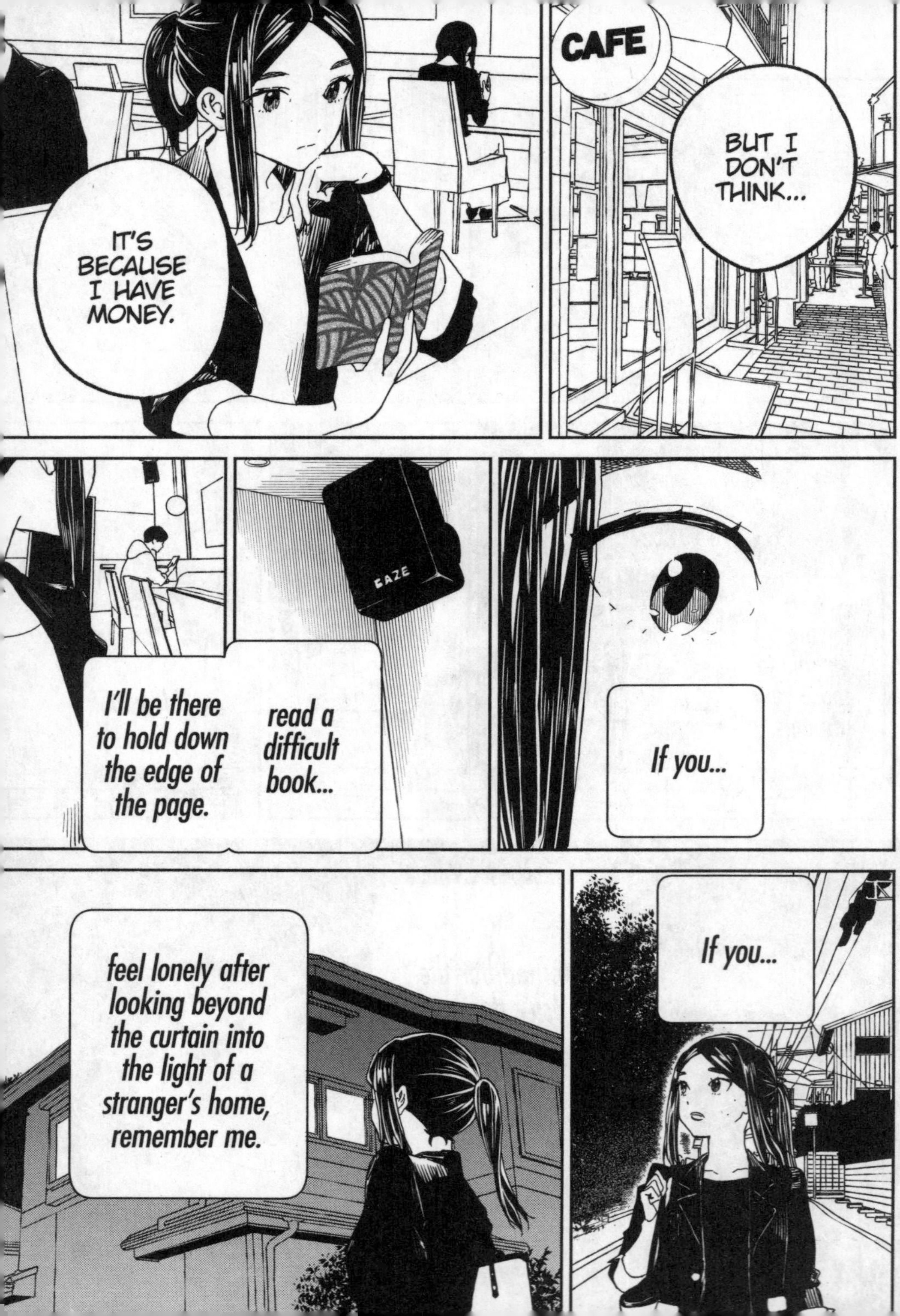
CAFE
BUT I DON'T THINK...
IT'S BECAUSE I HAVE MONEY.
If you...
read a difficult book...
I'll be there to hold down the edge of the page.
If you...
feel lonely after looking beyond the curtain into the light of a stranger's home, remember me.

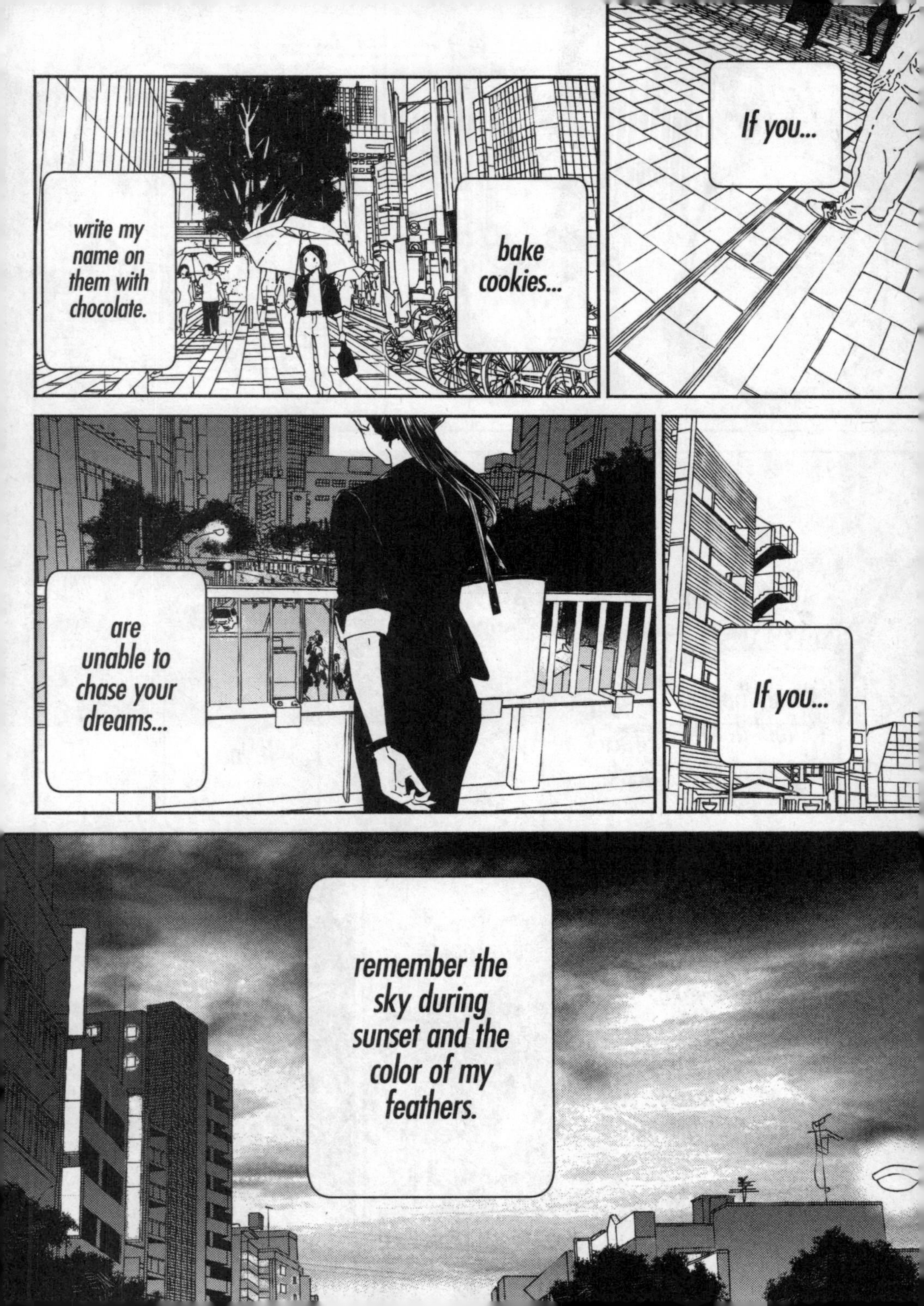

If you...
bake cookies...
write my name on them with chocolate.
If you...
are unable to chase your dreams...
remember the sky during sunset and the color of my feathers.

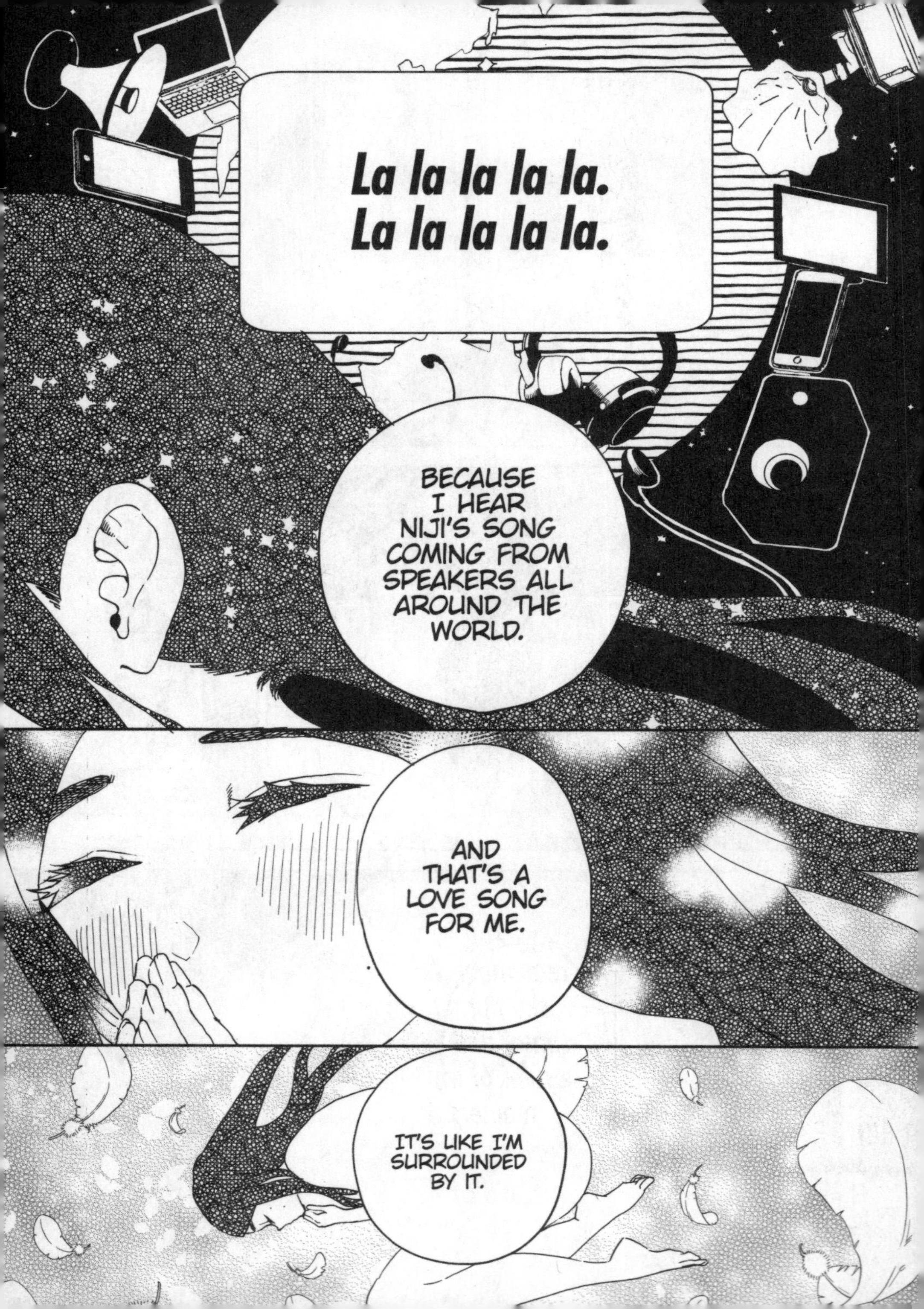
La la la la la. La la la la la.
BECAUSE I HEAR NIJI'S SONG COMING FROM SPEAKERS ALL AROUND THE WORLD.
AND THAT'S A LOVE SONG FOR ME.
IT'S LIKE I'M SURROUNDED BY IT.

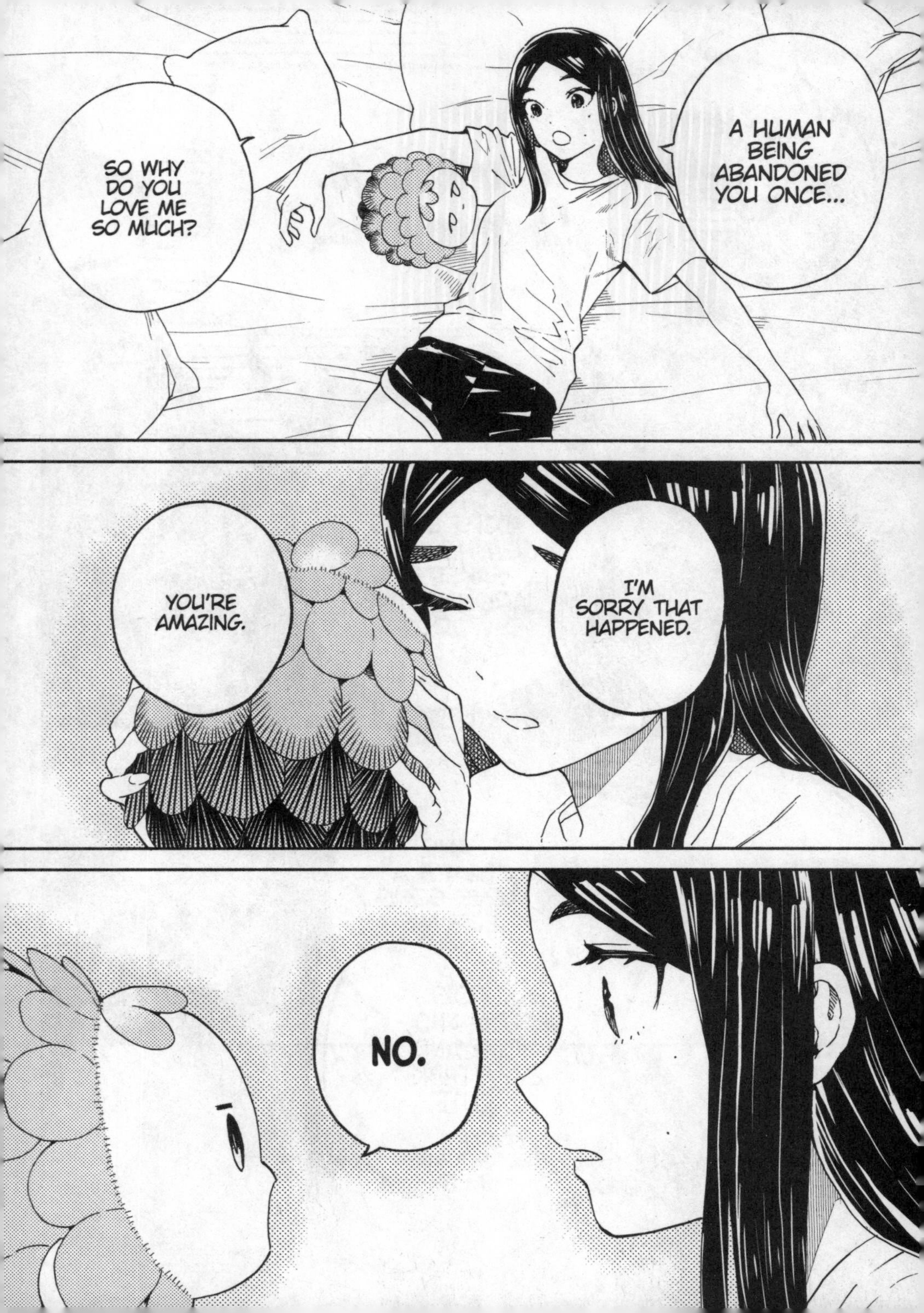
A HUMAN BEING ABANDONED YOU ONCE...
SO WHY DO YOU LOVE ME SO MUCH?
I'M SORRY THAT HAPPENED.
YOU'RE AMAZING.
NO.

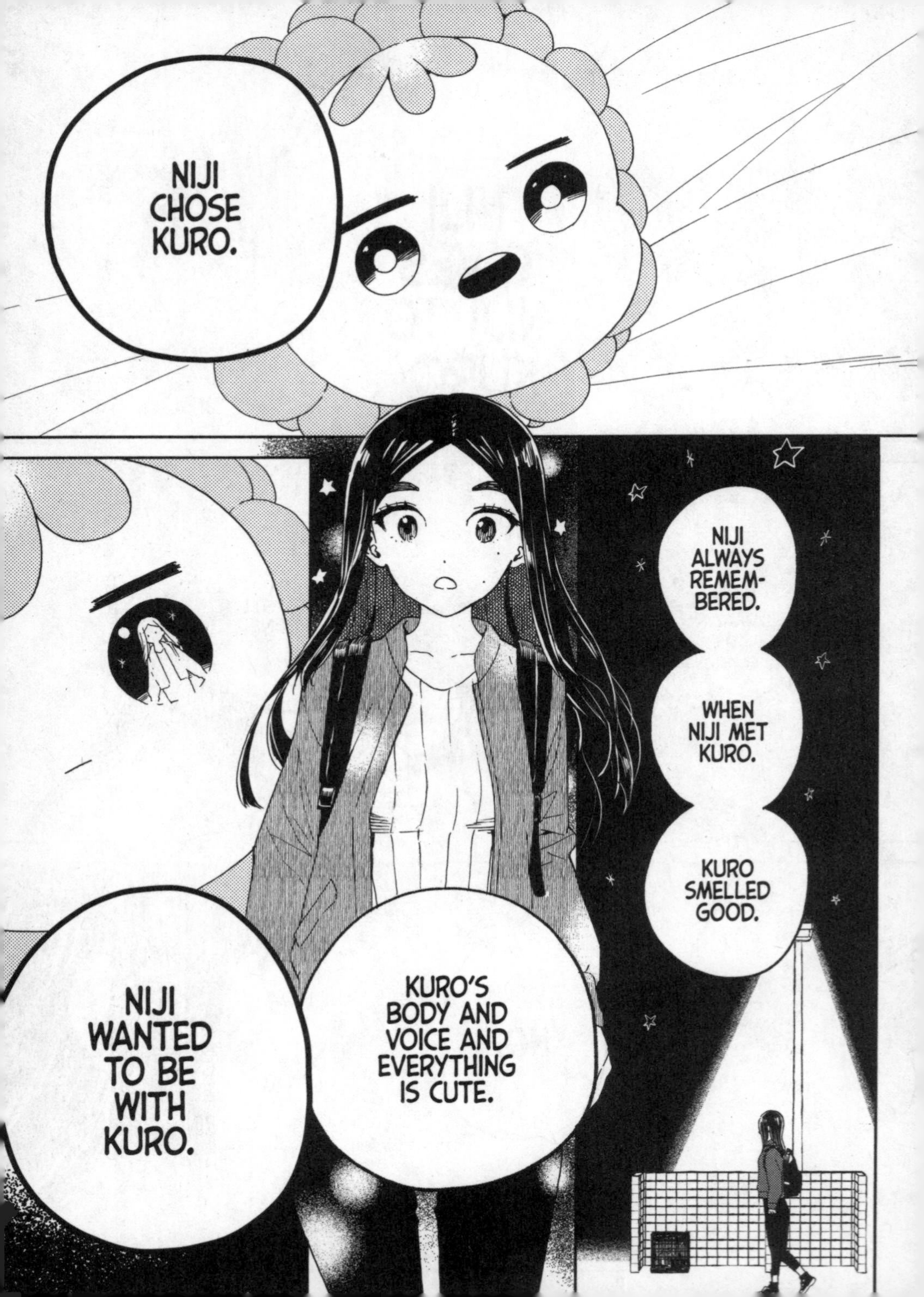
NIJI CHOSE KURO.
NIJI ALWAYS REMEMBERED.
WHEN NIJI MET KURO.
KURO SMELLED GOOD.
KURO'S BODY AND VOICE AND EVERYTHING IS CUTE.
NIJI WANTED TO BE WITH KURO.

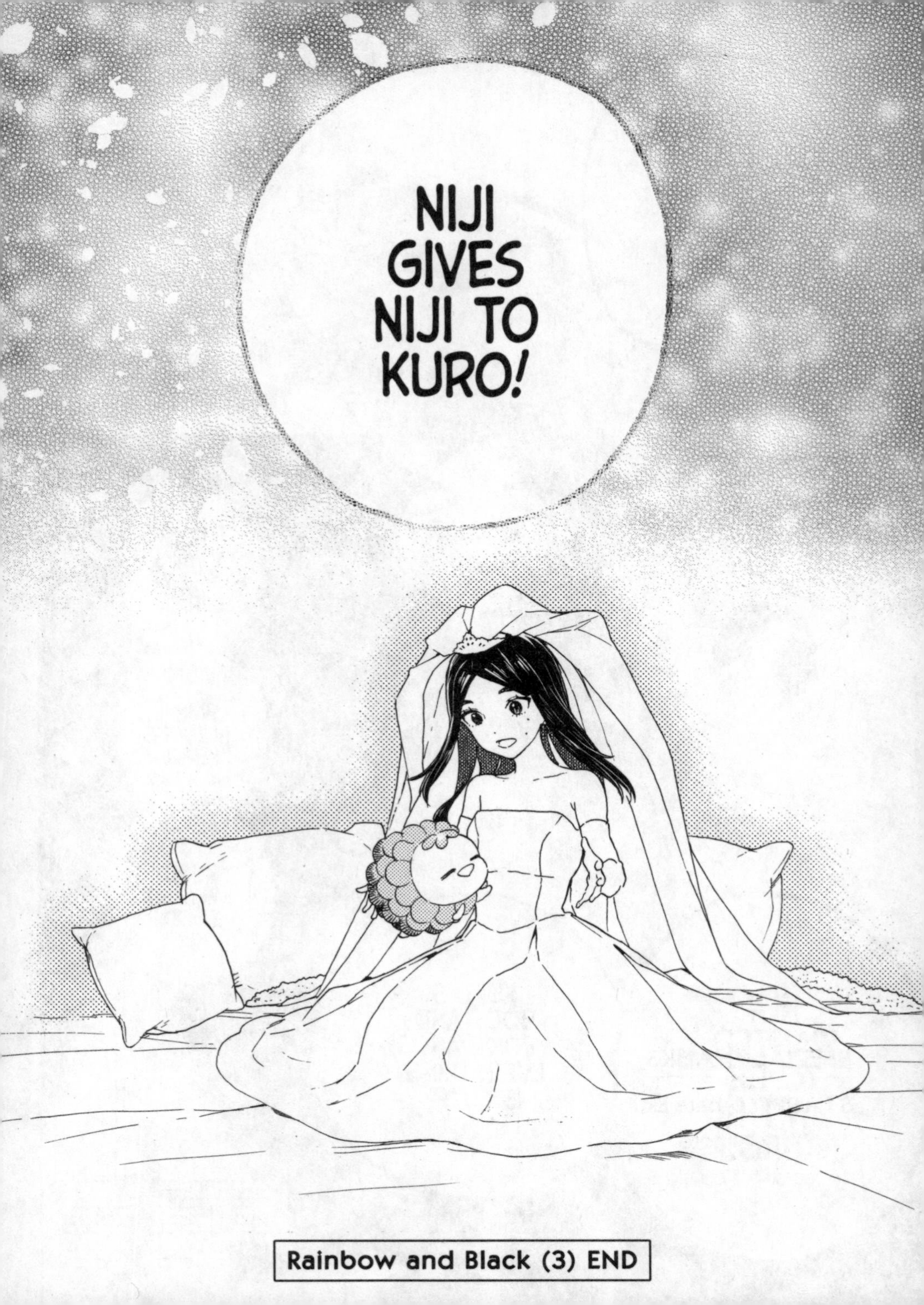
NIJI GIVES NIJI TO KURO!
Rainbow and Black (3) END

SPECIAL THANKS

STAFF: Abata Ekubo

Imoto

Katsuki Sae

Haseyoshi Eria

Fuji Koyomi

SEVEN SEAS ENTERTAINMENT PRESENTS

Rainbow and Black

story and art by **ERI TAKENASHI**

TRANSLATION
Jan Cash

ADAPTATION
Sam Mitchell

LETTERING AND RETOUCH
Ochie Caraan

COVER DESIGN
Hanase Qi

PROOFREADER
Kurestin Armada, Dawn Davis

EDITOR
Kristiina Korpus

PREPRESS TECHNICIAN
Rhiannon Rasmussen-Silverstein

PRODUCTION MANAGER
Lissa Pattillo

MANAGING EDITOR
Julie Davis

ASSOCIATE PUBLISHER
Adam Arnold

PUBLISHER
Jason DeAngelis

NIJI TO KURO VOL.3
©2021 Eri Takenashi. All ⬚
First published in Japan in 202⬚
Publication rights for this English edition arranged t⬚

Seven Seas press and purchase enquiries can be sent to Marketing Manager Lianne Sentar at press@gomanga.com. Information regarding the distribution and purchase of digital editions is available from Digital Manager CK Russell at digital@gomanga.com.

Seven Seas and the Seven Seas logo are trademarks of Seven Seas Entertainment. All rights reserved.

ISBN: 978-1-64827-284-4

Printed in Canada

First Printing: October 2021

10 9 8 7 6 5 4 3 2 1

FOLLOW US ONLINE: *www.sevenseasentertainment.com*

READING DIRECTIONS

This book reads from *right to left*, Japanese style. If this is your first time reading manga, you start reading from the top right panel on each page and take it from there. If you get lost, just follow the numbered diagram here. It may seem backwards at first, but you'll get the hang of it! Have fun!!

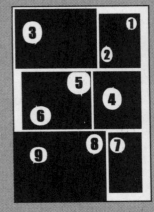